The Integration of Health and Social Care in the UK

Interagency Working in Health and Social Care
Edited by Jon Glasby

Aimed at students and practitioners, this series provides an introduction to inter-agency working across the health and social care spectrum, bringing together an appreciation of the policy background with a focus on contemporary themes. The books span a wide range of health and social care services and the impact that these have on people's lives, as well as offering insightful accounts of the issues facing professionals in a fast-changing organisational landscape.

Exploring how services and sectors interact and could change further, and the evidence for 'what works', the series is designed to frame debate as well as promote positive ways of interdisciplinary working.

Published titles
Baggott: *Partnerships for Public Health and Wellbeing: Policy and Practice*
Glasby/Tew: *Mental Health Policy and Practice 3rd edition*
French/Swain: *Working with Disabled People in Policy and Practice*
Kellett: *Children's Perspectives on Integrated Services: Every Child Matters in Policy and Practice*
Williams: *Learning Disability Policy and Practice: Changing Lives?*

The Integration of Health and Social Care in the UK

Policy and Practice

Derek Birrell and Deirdre Heenan

First published 2018 by
PALGRAVE

Palgrave in the UK is an imprint of Macmillan Publishers Limited, registered in England, company number 785998, of 4 Crinan Street, London, N1 9XW.

Palgrave® and Macmillan® are registered trademarks in the United States, the United Kingdom, Europe and other countries.

ISBN 978–1–137–40442–8 paperback

This book is printed on paper suitable for recycling and made from fully managed and sustained forest sources. Logging, pulping and manufacturing processes are expected to conform to the environmental regulations of the country of origin.

A catalogue record for this book is available from the British Library.

A catalog record for this book is available from the Library of Congress.

Contents

List of Boxes, Figures and Tables *viii*

Abbreviations *x*

Acknowledgements *xii*

1 Introduction and Content *1*
Introduction *1*
The wider context and challenge *7*
The implementation of integration *9*
Structure of book *9*
Sources *13*
Terminology *14*

2 Development of Policies and Strategies in England *15*
Policies and strategies pre-1999 *15*
Promoting partnerships and the Flexibilities agenda *16*
Transforming care and integration policies under New Labour *18*
NHS reforms and impact on integration *20*
Social care reform and integration *22*
Support for integration from non-statutory bodies *24*
Operation of integrated care in England *28*
Partnerships and use of Flexibilities *31*
Major themes in integrated partnerships *37*
Conclusions *42*

3 Reshaping Integration in England *43*
Introduction *43*
Clinical Commissioning Groups *43*
Health and Wellbeing Boards *46*
Partnership NHS trusts *50*
Integrated Care Pioneers Programme *50*
Government encouragement of integration *54*
Better Care Fund *56*
NICE: Standards for integration *57*
Vanguard sites, new care models *57*

City/region devolution and integration *59*
Integrated personal commissioning *60*
Conclusions *62*

4 Integration in Scotland *63*
Introduction *63*
Policy development and Joint Future *63*
Establishment of health and social care partnerships *64*
Support for integration *66*
Vision for integration *67*
Integrated Authorities *68*
Assessment of progress *71*
Integration activities *72*
Self-directed support *73*
Conclusions *74*

5 Integration in Wales *76*
Introduction *76*
The Welsh experience of integration *82*
Other promotional factors *86*
Assessments of integrated care *88*
Conclusions *90*

6 Integration in Northern Ireland *92*
Introduction *92*
Historical context *92*
Development of integrated structure *93*
Reorganisation of health and social care *96*
Transforming your care and its impact *97*
Integrated Care Partnerships *100*
Research on integration in Northern Ireland *101*
Operation of integration *102*
Conclusions *107*

7 Achievements of Integration *109*
Introduction *109*
Limitations of the findings *110*
Clinical outcomes *112*
Operational achievements *113*
Cost-effectiveness *116*
Rehabilitation and prevention *117*
User and staff satisfaction *119*
Integration and service groups *120*
The new initiatives *123*
Wider dimensions *124*
Conclusions *125*

8 Promoting Integration *127*
Financial support *127*
Leadership and management *129*
A shared vision and culture *130*
Education and training *131*
Co-location *133*
Flexible roles *133*
Person- and user-centred *133*
Legacy of joint working *135*
GP engagement *135*
Evidence and research *136*
Integrated teams *136*
Commissioning integrated services *137*
Other promotional factors *138*
Conclusions *140*

9 Barriers to Integration *142*
Introduction *142*
Professional differences *142*
Equity issues *143*
Funding difficulties *144*
Lack of clarity *145*
Staffing differences and problems *148*
Lack of training *148*
Other barriers *149*
Conclusions *151*

10 International Perspectives *153*
Care pathways *154*
Financial framework *158*
Information systems *160*
Leadership *163*
Decentralisation *166*
Conclusions *166*

11 Conclusions *169*

References *175*

Index *196*

List of Boxes, Figures and Tables

Boxes

1.1 Categories of Approach to Integration *5*

1.2 Processes of Integration *5*

1.3 Leutz's Five Laws of Integration *6*

1.4 Updating the Meaning of Integration *6*

1.5 Summary of Integrated Structures in the UK *10*

2.1 Government Strategies for Health and Social Care *18*

2.2 Governance Characteristics of Care Trusts *29*

2.3 Functions of Care Trusts *29*

2.4 Partnership Relationships *34*

2.5 Rapid Response Features *41*

3.1 Structure of the HWB in Oxfordshire *48*

3.2 Tool Kit for Integrated Working *48*

3.3 Potential Benefits of HWBs *50*

3.4 Pioneers' Integrated Practices *52*

3.5 National Collaboration for Integrated Care and Support Partners, 2013 *55*

3.6 Aims of the National Collaboration for Integrated Care and Support *55*

3.7 Types and Numbers of Vanguard Sites *58*

3.8 Assessment Criteria Framework for City Devolution of Health and Social Care *60*

3.9 Five Key Shifts of Integrated Personal Commissioning *61*

4.1 2020 Vision for Health and Social Care *68*

4.2 Structure for Delivering Integrated Health and Social Care *68*

4.3   Integrated Planning Principles *70*

4.4   Social Services to be Integrated 2015 *70*

6.1   Characteristics of Integrated Trusts *96*

6.2   Principles of Transforming Your Care *98*

6.3   TYC Included 99 Recommendations; Key Drivers for Change *98*

6.4   Enhancing Integration *102*

7.1   Main Sources *109*

7.2   Northern Devon Stroke Service *120*

7.3   Impact of Bracknell Forest Community Dementia Support Team *122*

7.4   Impact of the West Sussex Integrated Dementia Care Team *122*

7.5   Pioneer Projects: Examples of Best Practice *124*

8.1   Groupings of Factors Promoting Integration *139*

9.1   Primary Barriers *151*

9.2   Second-level Barriers to Integration *152*

9.3   Third-level Barriers to Integration *152*

Figures

2.1   Timeline 2010–2014 *22*

3.1   Pioneers and Programmes *53*

6.1   Structural Integration 1999 *96*

6.2   Structural Integration 2007–2016 *97*

Tables

3.1   Integration Pioneer Sites and Composition of Bodies *51*

6.1   Programmes of Care by Percentage Expenditure *103*

Abbreviations

A&E	Accident and Emergency
ADASS	Association of Directors of Adult Social Services
ASCOT	Adult Social Care Outcomes Toolkit
BCF	Better Care Fund
BMA	British Medical Association
CAAMHS	Child and Adolescent Adult Mental Health Services
CCC	Computerised Clinical Chart
CCG	Clinical Commissioning Group
CHP	Community Health Partnership
CPD	Continuous Professional Development
CQC	Care Quality Commission
DH	Department of Health
DHSS	Department of Health and Social Services
DHSSPS	Department of Health and Social Services and Personal Safety
FHTs	Family Health Teams
GB	Great Britain
GP	General Practitioner
HWB	Health and Wellbeing Board
HR	Human Resources
HSC	Health and Social Care
HSCB	Health and Social Care Board
ICASE	Integrated Care and Support Exchange
ICP	Integrated Care Partnership
IPC	Integrated Personal Commissioning
IRF	Integrated Resource Framework
IT	Information Technology
JSNA	Joint Strategic Needs Assessment
LGA	Local Government Association
MCN	Managed Clinical Network
NAO	National Audit Office
NHS	National Health Service
NHSCB	National Health Service Commissioning Board
NHSIQ	National Health Service Improving Quality
NICE	National Institute for Health and Care Excellence

OECD	Organization for Economic Co-operation and Development
PCP	Primary Care Partnership
PCT	Primary Care Trust
PRISMA	Program of Research to Integrate Services for the Maintenance of Autonomy
RCN	Royal College of Nursing
RPA	Review of Public Administration
SAP	Single Assessment Process
SCIE	Social Care Institute for Excellence
STPs	Sustainability and Transformation Plans
TCA	Team Care Arrangement
TCS	Transforming Community Services
TYC	Transforming Your Care
UAP	Unified Assessment Process
UK	United Kingdom
USA	United States of America
WHO	World Health Organization

Acknowledgements

We would like to thank everyone who supported us in the writing of this book. Particular thanks to Liz McNeill for her unfailing assistance in preparing the final manuscript and the staff at Palgrave Macmillan for their advice and patience. Special thanks also to Professor Jon Glasby for his helpful advice and feedback.

1 Introduction and Content

Introduction

The integration of health and social care has become a constant policy ambition in the UK. Closer integration has become the goal of successive UK governments for over 40 years (Humphries, 2015, has become established as a contemporary priority and endorsed by the devolved administrations in Scotland, Wales and Northern Ireland). It has been noted that the imperative to integrate and transform has never been greater (NHS Confederation/Local Government Association, 2016). The Barker Commission (2014) on the future of social care noted the compelling case for the bringing together of health and social care and called for far better integration built around people's needs and an alignment of the two systems of care. In 2015 much closer integration of health and social care was identified as one of the three major challenges faced by the NHS (Ham, 2015). The Nuffield Trust (2015) has identified five factors to pursue in improving UK health care, each of which relates to integrated approaches: the quality of care, new models of care delivery, older people's needs, complex conditions and workforce development. In their five point plan for the UK government in 2014 the Royal College of Physicians noted the need to remove the financial and structural barriers to joined-up care for patients and argued that it should be easier for hospitals, GPs and social care teams to work together than separately and shared practice and outcomes should become the norm. It is a matter for discussion how effective the rhetoric has been in reality (Glasby, 2016) although governments have been introducing legislative measures to support and promote integration. Other views have noted that as existing systems were not designed to deliver an integrated approach (Goldberg, 2014), it will take a long time for the ultimate goals to be reached. The UK government has confirmed its intention to achieve a more comprehensive integrated system between health and social care by 2020 (Care Quality Commission, 2016). Similar policy commitments to integration have also been made by the three devolved governments of Scotland, Wales and Northern Ireland. A main aim of this book is to compare the development of policies and systems of integration throughout the UK and present a detailed analysis of practice and structures of the four countries of the UK. This includes an assessment of achievements alongside a discussion of what can be identified as promoting integration or causing barriers to implementation. This provides material for an analysis of what each part of the UK can learn from each other.

Rationale for integration

There is considerable consensus on the case for promoting integration and the major rationales that have been identified in existing research and literature. These can listed as:

A holistic approach to care – it has become important to deal with the need for close coordination in the various aspects of care which the health services and social care services provide. This has become particularly important with the increase in chronic, complex multiple needs, the increase in frail older people with conditions such as dementia, and those with disabilities.

A seamless service – this may be regarded as something of a buzzword but provision of such services means easier access, quicker responses, better coordinated initial care and pathways to continuing care.

Ending and reducing fragmentation – a major argument for integration has been to remove the large structural barrier between the NHS and local government social services in Great Britain or at least to reduce its significance, with the potential to radically improve a fragmented system in a number of respects. Typically care has been provided by a range of organisations including hospitals, GP practices, community health bodies, social service or social work departments, independent providers and voluntary bodies.

Concern over fragmentation-this can include gaps in care and duplication of care. The problem also reflected the increasing complexity of health care and specialisation (Shaw and Rosen, 2013). Fragmentation is also demonstrated in different financial systems, different employers, regulations, and accountability processes. Integration has the attraction of less silo working and closer engagement and a more multidimensional approach.

Improved communication – integrated approaches have an advantage in improving communication and access to and exchange of information relating to service users, particularly between health and social care.

More efficient use of resources – demand for both health and social care has increased while resources have been limited. Integration contributes to efficiency through reducing duplication and unnecessary costs (Miller et al., 2016). New ways of working and practice, the pooling of budgets, sharing of management posts, unified assessment, all can save on resources. Integration may make a vital contribution to closing the funding gap the NHS faces.

Promoting prevention – with increasing demand on acute care and on care for older people there has been an emphasis on reducing the high level of dependence on institutional and hospital care. Improvements in the quality and range of services, integrated care, care in the community and the emphasis on public health have contributed to the advancement of prevention. Admissions to acute care may be avoidable by an increased emphasis on prevention, community based care and more personalised care along a social care spectrum (Goldberg, 2014).

Better outcomes for users – integration holds out the prospects of improved outcomes, in terms both of reduced hospital admissions or speedier pathways through care and of meeting service users' expectations and demands. Users are no longer content to be passive recipients and wish to be involved in decisions about their care and decisions, particularly relating to services in the community. There has also been an emphasis on delivering better quality services in health and social care responsive to user demands (NHS Confederation, 2014). This can be assessed through inspections, performance management, targets and value for money and through the use of outcomes-based frameworks to evaluate the user experience and impact on quality of life.

Many accounts of partnership working have focused on potential benefits and descriptive accounts of the processes involved rather than on evidence about outcomes (Glasby et al., 2011). The analysis in the book examines the evidence in support of the achievements and values of these rationales, in the context of research and evaluations from throughout the UK and wider sources.

The meaning of integration

A wide-ranging debate has taken place over the meaning of integration, with much less consensus than over the policy commitment and the rationales for integration. While it may be an exaggeration to hold the opinion that nowhere in recent literature is there a systematic, comprehensive examination of the concept of health and social services integration (Fisher and Elnitsky, 2012), there appears no one broadly accepted definition of integrated care. A review of literature in 2009 identified some 175 definitions and concepts of integrated care (Armitage et al., 2009). Most of these definitions referred to bringing together the organisation, delivery, management and outputs of services in a way which resulted in improved quality efficiency and user satisfaction. However, it seems that some of the references apply to largely health only services. El Ansari (2011) considered a number of the concepts associated with integrated care and noted there was considerable ambiguity and confusion in the literature which created a lack of clarity over what was being studied and how this related to other principles. He contended that inconsistent terminology in the literature led to conceptual chaos as meanings are implied rather than precisely articulated. Petch (2012) accepts that it is essential that in a discussion of integration of health and social care people define what they are talking about, noting the possibility of a terminological quagmire, methodological anarchy and definitional chaos. She notes the danger that people are either referring to a similar arrangement using different terms or using the same term to refer to different configurations. Working definitions ideally reflecting experience are essential. Curry and Ham (2010) specify that integration is concerned with the process of bringing organisations and professionals together with the aim of improving outcomes for patients and service users through the delivery of integrated care.

Collaboration or a continuum of collaboration across the organisational boundaries of health and social care was another approach, although leaving aside the question of the degree of collaboration (Edwards, 2010)

Edwards includes a distinction between cooperation, coordination and integration in addressing organisational forms. Leutz (2005) characterised three levels of intensity in integration: linkage, taking place between existing organisational units to facilitate communication and promote continuity of care; coordination, operating through existing operational units to share information and promote care; and full integration, pooling resources and allowing new organisations to be created to develop comprehensive services. Such an approach was more fully developed by Glasby (2005) mapping the depth of integration, covering shared pathways, jointly managed projects and formal mergers and the breadth of integration covering health, social care, housing and other specialist services. Such mapping could be amended to apply to current developments with the depth covering cooperation, partnerships and structural integration and breadth covering primary, community and acute health provision, adult social care and children's services, an approach useful with the development of four different systems in the UK.

Also used to suggest different levels within systems have been micro to macro concepts with micro the smallest unit of organisation, macro the largest and mezzo in between (Miller et al., 2016, p. 22). Macro can be described as at the societal level, micro at the individual service user level and mezzo at a service system level. Curry and Ham (2010) also suggested a distinction between integration at three levels: the macro level where care is delivered across the full spectrum of services to the populations they serve; the micro level at which providers deliver integrated care for individual service users and their carers; and the mezzo level at which providers deliver care for a particular group of people such as care for older people. A further popular distinction has involved drawing a distinction between vertical and horizontal integration. Vertical integration is used to describe the different levels of care that people may pass through as with moving through primary to secondary care in different settings from domiciliary to community-centred to hospital. Horizontal integration refers to working between services in parallel and possibly at the same stage of a care pathway.

Other types of definition have had more of a focus on organisation and functions. A distinction is often made between integrated organisations and integrated care. Reed et al. (2005) produced a typology of integration: between service sectors, health and social care; between professions; between settings; between statutory, private and voluntary sectors; and between types of care.

Definitions using organisational processes can go into considerable detail. Kodner and Swpreeuwenberg (2002) identify five categories of approach or activity contributing to integration:

Box 1.1	Categories of Approach to Integration

Funding – including pooling

Administrative – joint planning, purchasing, commissioning, needs assessment, decentralisation

Organisational – co-location of services, inter-agency budgeting, jointly managed programmes, care networks or mergers

Service delivery – joint training, centralised information systems, care management, multidisciplinary teamwork

Clinical – uniform assessment, standard criteria, joint care planning, shared clinical records, common monitoring and protocols, family and carer contact

Process-focused descriptions and definitions involve all practitioners, clinicians and back room staff. Miller et al. (2016) have adopted an earlier mapping (Fulop et al., 2005) of different mechanisms and approaches within services and organisations, called processes of integration.

Box 1.2	Processes of Integration

Integration of structures – organisations being merged together, new organisations formed, joint planning bodies

Integration of support functions – one organisation taking on functions on behalf of others

Integration of services – staff, funding and other resources being brought together into a single service that is jointly managed

Integration of practice – connecting work of different professionals, shared case management processes and pathways

Integration of learning – joint training and development opportunities

Integration of values – development of common vision and principles

Integration of systems governance – performance monitoring and incentives and common outcomes frameworks

The debate about definitions of integration has moved on somewhat to put more emphasis on the user experience so integrated care can be seen as not so much about structures, organisations, pathways and processes but rather about better outcomes for users and with a more patient- or person-centred approach.

The Scottish Parliament has stated what is meant by integration is that services be planned and delivered seamlessly from the perspective of the patient, service user or carer, and that systems for managing such services should actively support seamlessness (Robson, 2013). National Voices (2013) had put forward a similar view that integration means a user can plan their care with people who work together to support them and bring together services to achieve the outcomes important to the individual. This emphasis on the service user as the organising principle of integrated care reflects the influence of the user perspective, particularly in delivering social care (Beresford and Carr, 2012). Regardless of what definition is adopted, some interpretations have traditionally put more emphasis on some key principles governing the use of integration. These have included the still influential paper by Leutz (1999) who developed five laws of integration:

Box 1.3	Leutz's Five Laws of Integration

1. You can integrate some services for all of the people, all of the services for some people, but you cannot integrate all of the services for all of the people.
2. Integration costs before it pays.
3. Your integration is my fragmentation.
4. You cannot integrate a square peg and a round hole.
5. The one who integrates calls the tune, i.e. sets the agenda.

The five laws are more observations than the basis of an operational plan or a course and effect model. Leutz (2005) revised the five laws suggesting full integration may be appropriate for small numbers of people where linkage and coordination may be more widely applicable. Leutz (2005, p. 7) also suggests the value of a single point of contact, financial support, a dedicated leader and integration implemented locally and over time. An updated version was produced by the Department of Health (2010a) which suggested five principles:

Box 1.4	Updating the Meaning of Integration

1. Integration is not a panacea for all and should be targeted where it is most appropriate.
2. Integration is not a quick win, it requires investment in time and resources to underpin what may be complex change.
3. There are fundamental differences across organisations and these must be recognised and dealt with.
4. Integration should be designed in conjunction with the needs of service users.
5. If integration is to be sustainable it requires buy-in at all levels.

An interpretation by Goodwin (2012) of the five laws stressed the importance of targeting; possible financial risks; the need to broker partnerships; adapting to meet local circumstances; and a genuine coalition of interests.

The wider context and challenge

Across the world, governments and health care delivery systems are grappling with the need to balance competing priorities, meeting the increasing demand for services and addressing the escalating costs of those services. In the face of growing competition for resources, the strengthening of health care systems is a key public policy consideration and has been afforded the highest priority. Walshe and Smith (2006) suggest that in every developed country the health care system is subject to four inescapable challenges:

- demographic trends;
- technological innovation;
- increasing user and consumer demands and expectations;
- rising costs within a context of economic recession.

According to the United Nations, the world's population is expected to increase by 1 billion people by 2025. Of that billion, 300 million will be people aged 65 or older, as life expectancy around the globe continues to rise. Additional health care resources and innovative services are needed globally to deliver the long-term care and chronic disease management services required by a rapidly increasing older population. When the NHS was founded in 1948, 48 per cent of the population died before the age of 65; that figure has fallen to 14 per cent (Office of National Statistics, 2013). By 2030 one in five people in England will be over 65.

Whilst living longer is a good news story, it has implications for our health and social care system. As people age they are progressively more likely to live with complex co-morbidities, disabilities and poor health (Oliver et al., 2014). Older people are disproportionately much heavier users of health care systems. People may live longer, but they cost more to keep alive, they are more likely to have complex, chronic health conditions, and end of life care tends to be more expensive. Health and social care systems are struggling to keep up with these demands. They were not designed to address complex, multiple conditions in an integrated way and for service users this can translate into engaging with multiple services and providers. There is a high level of dependence on institutional and hospital care for older people, and inconsistencies in the quality and range of services. Social care is currently not meeting the needs and expectations of older people who have said that they want care, support and treatment in or close to home and support for independent living. The impact of the recession and government action which has reduced expenditure, particularly in adult social care, presents a major challenge in the UK. This has produced pressure on integrated practice to prove cost-effectiveness and reduce expenditure on the acute sector.

Main themes in integrated approaches

Transformational service reform is required to respond to growing demand with an increased emphasis on prevention services, community based services, and personalisation. The most effective method of delaying or avoiding the onset of debilitating and long-term conditions is prevention (Goldberg, 2014). Many of the conditions such as heart disease, obesity and diabetes dealt with by health care systems are preventable. In 2013, approximately 23 per cent (114,740 out of 506,790) of all deaths registered in England and Wales were from causes considered avoidable through good quality health care or wider public health interventions. Addressing these issues is problematic when the focus has been on assisting those deemed to be in greatest need. Clearly a prevention agenda is not solely in the domain of either health or social care but requires an integrated multi-agency approach aimed at reablement, rapid responses and community based holistic approaches to reduce the necessity for admission to acute hospital care.

A shift to community-based care from acute care has become a core aspect of policy development. This implies close effective collaboration, particularly with primary care, with GPs, community nursing, mental health nurses, physiotherapists, occupational therapists. It also means an emphasis on domiciliary care and supporting independent living, replacing residential care including effective and planned hospital discharge. Personalisation has also developed as a key theme, covering an emphasis on person-centred provision, moving away from institution-centred or provider-centred, towards strategies for person-directed care, direct payments and individual budgets (Needham and Glasby, 2014; Locke and West, 2016).

Another challenge relates to technological innovation as new provision is constantly being developed. Most obviously in pharmaceuticals, but also in surgery, diagnostics, telemedicine, we are consistently developing new methods to cure or manage disease. In some cases this translates into more effective treatments than the current ones and it also means developing new treatments for illnesses or problems which were hitherto deemed to be untreatable. New drugs, diagnostic methods, drug delivery systems and new devices offer the hope of dealing with diseases more effectively. Fragmented communication between and within health care services has been a perennial issue in the NHS. Advances in information technology (IT) can vastly improve the efficiency and effectiveness of health care delivery. Despite the fact that the world has never possessed such a sophisticated array of health care interventions and technologies, health systems remain unable to deliver services to those in greatest need, efficiently and effectively. Fragmentation, poor coordination, duplication and ineffective IT communication across services can result in poor outcomes.

Unsurprisingly these innovations and technological developments have influenced service users' expectations and demands. Each generation demands and expects more from the health service than the previous one. The reality is that in today's modern age the expectations of how health care is delivered are changing. Patients increasingly go online for health information and advice; they self-diagnose and create treatment plans (Ham et al., 2012). They are no longer content to be passive recipients of health care delivered by experts. The banking and retailing industries in particular have revolutionised the way in which they engage with customers and individuals expect similar treatment from their health care providers.

Consumers, particularly younger ones, increasingly expect health care to perform in a similar way to other markets with transparency, accountability and a range of choices available. They expect to be consulted and involved in health care decisions; be able to access clear information quickly and easily; find a solution or cure for conditions and illnesses; and experience an efficient, approachable and responsive service. These challenges combine to be largely responsible for the related issue of rapidly increasing costs. Within health care systems there is persistent pressure to increase funding, a pressure particularly keenly felt against the backdrop of a global recession. A reduction in the resource available for health care in many countries has led to a focus on efficiency, effectiveness, reconfiguration of services and value for money, transparency, targets and the quality of performance.

The implementation of integration

Under pressure to deliver quality services that are responsive to users' demands, policy-makers, clinicians, practitioners and academics have been grappling with the question of how to strengthen the health and social care system. What are the characteristics of a successful system and how can they be achieved? Whilst this may mean greater levels of investment, it also requires consideration of how resources could be used more effectively through different ways of working. The integration of health and social care is a long-standing public policy agenda as it is widely believed to have the ability to address many of the problems identified in the existing configuration of services. Working in an integrated way could improve the efficiency, cost-effectiveness and organisational aspects of the system and be centred on the needs of individuals. Integration and integrated initiatives have had to be implemented in England, Scotland and Wales in the continuing context of organisational division between the NHS and local government. Whilst uniquely in Northern Ireland health and social care are structurally integrated. Policies and integrated structures also have been implemented in different ways between the four countries of the UK. Particularly in England the implementation of joined-up care has taken place amidst complex, fragmented and changing structures. To date much of the integration agenda in England has been introduced on a piecemeal and individual programme basis with much use of national pilots and experimentation. Financial pressures and public expenditure reductions have had an impact on social care provision, especially in England, although also across the UK. Implementation of integration has also been taking place, strongly influenced by new agendas of personalisation, user participation, workforce development, inspection and regulation and more targeted financial investment.

Structure of book

The book is organised to give an account of developments in policy and practice in the integration of health and social care in the UK. There is a particular emphasis on the most current developments with the policy priority given to

Box 1.5	Summary of Integrated Structures in the UK	

Country	Form of structure	Main bodies involved
England	Partnerships (diversity of types)	NHS health trusts, community trusts, local councils, Clinical Commissioning Groups
Scotland	Partnerships (uniform system)	Health Boards and local councils, Integration Authorities
Wales	Partnerships	Health Boards and local councils, Public Service Boards
Northern Ireland	Integrated Health and Social Care	Health and Social Care Boards, Health and Social Care Trusts

integration and with initiatives in legislation, funding structures and experimentation in practice. The content of the book gives recognition to the significance of devolution as the four countries in the UK have moved to divergence in integrated policies, structures and provision. England has remained as the main centre for policy development and analysis, innovation and research, pilots and evaluation and as a location for some significant differences between localities. A theme of the book is the formulation and implementation of new legislation, along with the objectives, implications and outcomes. A major theme is also to assess the achievements of integration in the UK and subsequently examine what this demonstrates about factors promoting integration and what can be identified as continuing barriers to integration.

The introductory chapter explains the rationale for the book in terms of the increasing attention and government prioritising and gives a summary of the background to the government policy of integration and reasons for its growing importance. The rationales and factors justifying integration are discussed. This chapter also explores the definitions and concepts of integration and changes that have taken place in major commentaries and literature. The range of services included within concepts of integration and the scope of integration are explained. Organisational differences, between structural integration and partnerships, and other forms of collaboration are also discussed. The significance of a UK wide approach and analysis is explained. An account is also given of the main sources used in the book.

The next two chapters are devoted to an account of developments in England through the evolution of policies and the implementation of major strategies and initiatives. Chapter 2 covers the period up until 2012–14 from the late 1990s and covers the formulation of strong support for integration in a series of government reports and strategies. It deals with the introduction of the Flexibilities approach and the growth in collaboration and partnerships between local government and primary care trusts plus the rather ill-fated structural experiment with Care Trusts. The trend towards the use of local experimentation and pilots is also explained and the continuing pressure from different sources for new and expanded policies backed up by legislation. Chapter 3 continues with the focus on developments in England, particularly the impact of new legislation on health and social care and the Care Act 2014 and the role of new institutions, the Clinical Commissioning Groups and Health and Wellbeing Boards. New initiatives, the Integrated Care Pioneer Programme, the Better Care Fund, the Vanguard scheme and the devolution proposals for city regions in England are covered. Some attention is also paid to the growing importance of scrutiny, regulatory and inspection bodies, such as NICE, the Care Quality Commission and NHS Improvement, later incorporating Monitor. This chapter also examines some recent developments with expanded integration to include other services, for example, housing.

The next chapters deal separately with the development and provision of integrated health and social care in Scotland, Wales and Northern Ireland. Chapter 4 gives an account of the growth of partnership working in Scotland between local councils and NHS boards and its expansion over time. A number of health strategies and legislative measures have promoted integration and the breaking down of barriers and setting a vision for integration. Developments in the implementation of integration are traced through the New Future Strategy, community health partnerships, health and social care partnerships and the legislation establishing Integration Authorities. The expansion in scope of integrated services from the original focus on older people is described. An assessment is made of the performance of integration in Scotland and the focus on workforce development and GP involvement.

Chapter 5 outlines how the Welsh Assembly Government moved to take over full legislative responsibilities for integration and how partnerships were promoted between 22 local councils and seven local health boards. Local authority social services in Wales have retained a separate identity although a reduction in the number of councils is under consideration. The alignment between health and social care has developed within a strong Welsh policy commitment to reduce inequalities, improve services and encourage early prevention. There has also been a strong focus in Wales on joined-up services through 'Making the Connections' and other strategies. A number of strategies in the social care field have raised the profile of integration and the Health and Well-being Act 2014 has strengthened collaboration, with local councils required to promote integration between local councils and local health boards. It is noted that the Welsh government is committed to protecting expenditure on social care, rather than health care, and has given priority to older people, chronic conditions, intermediate care, and GP involvement. To date the format and arrangements for integration have operated with a degree of local discretion throughout Wales.

Chapter 6 provides an outline of the development of the structural integration of health and social care in Northern Ireland, the origins of the policy and its emergence as a unique example of comprehensive structural integration. The detailed operation of integrated provision and a policy of transformation through a shift from acute care to community based care are described.

An account is given of the main features of integrated working through integrated teams, a single employer, a single source of funding, integrated management and integrated commissioning. The Northern Ireland model has given rise to much discussion about the benefits and achievements of structural integration and an assessment is made of successes but also of difficulties in realising the full potential of structural integration. Attention is also given to concerns about the status of social care within the structure and the rationale for an initiative to set up internal integrated care partnerships within the existing structure.

Three chapters make an assessment of progress with the implementation of integration and the outcomes. Chapter 7 examines the achievements of integration and examples of integration working. This process means using a range of research reports, evaluations of pilot studies, Pioneer programmes, case studies and Vanguard experiments, from government, academic, voluntary sector and other sources of data. There is a certain reluctance to identify outstanding examples of successful outcomes and a recognition of the limitations in research to date. Evidence is examined in relation to clinical criteria, and the major areas of achievement such as integrated teams, care pathways, unified assessment and commissioning, reablement and intermediate care and sharing of information. Also discussed is evidence on cost reductions, user satisfaction and involvement of GPs. There is also an examination of any apparent differences between different user groups and types of services. Chapter 8 makes an analysis of the factors contributing to the promotion of integration and making it work. Evidence is analysed to determine the group of major factors which appear to make the most impact in fostering integration and integrated practice. Quite a wide range of factors advancing integration are identified including: financial support, information sharing, leadership, production of vision statements, education and training, co-location, GP involvement, and user and carer support. The research and literature also suggest some other relevant but less important factors. Some potential factors, such as structural integration, prompt more of a difference of opinion as to their importance in promoting integration. Chapter 9 examines the other side of this argument by focusing on what have been identified as barriers to the introduction and advancement of integration. The language of barriers is still frequently used and there is a degree of consensus on what are the major difficulties. Some of the obstacles can be of a complex nature. The major barriers to integration identified in this analysis include professional differences, lack of equity between health and social care, lack of information sharing, financial difficulties, lack of clarity in procedures and workforce and training issues. Some mention is made of other less important or more specialist or localist barriers that arise more infrequently.

Chapter 10 examines a different dimension in drawing upon international evidence, research and commentaries, and considers any lessons that might be applied to UK experience. It was not the intention to carry out a full comparison but some interesting comparative aspects can be analysed. The international lessons are drawn mainly from European countries, the USA, Canada and Australia. The dominant theme that emerges is the lack of a clear definition of integrated health and social care and instead a focus on a joined-up approach to chronic conditions and the care of older people. The term integration is often used to refer to integrated health care. It is also noted that the practice of integrated care often occurs at a local level within the jurisdiction of small local government councils. The conclusion, in Chapter 11 of the book, sums up the current state of progress to greater integration. A final general comparison is made between the four countries of the UK, commenting particularly on structural differences with structural integration in Northern Ireland, uniform partnerships in Scotland and more diffuse forms of partnerships in England and Wales. An assessment is also made of the consequences of the new legislative frameworks promoting integration in Great Britain. The main features of the operation of integration are identified, the main areas of expansion in activities, and consideration is given to potential future developments. Attention is drawn to the continuing importance of experimentation, research and evaluation of initiatives and the growing importance of workforce development. It is clear that integration will continue to be a major priority within health and social care with a key role in meeting future needs and reducing pressures on acute care.

Sources

As integration has become a topical issue and the subject of much government attention, debate and legislation, there has been a significant growth in the literature and the sources of material that can be drawn upon. A major source of material is government reports, publications of the Department of Health, and other UK government agencies, such as NHS England. The role of local government in delivering social care means that a range of local authority bodies, particularly the Local Government Association, publish reports on integration as well as individual local councils. The three devolved administrations through their government departments and agencies also produce separate reports, evaluations, and guidance. Other UK professional representative bodies are also frequent commentators, for example, the Association of Directors of Adult Social Care, the NHS Confederation, and the BMA, and they also operate and publish through devolved offices. The published output of the UK Parliament is also important through particularly select committee reports, the National Audit Office and parliamentary briefings. Again this work is replicated in the Scottish Parliament, and the Welsh and Northern Ireland Assemblies, and through the work of their research offices. There has also been a growth in the activities of regulation and inspection bodies, such as the Care Quality Commission. The scale and scope of research reports and policy evaluation have also continued to develop particularly from think tanks, led by The King's Fund but also by other bodies, the Nuffield Trust, the Social Care Institute for Excellence and the Health Foundation. Use is also made of traditional academic sources in terms of books, research reports, occasional papers, and journal articles, especially the specialist *Journal of Integrated Care*, as well as the *International Journal of Integrated Care and Health and Social Care in the Community*. A number of journals/magazines representing practitioners and professional organisations and the voluntary sector also produce contemporary commentaries.

Terminology

Throughout the book the term United Kingdom (UK) refers to England, Scotland, Wales and Northern Ireland, while the term Great Britain refers to England, Scotland and Wales. The term UK government refers to the Westminster government in London and UK departments to Whitehall departments but their responsibilities for health and social care apply almost wholly to England. The term devolved administrations, when used, refers to the systems of devolved governance in Scotland, Wales and Northern Ireland. Devolved governments are described individually as, the Scottish government, the Welsh government but formerly the Welsh Assembly government and the Northern Ireland Executive rather than the Northern Ireland government. The term social care is used in a comprehensive way to describe adult social care but some historical references or quotes may use the terms social services and personal social services or social work services. The terms local authorities, local councils and local government are largely interchangeable. Also the terms quangos, arm's-length bodies and non-departmental public bodies largely describe the same organisations. The terms partnerships and trusts are frequently used and their meanings explained in the text.

2 Development of Policies and Strategies in England

Policy development specifically related to the integration of health and social care has quite a substantial history, usually identified as going back to the 1970s. This process has normally been dominated by the UK government and the responsible government department, although some policy discretion was exercised by the Scottish Office, the Welsh Office and the Northern Ireland Office and local administrations. After 1999 policies produced by the UK government applied only to England although some of these ideas and strategies could still influence developments in the new devolved administrations.

Policies and strategies pre-1999

Policies on the integration of health and social care have occupied a central role in major government thinking, reports and inquiries and department papers, and through these the emergence of a clear commitment to integration and the priority given to it can be traced.

The divisions between social care and health had become more structured and identifiable following the implementation of the Seebohm Report in the early 1970s, with the creation of comprehensive social service departments in local government. A reorganisation of the NHS saw community health services move out of local authorities into the NHS. Policies involving health services were largely to emerge separately from social care. The direction of major policy development in social care in the following years related to community care and this debate did serve to highlight relevant issues linked to collaborative working. *Caring for People* (DH, 1989), a UK government White Paper, set out proposals for improving community care and a new strategic framework of care assessment, provision and management. These proposals were built on the Griffiths Report (1988) which had recommended the lead role in community care for local authorities. Griffiths had been critical of the failures of joint working; however, *Caring for People* did recognise that over the past 15 years policies designed to promote collaboration between health and local authorities had emerged, focused on mechanisms for joint planning and joint finance. The *Caring for People* White Paper noted that its proposals would substantially strengthen the underlying incentives for health and social services to work closer together and a whole chapter was devoted to collaborative working. The approach to collaboration was based on three elements: clarifying who does what; redefining joint planning to suit local authorities more; and joint finance which shifted resources across the boundary between health and social care (DH, 1989, p. 51). It has been suggested that despite the record of shortcomings and failure, interagency cooperation at this time was put firmly on the agenda (Hudson and Henwood, 2002). However, it has also been argued that despite the recognition of the need to collaborate, the actual principle of health and social integration hardly got a look-in (Greig, 2012). In 1990 the NHS and Community Care Act enacted proposals giving local authorities major responsibility for social care, rather than the promotion of integration. Under this legislation social service functions in local government expanded considerably, with a substantial transfer to local authorities of resources from the social security programme (Hill, 2000, p. 182). The NHS and Community Care Act also enacted proposals from a government health White Paper *Working for Patients* to extend choice and value for money. An internal market in the health service was created by separating the purchasing function from the provision of services by hospitals and GPs. The purchaser–provider split was extended to social care with local authorities no longer obliged to directly provide services (Johnson, 1990). In general, therefore, during the 1990s the boundary between health and social care tended to develop with a focus on competition rather than collaboration (Hudson and Henwood, 2002). This view was endorsed by Glendinning and Means (2004) arguing also that the delivery of the purchaser–provider system did not produce better collaboration as quasi-markets created new barriers. Lewis (2001) adds the view that at the time social care delivery was not at the forefront of government thinking.

Promoting partnerships and the Flexibilities agenda

With the election of a Labour government in 1997 a change in policy direction took place and the development of partnerships was seen as the key to more effective delivery. Hudson and Henwood (2002, p. 157) refer to a shift in values so that collaboration was not simply back on the agenda but was to be at the heart of new policies on health and social care in the form of partnerships. A major debate was prompted by a discussion document, *Partnership in Action* (DH, 1998a). This fulfilled a commitment to consult on ways to improve partnership working between health and social care. This paper discussed a statutory duty of partnership working, the removal of legislative constraints and declared training and education, as all important in order to support and develop competences for collaborative working. A background factor was a strong government commitment to also improve inter-agency collaboration in child protection. *Partnership in Action* also referred to policy options including the introduction of incentives to allow more flexibility in the transfer of funds between partnership authorities, as well as a statutory duty of partnership. A government White Paper on social service provision in its totality quickly followed. *Modernising Social Services* (DH, 1998b) promised action with a strong emphasis on performance, improving standards, inspection and training, and created a new Social Services Modernisation Fund. *Modernising Social Services* identified a New Labour third way for social care, based on a number of key principles around the quality of services and supporting people's independence to live in their own homes. Improving partnerships between social care and other services, such as the NHS, was not described as a key principle but was treated as a mechanism for more effective delivery. A chapter of the White Paper was devoted to improving partnerships and quoted examples of good practice in joint working: local hospitals appointing discharge coordinators to work closely with local social service departments and creating community care multidisciplinary teams for patients in their own homes. The White Paper called for a new spirit of flexible partnership working which moved away from sterile conflicts over boundaries, although a major reorganisation of service boundaries was ruled out (DH, 1998b, p. 97). There was a declaration that the government had made it one of its priorities to bring down the 'Berlin Wall' that divides health and social services and to create a system of integrated care. The NHS was seen as a crucial partner in almost all social services work. Three key proposals were mooted to make it easier for health and social services authorities to work together: pooled budgets, lead commissioning and integrated provision.

The proposals outlined in *Modernising Social Services* were enacted in the Health Act 1999. In section 31 it introduced what became known as the Health Act Flexibilities, enabling local councils and the NHS to work more closely together. The three Flexibilities related to:

- pooled budgets, involving local health and social services putting money into a single dedicated budget to fund a wide range of care services;
- lead commissioning, with either the local authority or the primary care group taking the lead in commissioning services on behalf of both bodies;
- integrated provision, with local authorities and health authorities merging their services to deliver a one-stop package of care. (DH, 2000)

The NHS Plan (DH, 2000) was surprisingly to add a further major element to the promotion of integration with the most radical proposal to date from the Department of Health. *The NHS Plan* restated a belief in partnerships as the means of overcoming the old division between health and social care. It was noted that only a minority of bodies were using Flexibilities together and many people were being denied access to seamless services. A more fundamental reform was needed to tackle such problems (DH, 2000, p. 71). Proposed was a new level of Care Trust to provide closer integration of health and social care. Care Trusts would be single multi-purpose legal bodies to commission and be responsible for health and social care. They would deliver primary and community health and social care for older people and other client groups and would deliver under delegated authority from local councils. It was recommended that Care Trusts would be established where there were joint agreements at local level (DH, 2000, p. 73). They would be part of the NHS although local councils would have representation on the governing board. NHS Primary Care Trusts (PCTs), only formed in 2000, were to be the basis for closer integrated working. Legislation to permit the creation of care trusts was included in the Health and Social Care Act 2001. At one stage it looked as if the minister would assume powers for the compulsory creation of care trusts but this was not pursued. However, there was an expectation that by 2004 all PCTs would have moved to care trust status with all adult care services commissioned by care trusts within five years (Hudson and Henwood, 2002, p. 162). It seemed possible that Care Trusts represented a new policy to replace partnership working through section 31 notifications and use of Flexibilities. Initially 15 pilots were started, leading to only five care trusts being launched, and the total number in operation was never to grow beyond 10 or 11 in operation at any one time, out of a possible 152. The lack of a specific blueprint meant that there could be considerable variation in what services were covered (Glasby and Peck, 2003). The original expectation was that Care Trusts would focus on mental health and older people's services, but a range of logistical difficulties emerged in IT, finance, human resources and governance (Miller et al., 2011). Local authorities were to fail to actively endorse the concept and its structural implications. Issues that arose included: a fear of losing all their social care responsibilities to the NHS; worries that the NHS was colonising social services; doubts about the evidence that the structures would work; and concern that care Trusts would promote a medical model rather than a social model of care (Glendinning and Means, 2004, p. 445). Local authority attention and resources had also soon to be directed away towards the internal changes required by government policy for the separation of adult social care from children's services. Care Trusts did remain an option for a number of years and an operating model of a more structural form of integration of health and social care in England (see below).

Transforming care and integration policies under New Labour

Post 2002 the New Labour administration and subsequently the Coalition government were to regard joint working as a key feature of developing strategies for health and social care. This was driven by the needs of an ageing population, the increase of long-term conditions and a policy of shifting resources from the acute health sector to prevention, and primary and community care. This approach and its development under New Labour can be seen in a number of strategy and policy papers which covered both health and social care.

Box 2.1	Government Strategies for Health and Social Care

Delivering the NHS Plan (DH, 2002)

Although dealing mainly with health and tackling major capacity constraints suffered by the NHS, the NHS Plan called for a radically different relationship between health and social services to fundamentally change the way jobs are designed and work organised.

Independence, Well-Being and Choice: Our Vision for Future Social Care (DH, 2005)

This Green Paper proposed a continuation of a transformation across social care primarily relating to the organisation of social care by government agencies and voluntary bodies, with more focus on preventative services. The vision included social care and the NHS working on a shared agenda to maintain the independence of individuals. The discussion underlined a vital leading role for local government working in partnership with other agencies, particularly the NHS, to ensure a range of provision. The Green Paper explored mechanisms for strengthening collaboration and partnership working.

Our Health, Our Care, Our Say: A New Direction for Community Services (DH, 2006a)

This White Paper, following the Green Discussion Paper, came out with a commitment to move to an emphasis on better and early prevention and delivering social care in a more integrated way with the NHS. It called for a fundamental shift towards integrated services provided in local communities. There was a new emphasis on personalisation with more choice and voice and putting the needs of patients and service users at the heart of service improvement. Local health and social care communities would work together to address inequalities.

Our Health, Our Care, Our Say: Making It Happen (DH, 2006b)

The paper on implementation saw increasing opportunities for partnership working between local authorities, the NHS and the third sector. Some 70 per cent of PCT boundaries were co-terminous with local authorities, offering better opportunities to strengthen partnership working. It called for much more joint care planning commissioning between PCTs and local authorities and for joint networks and teams to support people with complex needs. Also to be implemented were plans for workforce planning responsive provider initiatives and a joint outcomes focused framework with performance assessment and inspection regimes.

Putting People First: A Shared Vision and Commitment to the Transformation of Adult Social Care (HM Government, 2007)

This was the government's vision, outlining the shared aims and values for transforming social care. Basically the document was a protocol, signed by government ministers, local government associations, the NHS and other statutory bodies. The aim was to support social care working in partnership with health to create a shared and high quality system. *Putting People First* confirmed that reform can only be delivered through a collaborative approach which could secure responsive and seamless services. Local authorities would take the leadership role, accompanied by authentic partnership working with the local NHS and voluntary bodies.

High Quality Care for All, Darzi Review (DH, 2008)

Although the Darzi Review was focused on improving health and the NHS and empowering patients, it did call for services to be better coordinated and integrated to provide supportive, person centred services based on earlier and cost-effective intervention. Darzi wished to ensure that every Primary Care Trust commissioned comprehensive well-being and prevention services, in partnership with local councils, to offer personalised services to the local population.

Shaping the Future of Care Together (DH, 2009)

This Green Paper had a background of the vision of *Putting People First*. A major subject for discussion was options for funding adult social care in the future. However, the paper also produced a radical advance in thinking with a proposal for the development of a National Care Service. Services would be fully joined up between the NHS and the National Care Service. As it was expressed all the services you needed would work together smoothly. Particular attention was given to a common assessment framework. The Green Paper stated that although services must work together this did not mean structural change was necessary. The potential importance of the proposal for a National Care Service was demonstrated by the establishment of a ministerial group on the integration of health and social care services. This would identify what has worked well, identify barriers and help push forward integration.

These government papers show the development of a strong commitment to a key role for integrated strategies and the priority given to them. However, it has been argued that the aspirations expressed in these strategies were largely unfulfilled (or successful in only some areas (Wistow, 2011, p. 106)), or only partially implemented. The mid to late 2000s saw a renewed focus on competition in the NHS based on an assumption that competition and choice would drive up quality in a diverse social care market (Lewis and West, 2014). The Transforming Community Services Programme supported the separation of NHS commissioning and provider functions, disrupting integrated health and social care arrangements. PCTs began to divest themselves of their provider role to concentrate on commissioning. A care trust in Solihull ceased to exist as it was no longer viable when its community services were separated from its commissioning functions and the services to an NHS Trust and a local council.

NHS reforms and impact on integration

The existence of a political consensus on the promotion of integration continued to be underlined by the priority and profile given to the policy by the Coalition government in papers and proposals. Integration was to feature as a significant component in the vision and plans of the coalition for both health and social care. The coalition set out its long-term vision for the future of the NHS in a White Paper, *Equity and Excellence: Liberating the NHS* (DH, 2010a). It envisaged the removal of PCTs which had been the main partner for councils in developed integrated services (Humphries and Curry, 2011, p. 8). The focus was on clinical outcomes, and empowering health professions and patients. The White Paper did recognise the critical independence between the NHS and the adult social care system in securing better outcomes for people, including carers. It declared 'we will seek to break down barriers between health and social care funding to encourage preventative action' (DH, 2010a, p. 10). It was seen as essential for patient outcomes that health and social care are integrated at all levels of the system. A further government paper *Local Democratic Legitimacy in Health* (DH, 2010b) proposed expanding the role of councils in decision making in health, seen as highly significant in joining up and bridging health, social care and public health (Wistow, 2011). A core element of the reform proposals, however, was the creation of GP commissioning consortia which would replace Primary Care Trusts (PCTs), who had a key role in existing integrated partnership working. Following the White Paper the Coalition proposed to put the reforms into practice through a major Health and Social Care Bill. A government paper on implementation accepted the new GP consortia would work together with local government and have an equal and explicit obligation to do so. Thus the promotion of integration across the NHS and social care was seen as critical and it was stated action would be taken to free-up structures to support joint working and also to remove barriers (DH, 2010c). This meant that the health reform measure, the Health and Social Care Act, 2012 was to become a major vehicle to promote integrated working. With considerable criticism of the health reform proposals and the health minister, especially on the issue of competition, the Coalition government decided on a break; to pause, listen and reflect on modernisation and improvement plans. There was evidence that the more commercially minded policy approaches of Labour's Transforming Community Services Programme and the proposed new Health and Social Care Act could destabilise existing partnerships, thereby creating new tensions across the health and social care divide. Farnsworth (2012b) discussed the possible damaging consequences for Torbay's Integrated Care Trust, relating to the lack of leadership, fragmentation of funding, and a change in commissioning responsibility, likely leading to the abolition of the Trust. The listening exercise, conducted by a large advisory panel, produced a set of recommendations accepted by government (National Institute for Health Research, 2011). Messages from this *NHS Future Forum* (DH, 2011) stated it was clear that the health service needs to drive integration in a way that has simply never happened to date. Integration was seen as a virtually important aspect of the experience of health and social care for millions of people. The NHS Future Forum's recommendations included giving commissioners and providers freedom and flexibility to 'get on and do' and make integration commonplace.

The better integration of commissioning across health and social care was proposed to be a key vehicle for integration in all areas. It was also recommended that local commissioners should fully and properly explore the potential benefits of joint commissioning and pooled budgets for key populations. The proposed centralised NHS Commissioning Board would work with local commissioners to introduce measures of service interoperability in contracts. It also recommended that the Department of Health should seek greater alignment and coherence between the national outcomes frameworks, the NHS, public health and local authorities. A further recommendation proposed that Health and Wellbeing Boards (HWBs), located in local authorities, should become the crucible for health and social care integration (NHS Future Forum, 2012, p. 6). They were envisaged as providing the basis for better collaboration, partnership working and integration across local government and the NHS. The main drivers of integration would be the GP consortia (now known as Clinical Commissioning Groups or CCGs) and the NHS Commissioning Board. The Act created a duty for CCGs, the NHS Commissioning Board and Monitor, the regulatory body, to promote integrated services between the NHS and social care where this would improve quality and efficiency and reduce inequalities. One of the main objectives then of the Health and Social Act was to encourage and enable more integration between services and the recommendations of the NHS Future Forum on how to strengthen integration were accepted in full. Local councils were not to be empowered to oversee CCG plans but the proposals were seen as representing the first weakening of silo structures since the creation of the NHS (Wistow, 2012, p. 107). This legislative package of proposals for integration was viewed as demonstrating substantial learning from earlier evaluations and experience (Wistow, 2012, p. 107), although the author noted the potential of working across local authorities, and NHS services had yet to be fully exploited. He suggested integration had remained at the margins of NHS and local government business (Wistow, 2012, p. 110). Additionally, it was suggested making the arrangements work would depend on trust, building relationships, and investing time, rather than legislation (Hudson, 2011).

Social care reform and integration

The Coalition's vision for social care was set out in the paper *The Vision for Adult Social Care* (DH, 2010d). This contained a commitment to a new direction for adult social care, putting prevention, personalised services and best outcomes central stage. The first of three specific commitments was to 'break down barriers between health and social care funding to incentivise preventative action' (Figure 2.1) (DH, 2010d, p. 6).

Liberating the NHS provided an opportunity for a much greater degree of coordination and integrated working to shift the balance of power. The vision paper proposed that local councils would have a lead role in ensuring local services are more coherent, responsive and integrated. The government would

Figure 2.1	Timeline 2010–2014			
A Vision for Adult Social Care	Law Commission Social Care	Caring for Our Future	Health and Social Care Act	Care and Support Act
Nov. 2010	May 2011	Sep. 2011 *Act*	Sep. 2011	Jul. 2014

identify and remove barriers to collaboration and to the pooling or alignment of budgets across health and social care. Local councils would work with the NHS and other partners to pool funding streams at local level.

This vision paper was followed by the White Paper *Caring for Our Future* (DH, 2012a) which was published alongside a draft Care and Support Bill. Given the treatment of integration in the Health and Social Care Bill, the White Paper had not an immediate focus on integration. Two principles were put forward as core to the White Paper: firstly, preventing and maintaining independence and, secondly, that people should be in control of their own care and support. However, the foreword to the White Paper recognised that the transformation it envisaged and had set out in the Care and Support Bill would only come about were it a genuine collaborative endeavour and transitional boundaries dissolved. *Caring for Our Future*, in discussing integration, noted the clear objectives in the Health and Social Care Act and its relationship with the Care and Support Bill. It also noted that the NHS Commissioning Board, Clinical Commissioning Groups, Monitor and HWBs all have duties to promote and enable integration. It added that integrated services were expected to be person-centred, to improve outcomes and to reduce inequalities. The declared ambition was for everyone who uses health, care and support to experience joined-up services. The draft Bill set out a duty on the local authority to promote the integration of services, along similar lines to the duty on the local NHS already enacted by the 2012 Act. It was anticipated that modernisation would create greater opportunities and freedoms to work across systems to develop innovative services. A promise was made that the government would publish a framework to support the removal of barriers to making evidence based integrated care and support the norm. A range of ideas were suggested, measuring users' experience of integrated care, sharing tools for integration, aligning incentives, models of coordinating care and better integration at transitional points (DH, 2012b).

The Care and Support Bill sought to deliver the vision in the White Paper, although circumstances meant that the Bill was used to introduce specifically health measures to address issues arising from the failings in care at Mid-Staffordshire Hospital. The main focus in the Bill was taking forward the recommendations of the Law Commission for the reform and modernisation of adult social care legislation. The first part of the Bill contained reform measures aimed at achieving the aspirations of the White Paper *Caring for Our Future*. Measures included treating carers as equal to the cared, developing national eligibility criteria, adopting preventative approaches, and placing a cap on care costs. Integration was regarded as one of the main topics of part one of the Bill. A key aim was described as 'providing the freedom and flexibility needed by local authorities and care professionals to integrate with other local services, to innovate and achieve better results for people' (DH, 2013a). Clause three placed a duty on local authorities to carry out their care and support functions with the aim of integrating services with those provided by the NHS and other health-related services, and to work together to provide improved outcomes. This clause was intended to apply broadly across local authority functions and to reflect the partner duty on the NHS to provide integration, contained in the Health and

Social Care Act 2012. The general duty to promote coordinated health and social care as a matter of course was backed up by a more specific duty to cooperate in relation to individual cases. A local authority can request help from partners or vice versa to help with a specific issue to do with a user or carer. This duty to cooperate did not cover independent providers and cooperation with the private and voluntary sectors was left to be achieved through the commissioning process. Notwithstanding the focus on a statutory duty to cooperate, the existing boundaries between the care and support system and the NHS were to be maintained. The Health and Social Care Act became operative in 2013 bringing into being a range of significant new structures including the National Commissioning Board (which was to be known as 'NHS England') and HWBs with duties to make it easier for health and social care to work together. The Care and Support Act became law in 2014 for implementation in April 2015.

Support for integration from non-statutory bodies

The policy of integration has received much support and attention from a wide range of organisations which have conducted policy analyses, research and evaluation, collected evidence and published reports with recommendations on policy and practice. Some of these views which were significant are described from four categories of such bodies: Parliament; professional and representative bodies; research and policy institutes; voluntary organisations and other statutory bodies.

Parliament

The most major parliamentary study of integration was undertaken by the Health Committee in 2012 (House of Commons Health Committee, 2012). The Committee came to the view that the separate systems of the NHS and social care are inefficient and lead to poorer outcomes. The Health Committee recommended that while integration was not an end in itself it can be a very powerful tool to improve outcomes for people. It was seen as especially valuable for people with disabilities, long-term conditions and those who need multiple services. It noted that real progress had been made with a fully integrated approach to commissioning. They paid particular attention to the value of having a single pot of money from different sources to deploy to meet people's needs. In making the case for integration the Health Committee said that integration should become the main business for health and social care. However, it can be noted that the Committee put forward the view that a precise institutional framework was not important and admitted that it was wary of recommending a solution based on a single structure.

The views of professional and representative organisations

The Association of Directors of Adult Social Services (ADASS) recognised rising demands and scarce resources had led to renewed interest in integrated care as a solution (ADASS, 2010). It noted the benefits of integration in relieving pressures on the NHS. There was also a commitment in 2012 to bring forward the further integration of services and support. A specific commitment was an agreement with the Royal College of Psychiatrists to facilitate working together, with integrated budgets and integrated assessment (ADASS, 2013). Statements by ADASS noted that furthering integration was not necessarily about changing structures or bureaucracy but about culture, behaviour and values. The NHS Confederation stressed that developing integrated care was critical to keep pace with today's changing needs. It also stressed the case for redesigning models of health care to integrate with social care in one comprehensive service. At macro-level it called for a more coordinated approach to policy development between health and social care nationally, and at micro-level for mixed professional teams to enable further integration. Community health care has been seen as an important area for collaborative approaches, particularly in discharge services (NHS Confederation, 2013). However, the NHS Confederation stated integrated working was not solely about organisational mergers, and was more about cultures, not structures. In 2016 the NHS Confederation with the Local Government Association published 'Stepping Up to the Place', examining the key to successful health and care integration and the imperative to integrate and transform and to put integrated systems and services to the test.

The Local Government Association (LGA) has also been supportive of integration but has warned that integration should not be seen as an end in itself. Instead it should be seen as part of the bigger goal of successful adult social care and support reform. It has emphasised the importance of integrated commissioning. Again there has been a caveat about the government dictating structural solutions. The Local Government Association has recognised that local councils have worked increasingly closely with health bodies and there is the basis for developing even closer, more effective working at both a national and a local level in future (Local Government Association, 2013a).

The British Medical Association (BMA) as an organisation supports collaboration between health and social care services and the breaking down of burdensome barriers that do not benefit patients. It has noted that boundaries are becoming increasingly blurred between health and social care and has identified a general agreement that closer integration of services and resources can secure long-term gains in efficiency, quality and productivity. However, surveys of BMA members have demonstrated some uncertainty about the beneficial outcomes of integration and also little support for organisational mergers (BMA, 2011).

Policy and research institutes

The King's Fund and the Nuffield Trust have both conducted and published a succession of reports, papers and evaluations around the subject of integration. The importance attached to the subject reflects the view that the integration of health and social care is central to meeting the challenges faced by the NHS and the social care system. A further report specified benefits in terms of better outcomes, efficient use of existing resources and improved access to services

(Humphries and Curry, 2011). A survey of evidence produced by the King's Fund was held to show that moves to achieve closer integration should continue (Curry and Ham, 2010). The overall position of the King's Fund was described in the view that integrated care offered the most promising approach to improving care and meeting the key financial and demographic pressures facing both local government and the NHS. Progress was assessed by the House of Commons Health Committee as patchy so far, despite evidence that it offers opportunities to deliver better outcomes and financial savings (House of Commons Health Committee, 2012). Recommendations to Parliament were made that it was necessary for local authorities and the NHS to pool resources and adopt a more ambitious approach. It was also suggested that structural or organisational routes to integration would not work unless accompanied by other changes such as new ways of working or integrated service delivery. A paper on transforming the delivery of health and social care advocated the need to integrate care around the needs of people and populations (Ham et al., 2012). The Nuffield Trust has also made integration a major subject for investigation, in evaluation reports, briefing papers and seminar proceedings. A major report in 2009 had advocated a coherent health and social care reforms narrative for partnership working (Ham, 2009). A joint paper by the Nuffield Trust and the King's Fund was produced as a contribution to the work of the NHS Future Forum and in support of the government aim of placing integrated care at the heart of the programme of NHS reform (Goodwin et al., 2012). The message asserted that integrated care was essential to meet the needs of the ageing population and it could be delivered without further legislative change or structural upheaval. This report also stated that proposals for promoting and improving integrated care were widely supported by NHS staff as well as patient groups and other key stakeholders.

The Social Care Institute for Excellence (SCIE) is government sponsored and integrated care has been a major subject for investigation and the theme for many publications, including research briefings, short guides and fuller research and policy reports. There is an emphasis on expanding the evidence base underpinning what works for integration. The SCIE endorsed the position that finding ways of making integration a reality was central to delivering improved outcomes for people. The organisation has also reported that there is a broad consensus from people who use, provide and commission services that more integrated care is better and more effective (SCIE, 2013).

Voluntary organisations

Voluntary bodies have also been generally supportive of the promotion of integration. Quoting some examples, Parkinson's UK has stated it is essential that councils and the NHS use every opportunity to close the gap between health and social care and build services based around the person. They saw this as especially important for conditions such as Parkinson's where integrated care, planning and delivery is essential. Age UK has taken the position that care and support should be better integrated and suggested that frameworks have to be adjusted to help deliver the integration that is required. National Voices, the coalition of health and social care charities, has said that achieving integrated care would be the biggest contribution that health and social care services can make to improving quality and safety and is the biggest step forward people who use services want to see (National Voices, 2013). National Voices also produced a person-centred coordinated care model based on what matters to patients and service users. The model had five dimensions of goals, information, communication, decision making, care planning and transition (National Voices, 2013).

Other statutory bodies

A range of bodies have been supportive of integration as part of their work. Particularly important have been views expressed by The National Audit Office, Monitor, the Law Commission and NHS based bodies. The National Audit Office, having reported on many aspects of health and social care provision, has taken the view that integrated working offers the potential for efficiency savings and improving outcomes for people, although it noted that integrated arrangements can be complex. In an overview of adult social care, the view was expressed that there is a need to think clearly and in a joined-up way about the growing challenges (National Audit Office, 2014). Monitor, the NHS regulatory body established under the Health and Social Care Act, had a duty to enable integrated health care and integrated health and social care. Monitor gave a degree of priority to integration and identified four types of benefit in terms of patient experience, clinical outcome, patient safety and cost efficiency (Monitor, 2012). Monitor also committed itself to ensuring that its actions did not create barriers to integrated care and supporting integrated care by addressing the financial benefits as shared by providers (Monitor, 2012, p. 56). From 2016 Monitor became part of the NHS Improvement organisation.

In 2011 the Law Commission, a government body, carried out a review of existing law on adult social care. It found the current legislative provisions to be outdated, disparate, complex and fragmented. The review was not a policy exercise and the Law Commission was not expected to come up with proposals for law reform which would deliver greater integration of social care services with health (Dow, 2010). However, some of the recommendations had implications for integration. The recommendation on community care assessment proposed that the assessment could be carried out by local authorities in cooperation with other agencies (Law Commission, 2011). The review did examine the legal implications of the health–social care divide and reported that the consultation process had produced an overwhelming message that the divide was contentious and lacked transparency for users. A recommendation was made that there should be an enhanced duty imposed on each social service department to cooperate with other organisations (Law Commission, 2011, p. 149).

Operation of integrated care in England

The operation of integrated care since 2000 can be classified under a number of headings, although in practice the more open and diverse category of partnerships and use of Flexibilities has been dominant.

Care Trusts

The experiment with Care Trusts stands as a unique example of formal structural integration. The organisational form of a Care Trust had been proposed by the NHS Plan (DH, 2000, p. 73). They would be built on existing partnerships but Care Trusts would each be a single, multi-purpose legal body. This would be based on a linkage between a Primary Care Trust and/or NHS Trust and local government functions. Care Trusts were modelled on NHS Trusts and would be within the NHS, with local authorities delegating services to them, but not transferring functions. The governance arrangements would reflect the shared responsibilities. The Health and Social Care Act set out the necessary legal framework based on a partnership of equals (DH, 2002). Otherwise there was a degree of flexibility in the possible arrangements which allowed responses to local situations. Care Trusts would be established through a joint local agreement. They could be provider bodies or combine provision or commissioning but it was not specified which client groups they could focus on (Glasby and Peck, 2003). Spelled out in the NHS plan was the possibility that the minister could make the formation of a Care Trust compulsory where local health and social care organisations had failed to establish effective arrangements for Care Trusts (DH, 2000, p. 73). This threat was not to be pursued (Glasby et al., 2005). The take-up from the opportunity to form Care Trusts was slow and limited. By 2001, 17 applications had been made to the Secretary of State, but by 2002 only five Care Trusts had been launched. These were followed by another three in 2003 and a further three between 2005 and 2007, and then none until 2010 (Miller et al., 2011). This stands against the total of 152 local authorities. Restructuring into Care Trusts did not prove popular, especially with local authorities. Hudson (2002) has referred to reasons for the lack of development: the absence of evidence that the scheme would work; financial difficulties; different cultures and values; problems with different IT and HR systems; and concerns over democratic accountability. Some moves to create Care Trusts broke down over disagreements related to management structures, finance and accountability (Baggot, 2004). Local authorities were concerned at losing their social care responsibilities and anxious about a takeover of functions by the NHS (Glendinning and Means, 2004). The requirements of reorganisation were a further deterrent, especially when local authorities also found they had to undertake a compulsory internal reorganisation of social services under the *Every Child Matters* agenda and set up separate children's trusts (Gray and Birrell, 2013). The total number of Care Trusts remained small and only 11 existed in total at any one time.

All the Care Trusts developed with similar characteristics related to governance.

Box 2.2	Governance Characteristics of Care Trusts

- An NHS Board with health and social care functions
- Set up by a partnership agreement and contract
- Council delegates adult social care functions
- Council representation on Board
- Financial agreement
- One management structure and employer
- Single or shared directors of social services

In practice no Care Trust became a comprehensive provider of community health and all adult social care. From the beginning Care Trusts included different combinations of services.

Box 2.3	Functions of Care Trusts

1. Mental health, learning disability, substance abuse   : 5 Care Trusts
2. Community health, adult services, not mental health : 3 Care Trusts
3. Community health   : 2 Care Trusts
4. Older people and physical disability   : 1 Care Trust

The most popular combination of functions was based around mental health which was attractive as an area of existing collaboration and joint working. The original expectation was that most Care Trusts would focus on older people but this was not to be the case (Miller et al., 2011). Five Care Trusts had similar services over mental health, learning disability and substance abuse. The perceived advantages were described by Camden and Islington Care Trust as: providing access to all mental health services through a single route; a fuller sharing of skills and expertise; quality improvement in both health and social care; and a single complaints procedure (Camden and Islington NHS Foundation Trust, 2013). Within the five Care Trusts organisational differences did exist. Manchester Mental Health and Social Care Trust developed 10 community mental health teams, with the main groups organised under four headings of, later life, adult community, adult inpatient, and psychological services. Sheffield Care Trust emphasised extending integrated approaches in working with GP health centres and housing associations. The Black Country Partnership Care Trust extended its service coverage to community health care for children and families.

Three Care Trusts had a more wide-ranging and different combination of community health services and adult social care but excluded most of mental health. Northumberland Care Trust was the first body to have these more comprehensive functions. It provided a wide range of primary health, community and intermediate health care services, including community nursing, child health services, occupational therapy, palliative care and a wheelchair service. Social care included care management services for older people with mental health problems and for adults with physical or learning disabilities, plus all day care, home care and residential care. Solihull Care Trust delivered community health and social care services by teams which brought together nursing, social care and occupational therapy staff based around GP practices, as well as integrated disability teams and out of hospital services. The commissioning and provision of adult social care as a key function was delivered mainly to older people, or people with a disability, mental illness or dementia. Domiciliary, residential and nursing care was purchased from independent providers and increasingly through direct payments from, local authority departments. Torbay Care Trust developed with a wide range of functions in health and adult social care and went on to develop a high profile model of integrated care. Integrated provision was delivered by health and social care zone teams, clustered around GP practices. They provided comprehensive integrated services, coordinated social care, district nursing, occupational therapy, and physiotherapy, as well as a reablement service with links to other services such as housing. The multidisciplinary teams were co-located which facilitated access and assessment. There were also specialist learning disability teams and complex care teams. The Torbay integrated teams operated seven days a week, were rapid response, had a focus on prevention, elderly people with complex needs, and early discharge, and had a commitment to working with GPs. The Torbay model was supported by pooled budgets, a single HR and financial system, shared IT and integrated commissioning.

The North East Lincolnshire Care Trust Plus was the first of its type with expanded responsibilities for health and social care. It funded the NHS services provided by a local hospital, mental health services and adult social care as well as more specialist services in hospitals and independent providers of care. The Care Trust Plus also provided services such as health visiting, district nursing and learning disability and worked in partnership with GPs. A further development was a change in status of some Care Trusts as they became NHS Foundation Trusts. Four of the five mental health centred Care Trusts achieved Foundation status. This was to be significant following the proposals to replace Primary Care Trusts, which created a question of how a separate model of a small number of Care Trusts could continue. The four trusts were able to plan to continue as NHS Foundation Trusts: Camden and Islington, Manchester, Sheffield, and the Black Country Partnership. The fifth Care Trust with a mental health focus, Bradford District Care Trust, found its contract with Bradford Council ended because of financial cuts. All the other Care Trusts came to an end with the exception of Torbay, which in 2012 changed to Torbay and Southern Devon Health and Care Trust NHS Trust. The new restructured Torbay Trust took on responsibilities for providing community health services in Torbay and South Devon and providing and commissioning adult social care.

The small number of Care Trusts brought into existence has led to some scepticism about the value of an organisation along these lines (Hudson, 2003) and this view appeared to be valid given their abolition or transformation into NHS Foundation Trusts. Care Trusts faced difficulty in getting established and never devolved fully. It has been noted that the experiment worked better where there was a local history of partnership working Glasby et al. (2005) suggest the limited focus of Care Trusts created an obstacle to their adoption. However, the continuation of some Care Trusts over a decade showed the model did function and could have had potential. The experience did, for example, offset concerns of an automatic NHS takeover (Thistlewaite, 2011).

Benefits from the totality of the Care Trust experiment have been identified in research by Miller et al. (2011) in a study based on interviews with chief executives. The main benefits were seen as better joint working between professions, multidisciplinary teams, and more career opportunities for staff. However, half the interviewees said they would not recommend the structure. Difficulties were identified as too many costs, financial and lost opportunities, adult social care being separated from other local government services, HR and staffing issues, professional conflicts, a need for a culture of integration, and Care Trusts being caught between the demands of the council and those of the health authorities. Considering whether the concept was a failure as a model for the promotion of integration, the authors of this research concluded that Care Trusts had, to a lesser or greater extent, made some improvements in integrated working (Miller et al., 2011, p. 20). A major impression was made by one Care Trust, Torbay, in terms of its experience with integration. Statistics have been produced to show the difference the Torbay structure made to outcomes, with reductions in occupied beds; emergency bed day use for older people; delayed transfers reduced; more quickly available care packages; and reduced numbers in residential care (Torbay Care Trust, 2013). However, the Trust was to leave more of a legacy through the Torbay model – Mrs Smith. To guide its integrated work Torbay invented Mrs Smith, a typical older lady who needed a range of services. Mrs Smith wanted: a single point of contact; to tell her story only once; a quick responsive service; and professionals talking to each other. This was to be seen as a powerful approach and continued to be held up as an example of excellence and of genuine innovation (Farnsworth, 2012a). Although Torbay Trust was to acknowledge some shortcomings, in relation to public involvement and the problem of an integrated Trust operating in a largely non-integrated system, the success of Torbay has meant that it has been able to continue to operate after the restructuring of PCTs with its particular values and integrated approach (Farnsworth, 2012b).

Partnerships and use of Flexibilities

The Flexibilities of the 1999 Health Act, section 31, facilitated partnership working between NHS bodies and local authorities in the three areas of pooled budgets, lead commissioning and joint projects and services. The provisions were restated in section 75 of the 2006 NHS Act. These provisions allowed formal collaborative working but without using the Care Trust model and the restructuring involved. The measures did support voluntary formal partnerships and there was discretion to use the legislation in innovative ways. Most partnerships were set up between a PCT and a local authority but some involved NHS Trusts, whether Mental Health Trusts, Acute or Foundation Trusts. Some developed as a PCT with two local authorities or a single local authority with a PCT and an NHS Trust, as in Barnsley. And in a few cases some partnerships had a larger membership, for example, Avon and Wiltshire Mental Health Partnership included five local authorities, a Mental Health Trust and a PCT. The names of partnerships varied and did not always indicate their origins or functions. Cambridgeshire and Peterborough Mental Health Partnership NHS Trust brought together staff groups from the mental health elements of seven former health care and social service organisations. In practice it has been suggested some Mental Health Partnerships did not actually differ greatly from Care Trusts, for example, East Kent NHS Trust which was formed when social services staff were seconded from Kent County Council to the Trust to form an integrated Mental Health And Social Care Trust. Somerset Partnership NHS and Social Care Trust was formed from the integration of existing mental health and learning disability services in Somerset with the mental health component of Somerset Social Services (Weekes, 2006). For the first time in England the majority of social services mental health staff transferred their employment (Peck et al., 2001). These partnerships were established with a formal written agreement, but were voluntary and could be terminated and could be time limited or subject to alteration. The normal form of governance was through a partnership board to provide overall direction. The local authority would have representation on this board and this normally included elected councillors. There could also be joint chairs, for example, with the partnership board chaired by the PCT chair and the local council leader. A form of partnership management board could take responsibility for the day-to-day operations. In Knowsley Partnership this board included managers, clinicians, elected councillors, user representatives and non-executives. Some partnerships also built in operational service or group sub-levels of administration and delivery.

Pooled budgets

Under the Flexibilities provisions health and social care authorities could transfer resources into a single budget which was managed by one of the authorities on behalf of the other(s). Section 75 of the 2006 Act gave the power to transfer money between NHS bodies and local authorities. Thus a local authority could transfer funds to a PCT to support service provision and vice versa. Pooled budgets meant that NHS money could be transferred to fund, for example, home care. The early take-up of Flexibilities was slow but pooled budgets were the most popular initiative (Glendinning et al., 2011). However, this represented only a small proportion of the total NHS and social care expenditure. The reasons have been noted as the slow development of joint funding despite the flexibility of the system; the perception that the arrangements were complex; the misalignment of financial systems, data collection and information sharing; and the growing impact of personal budgets (Petch, 2011). Reference has also been made to some confusion about the system, the joint options available and difficulty in desegregating the money to be transferred (Goldman, 2010). The main areas of use for pooled budgets were mental health, learning disability and equipment, but large areas of potential pooled expenditure were excluded. Primary Care Trusts were less likely to host a pooled budget compared to the number of partnerships they were involved with. In 2010 the Coalition government encouraged the greater use of Flexibilities to commission services and called upon local authorities to work with the NHS to pool and align funding streams at the local level (DH, 2010d, p. 24). It was suggested that the government should be alerted if barriers to local flexibility emerged and it was also suggested commissioning pooled budgets should be seen as compatible with increased personal budgets and with the growth of the market.

Lead and joint commissioning

The flexibility of lead commissioning originally meant that one body in a partnership would take the lead role in commissioning the partnership activity. The lead body could purchase the provision irrespective of whether classified as health and social care and thus a social services department could commission nursing or services for a learning disability group. In practice the lead role became a more technical point as there was a focus on the value of joint commissioning between health and social care coming together Collaboration could take place to jointly assess the needs of the local population, decide what holistic services were required and secure them from providers. There were also options to contract the commissioning system by linking back office services and making further savings. It has also been suggested that priority setting in commissioning was important and could be seen in terms of joint allocation decisions (Williams et al., 2010). Pressures for joint or integrated commissioning increased in the light of efficiency drives and expenditure cuts plus prevention, personalisation and care closer to home agendas (Hudson, 2010). The government paper *Our Health, Our Care, Our Say* (DH, 2006b, p. 9) recommended much more joint commissioning. The need to make rationing decisions, and traditional differences in approach, in mechanisms and evidence used by the NHS and local councils, can be seen as obstacles to agreed principles (Williams et al., 2010, p. 7). It has been pointed out that complicating factors challenge the development of integrated commissioning (Hudson, 2010, p. 13). These factors include tension between commissioning and personal budgets, separate performance and accountability arrangements, and NHS preoccupation with internal commissioning. A study of best practice and processes of joint commissioning in five English localities found there was not a coherent model of joint commissioning and there were a variety of different definitions and meanings (Dickinson and Glasby, 2013). Problems identified included what was left out in joining up. Where sites had provider and commissioner functions it was very difficult to tell when one activity stopped and another started. While there was evidence of formal and structured processes including pooled budgets and lead commissioning, in practice a lot of joint working was essentially relational and informal (Dickinson and Glasby, 2013, p. 227).

The relationship between statutory health and social care bodies involved in partnerships can be described as follows:

Box 2.4	Partnership Relationships

Local authority and Primary Care Trust
Local authority and Acute/Foundation NHS Trust
Local authority and Mental Health Trust
Local authority and GPs/GP practice
PCT and Acute/Foundation NHS Trust
PCT and Mental Health Trust
PCT and GPs/GP practice
Acute/Foundation NHS Trust and Mental Health Trust
Acute/Foundation NHS Trust and GPs/GP practice
GPs/GP practice and Mental Health Trust

This description is organised on a one-to-one basis and two further dimensions can be noted. Firstly, the number of bodies involved in a partnership could be of more than two categories, for example, a local authority with a PCT and a Mental Health Trust. In practice, until 2013, because of co-terminosity, the one local authority and one PCT linkage did dominate health and social care partnerships. Secondly, more than one type of organisation can be involved with two or more NHS Trusts or local authorities. Multi-body partnerships have become more common with some 211 Clinical Commissioning Groups replacing PCTs.

Scope of integrated services

The process of merging services under Flexibilities measures was subject to much interpretation and variation. It could mean that one authority took responsibility for the provision of both aspects of health and social care, or the partnership could create new joined-up management and delivery structures. Consequently integrated care teams could provide services from one site with social care staff seconded to work as part of an integrated specialist mental health team. Alternatively the service could be jointly provided such as a community based intermediate care team. Partnership working was service orientated but the actual range of activities can be classified in a number of categories:

- firstly, by major service and users in terms of mental health, learning, disability, older people, learning disability, physical disability;
- secondly, by areas of specific services or problem defined services, for example, intermediate care, reablement, long-term conditions, dementia, pregnancy, frail elderly, obesity, alcoholism;
- thirdly, by more narrowly defined projects covering a locality or a smaller group of people, for example, Telecare;

- fourthly, by a whole systems approach to attempt a more comprehensive coverage among partners.

A further dimension of the scope of integration relates to connections with services outside health and social care as some partnerships were extended to include social housing support, children's services, voluntary organisations or bodies relating to youth services, community services, children or offenders. Partnerships did not carry with them a need for structural change to initiate collaborative agreements and work. A tendency developed particularly for the formation of Mental Health Partnership Trusts. With the closure of mental hospitals, trusts could use partnership agreements to incorporate services from social service departments. This may also occur with formation of Community Health Trusts incorporating parts of social care. This does mean that they are formally all NHS bodies.

Joint posts

As partnerships developed one of the most common actions taken was the establishment of joint posts at senior level. A study of 97 PCTs has shown the most common initiative, with 39 examples, was joint posts. Some, such as Knowsley, created a joint post of PCT Chief Executive and Council Executive Director. Barking and Dagenham Borough and PCT created a joint post of PCT Chief Executive and Council Director of Social Services , thus combining commissioning and delivery. In other areas a single senior executive position was created to lead the partnership. A study of joint post holders found they felt strongly that combined leadership has been instrumental in bringing improvements, but there were tensions between structures and cultures Wistow and Waddington, 2006. There was a view that each locality had to develop its own solution rather than accept a centrally mandated plan. Some differences emerged over the benefits of structural interaction and styles of leadership but discretion to implement strategic visions was seen as important (NHS Confederation, 2010). It was also an option to have middle tier joint appointments. However, resistance to integrated working and the implicit changes have been identified as more common among middle management. Consequently in some partnerships middle management structures were kept separate to avoid disruption (NHS Confederation, 2010).

Integrated teams

The actual delivery of integrated services was most clearly demonstrated by the establishment of integrated care teams, although at times these were slow to develop. A study of Sedgefield in County Durham traced the development of frontline teams in five localities (Hudson, 2007). Each consisted of social workers, district nurses and therapists under a single management. Once in operation efficient team operation was built on the principle of inter-organisational commitment and respect overcoming professional or hierarchical differences. In Salford a similar system of integration was built around eight teams, all co-located and with one point of entry to each for use, again with a single line manager (Syson and Bond, 2010). More specialist mental health teams were easier to establish and some predated the Flexibilities initiative. Later developments have seen the development of more specialist integrated teams, particularly rapid response teams, reablement dementia teams and neurological rehabilitation teams. The co-location of teams has been put forward as a key factor in building a team drawn from different partner organisations with face-to-face contact a valuable feature. Co-location is seen as crucial, even necessary, in integrated working. It helps avoid a silo mentality and helps integration through the sharing of knowledge and expertise, improving coordination and delivering a quicker response (Hudson, 2006). Staff normally remained employed by their current employer but came under the management of the partnership. Staff may find themselves managed by people from other professions and even working under different disciplines, procedures or traditions. In multidisciplinary teams, arrangements were usually made for a professional line of accountability, for example, for senior social work staff. This operated for reasons of professional development and to maintain professional identity. Different professions were also able to meet as a separate group, perhaps in a professional forum. The agenda for such forums covered training, professional governance, professional recognition, advice, research and education. In practice most staff in integrated settings under section 31 partnerships worked under secondment arrangements. As integrated and multidisciplinary working became established, some attention was paid to 'role bending' and sharing the performance of tasks. Examples of flexible working could include social work members of an integrated team participating in the administration of medication and hygiene procedures. Integrated working is promoted if the whole team is following the same care pathway and aims and if the elements of professional care are not that far apart (Hudson, 2007).

Social enterprises

The Coalition government continued the Labour government's commitment to develop social enterprises and allow them to deliver health and social care. Social enterprises are business enterprises guided by social objectives where profits are invested in services or the community and there are no shareholders or owners. Most of their income is generated through service contracts. Different models of governance are used but staff involvement is a feature. Social enterprises are regarded as having the freedom to innovate, deliver new services and reduce formal bureaucracy. There has been a very rapid growth in social enterprises and as many as 6,000 are believed to be involved in health and social care. This growth has been promoted generally by government policies on outsourcing, the Big Society agenda and Social Value legislation and more specifically by local authorities withdrawing from services, the winding down of PCTs, the separation of purchasing and provision, and the increase in health and social care initiatives. The Coalition government also pushed the right of public sector employees to form mutual and social enterprises. Schemes in health and social care ranged from single GP projects to all PCT provider services and were usually funded through NHS funded contracts (Addicott, 2011). Activities are often spun out from existing statutory provision. In one example a range of adult social care services were spun out from Bath and NE Somerset Council Social Services and the local PCT. Some 1,700 staff transferred to the Bath and Somerset project. This has been described as the transfer of integrated community health and social services to a social enterprise (Bath and NE Somerset Council, 2014). However, some proposed developments have been highly controversial such as a spin-out from a PCT in Gloucester to form a Gloucester Community Interest Company when the organisers were accused of not consulting employees in the local population and of back door privatisation. Social enterprises can often be involved in innovative projects and practices and schemes can be adopted on a larger scale by other organisations.

Major themes in integrated partnerships

Hospital discharge

Problems caused by delayed discharge from hospital have been identified as 'something of an acid test of the relationship between local partners' (Glasby, 2007) and one of the clear indications of failure by health and social care professionals to work together. Delays in discharge and the unavailability of appropriate care packages or residential care or intermediate care led to 'blockages' in bed releases in acute hospitals. This was seen as an example of problems caused by rigid institutional boundaries and the absence of a joined, responsive and seamless service. The needs of the individual user were not at the centre of the system of provision. Despite the formation of partnerships, delayed discharge and resultant blockages and costs continued to be an issue. Relatively few partnerships between acute hospital trusts and local councils had been formed or were focused on hospital discharge. Some integrated practice had developed, such as ward based coordinators or discharge teams. However, competing norms of good practice between health and social care continued to be a problematic area of policy and practice (Glasby, 2007, p. 78) and it was difficult to isolate a discharge management process. The strength of concern expressed by government led to the introduction of a radical scheme of financial penalties or reimbursement under the Community Care (Delayed Discharges) Act 2003 which imposed fines on social service departments in local government if they were judged responsible for delays as a form of reimbursement to hospitals. This proved controversial as the provisions placed blame and penalties on councils, caused tensions between health and social care bodies, did not encourage partnerships and did not address the core issues. Problems continued as the responsibility for the provision of care on discharge was usually still outside the hospital system (Swinkels and Mitchell, 2009). Hospital discharge has for some time been seen as epitomising the challenges which beset partnership working (Henwood, 2006). A seamless service requires effective integrated management and practices but also an alignment of decision-making and resources. Increasing emergency admissions and pressures on social care provision in 2015–16 has brought the issue to the forefront again.

The interface between acute hospitals and community based services was seen as a core part of integrated care (Naylor et al., 2015).

Unified assessment

Unifying the assessment process for care in the community was a clear potential benefit of partnership working. The process had been largely divided with social care assessment the responsibility of the local authority while health authorities remained responsible for their elements. A single assessment process had been recommended by the National Service Framework for Older People and by 2001 community care assessments had been introduced which could be shared across the relevant services (Miller and Cameron, 2011).The adoption of a single assessment meant an improvement in joint working between community health and social care. The key professionals involved in shared assessment were social workers, community nurses and occupational therapists and the joint training required on assessment promoted inter-professional understanding, increased expertise and overcoming professional boundaries (Miller and Cameron, 2011, p. 42). In a practical example social care and health care teams in Staffordshire and Stoke use a single assessment process. In this area the Single Assessment Process (SAP) was available to all adults, not just older people. National guidelines were followed with four different levels of assessment' a contact assessment, an interview assessment, a specialist assessment, and a comprehensive assessment for more complex cases, which were coordinated by one agency. Government guidance stressed the importance of multi-agency working, cooperation, and integration developed through working procedures and practices. Research studies have thrown more light on the relationship between assessment and integration. A study of unified assessment of older people (Abendstern et al., 2011) found that while there was a commitment to an integrated approach the extent of integrated assessment between social care and health professionals had been realised in only a limited fashion. Progress had been hampered by disjointed sharing initiatives and the lack of involvement of some sectors. This study investigated three dimensions of integration: strategic integration, process integration, and practice level integration. The predominant linkage was between local authorities and PCTs, reported by 70 per cent of the sample. Most of the leads on assessment were from social service departments. There were few formal linkages with GPs. The main criticisms in this study concerned the limited use of an integrated IT system, inappropriate IT systems, difficulties engaging GPs and acute sector clinicians, and also that in only one-third of cases was a single care plan produced (Abendstern et al., 2011, p. 476). Another study of leads in local authorities and local health boards (Seddon et al., 2010) found the link between primary care practice and united assessment processes poorly established. Other problems identified were: the limitations of GP engagement; frustrations over protocols for sharing of information and computing difficulties; distrust about eroding professional roles; differences of opinion about tools which would facilitate assessment; and the challenge of translating the aims of united assessment into practice. On the positive side most health and social care staff reported improvements in the evidence provided to inform care planning and service delivery; the adoption of a person-centred approach and improvements in considering risks to independent living. Seddon et al. (2010, p. 222) found broad agreement that unified assessment had facilitated positive changes to practice. Inter-agency assessment facilitated interventions which reflected the interconnectedness of people's needs. The single assessment process made a contribution to the development of integrated working but there are still operational difficulties and conflicts to resolve.

Legislation placed an obligation on local authorities and PCTs to prepare a Joint Strategic Needs Assessment (JSNA) which assessed the needs of the local population. One research study did suggest that many assessments were joint, with various joint strategies, governance structures, and projects (Ellins and Glasby, 2011). In some cases this was putting on a statutory basis what had been more informal collaborative working. Other evidence has confirmed the establishment of a joint process which had a demonstrable impact on commissioning, investments and service design (Harding and Kane, 2011) but some issues about inadequate JSNA capacity remained. As the process has developed, more partnerships have aimed at supplying more qualitative insights and taking a wider approach to determinants of need. Some outstanding issues and problems have been identified. Harding and Kane (2011) suggest a need for more structured approaches and embedding JSNA in joint commissioning to reflect the needs assessment; poor participation by GPs and wider partners and cuts in public services have put pressure on evidence based decision-making. Overall JSNA has been seen as raising the importance of jointly agreed approaches to needs assessment and to partnership working more generally (Ellins and Glasby, 2011, p. 38).To date JSNA has on balance been evidence for the value of a shared integrated approach, justifying stronger action to use the process, information and findings it produces. Following restructuring from 2013 JSNA became the responsibility of Clinical Commissioning Groups and local authorities.

Intermediate Care

Although not a new idea a formal policy of intermediate care was introduced following the NHS Plan in 2000. Intermediate care was a policy of rehabilitation aimed at breaking the cycle of hospital admission, discharge and readmission. Intermediate care was located between hospital inpatient care and recovery to live independently at home. This transitional care from acute hospital could take the form of a short-term stay in a residential setting or in a community residential rehabilitation unit, or set in day hospital or rehabilitation services in their own homes (Moore et al., 2007). The aim was to assist a person to regain or relearn capabilities lost to illness or disease. Using intermediate care to assist rapid recovery from acute illness required removing barriers between health and social care and adopting an integrated approach. Key aspects of intermediate care have been described as: focusing on people facing unnecessarily prolonged hospital stays; having a plan to enable people to live at home and to live independently; basing decisions on a comprehensive single assessment; limiting time to a short period; and involving integrated cross-professional working (Regen et al., 2008).

Most intermediate care provision was based on a form of partnership and involved local authority social service departments working alongside NHS Community Trusts or PCTs. Bed-based intermediate care was often organised through specific projects and involved voluntary and private providers. An early example was Camberwell Green Intermediate Care Project in London which involved two NHS hospital Trusts, a community NHS Trust, a health authority and two local borough councils. The actual commissioning agreement was between one NHS Trust and an independent provider. Integration should have produced benefits in terms of interdisciplinary and multidisciplinary working supporting flexible responses, person- and home-centred approaches and access to a range of expertise. Salford has integrated intermediate care teams, as has Islington, with a team comprising social workers, care workers, occupational therapist, physiotherapist, nurses and GPs. However, a research study reported that a lack of effective joint working between health and social care was a major impediment to the implementation of intermediate care (Regen et al., 2008, p. 633).

Reablement

Issues remained unresolved concerning intermediate care, including a lack of capacity and poor relationships between mainstream services and intermediate care (Allen and Glasby, 2010) and there were continuing debates about how prevention and rehabilitation should best be organised. In this context the concept of reablement emerged. Reablement is designed as a short and intensive intervention, usually delivered in the home, which can be offered to people recovering from an illness or injury or people with disabilities and those who are frail (Social Care Institute for Excellence, 2012a). The aim is to help people with increased support needs to regain the skills necessary for restoring independent living. It is the focus on assistance to regain abilities and functioning that makes reablement distinctive from intermediate care. Referrals for reablement can come from hospitals, GPs, social services and carers, on the basis of health and social care needs rather than on the basis of clinical diagnosis (Social Care Institute for Excellence, 2012ac). The support is usually available for six weeks and is free of charge but the period can be extended and equipment and adoptions may be supplied. The actual tasks cover relearning skills, regaining physical functions, doing daily tasks such as dressing, washing, and cooking. Reablement services have been provided mainly by local authority services but can be in partnership with the NHS. Care workers are usually supported by occupational therapists and physiotherapists. There is no single model of reablement and procedures can differ from area to area but the initial assessment is carried out by a senior care worker or care manager. About 80 per cent of local councils operate the scheme with such assessments but only about one-quarter of councils co-fund reablement with health (Social Care Institute for Excellence, 2012c).

An example of a formal partnership is Central Surrey Health Integrated Rehabilitation and Reablement Service which consists of Central Surrey Health and Surrey local authority adult social care. Multidisciplinary working is appropriate to implement a reablement strategy and could, for example, be built around clusters of GP practices. More investment could lead to better joint working and funding between health and local government (Social Care Institute for Excellence, 2012c). The government transferred funding of £70million to PCTs for 2011/12 to develop local reablement services in partnership with councils. Increasingly local councils have been outsourcing the service to independent providers and home care providers can work with councils to develop reablement services. A survey of evaluations has shown strong support for reablement among users and managers (Francis et al., 2011). Local councils in Nottingham and Lancashire reported 90 and 85 per cent satisfaction. People using the service have experienced improvements in physical functioning, quality of life and better social care compared to standard home care. In relation to outcomes it has been reported that 60 per cent of people leaving reablement did not require a care package (Social Care Institute for Excellence, 2012a). It has also been reported that from a social care perspective there is a high probability that reablement is cost-effective (Francis et al., 2011, p. 9), despite some gaps in research to date. One of the problematic areas in this relatively new service is the handover when the user may be passed over to a more traditional package of services and providers. The Care Act 2014 in England meant that from 2015 reablement requiring minor aids and adaptations up to the value of £1,000 was available free (Local Government Association, 2015a), although this implies more of a balance towards an occupational therapy based service.

Rapid Response

Rapid response teams are another relatively new approach making use of a clinical or care approach. Rapid response teams have been set up in most local authority areas to step into crisis situations. Such interventions are occasioned by people experiencing a crisis through the onset of a sudden illness or following an initial assessment of a need for support to avoid an unplanned admission to hospital or due to the sudden illness of a main carer. The actual composition of a rapid response team may vary and some are more social work dominated but others are multidisciplinary, including social workers, nurses, reablement workers, occupational therapists, and physiotherapists, and possibly a community pharmacist, under a team leader with administrative support. The nature of a rapid response is as follows:

Box 2.5	Rapid Response Features

- Referral, by GP, community health, family
- Contact within 2 to 4 hours
- Assessment in own home or sometimes in Emergency Department or assessment unit
- Normally 24 hour, 7 day service
- Tailored social package, team working, hands-on support or equipment, over 48/72 hours
- Continue to domiciliary maintenance package or reablement or health care

The advantage of rapid response has been judged in terms of success in avoiding emergency ambulance calls, A&E attendance, acute admissions, or emergency residential care. Ideally users may be enabled to return to independent living. Rapid response mainly operates in relation to older people but there are examples of more specialist initiatives, a dementia rapid response and home treatment team. Some challenges have been encountered in establishing rapid response teams concerning: joint funding; creating multidisciplinary health and social care teams; and introducing single-line management. The schemes have demonstrated the identification of the opportunity to manage health and social care crises in a joined-up and innovative way (Clift, 2015).

Conclusions

This period was marked by both the development of a policy of promotion of integration through a series of top-down strategies and the implementation of a series of management and delivery practices. The attempt at structured integration through the Care Trust services had a limited uptake and the main vehicle for the advance of integration was through partnership working. This was facilitated through the statutory flexibility measures of pooled budgets, joint commissioning and joint projects. These partnership arrangements allowed extensive local discretion and innovation. It has, however, been suggested that overall the model of promoting bridges between two hardened organisational silos was fundamentally flawed (Wistow, 2011). Policy analysis, research, evaluation and Parliamentary reports led to a strong support narrative and lobbying for integration particularly through the NHS Future Forum. A consequence was legislation in England promoting integration as well as the more general development of adult social care, with a focus on competition and choice to improve outcomes whilst sitting alongside integration. This underpinned the continuing development and experimentation with integrated practices in the areas of integrated teams, unified assessment, delayed discharge, intermediate care and reablement. Despite government management and professional commitments and a range of local initiatives the overall view remained of disappointing outcomes with the potential of integration not fully realised.

3 Reshaping Integration in England

Introduction

The period since 2012 has seen a remarkable move forward in the UK with integration put on a statutory footing and having an enhanced status following new legislation in England, Scotland and Wales. Two pieces of legislation in England were of significance: firstly, the Health and Social Care Act 2012, which introduced institutional changes, particularly Clinical Commissioning Groups and Health and Wellbeing Boards; and secondly, the Care Act 2014, which makes integration, cooperation, and partnership a legal requirement for local authorities and also for all other agencies involved in public care and including private and voluntary organisations. Innovations introduced included joint commissioning teams, sharing of information, pooled budgets, and combined approaches to a market (Local Government Association, 2015, p. 16). To reinforce the focus on joint working at a local level the NHS was no longer obliged to seek reimbursement for delayed discharges attributable to the local authority. The joint programme management scheme offered support in local areas on the implementation of the Care Act and associated reforms through case studies, templates, self-assessment frameworks, and tool kits. The major institutional developments impacting upon integration in England can be listed as: Clinical Commissioning Groups; Health and Wellbeing Boards; Healthwatch; and the new city devolution structure covering health and social care. The continuing significance of innovations, the Pioneer and Vanguard initiatives, the Better Care Fun, Sustainability and Transformation Plans, and the increasing role of inspection and scrutiny through the Care Quality Commission, audits, NICE, and more focused research and evaluation are assessed.

Clinical Commissioning Groups

The implementation of the Health and Social Care Act 2012 meant that in 2013 PCTs were replaced by GP led Clinical Commissioning Groups (CCGs). This implied significant change, given that PCTs had had a leading role in integration, partnerships, and collaborative arrangements. In future, joint working would have to take place mainly between the new and emerging CCGs and local authority adult social care departments. Some commentators interpreted this as requiring not just incremental adjustments but also a paradigm shift (Farnsworth, 2012b).

Future integration would be driven more by clinical engagement and local action with GP consortia centre-stage as a set of new players, responsible for commissioning the majority of NHS services (Humphries and Curry, 2011, p. 8). A number of critical questions arose. The changes meant a strict separation of commissioning and provider functions so CCGs, unlike PCTs, would not have any provider role. Many PCTs had developed a leadership role in promoting integration and had been established as the lead body for joined-up mental health services. CCGs were GP led and dominated but GPs had traditionally not been heavily engaged in integrated working or with adult social care. GPs also had a different contractual relationship from other health and social care professionals. Would GPs commit strongly to the integrated agenda? While CCGs did demonstrate an appetite for fostering clinically led collaboration and new solutions, much time had to be devoted to issues of organisation and governance. A pressing concern was that almost all existing partnership agreements would have to be adjusted or renegotiated to take account of the new NHS commissioners. Local councils would have to work with CCGs to protect existing arrangements or build new ones. There were further potential difficulties. PCTs and local councils in England had almost complete co-terminosity in boundaries with 152 local authorities which facilitated integrated working. However, it appeared that there would be some 211 CCGs. All GP practices had to be a member of a CCG. A requirement of the new legislation governing commissioning was a market principle that services could be awarded to any qualified provider, which could potentially have an adverse effect on the quality and scale of integrated provision.

The final Department of Health guidance on the legislation did address the issue of integration more specifically (DH, 2012c). CCGs were required to act with a view to secure that health services are provided in an integrated way, and that provision of health care is integrated with provision of social care services if the CCG considers that this would improve the quality of services. This was seen as likely to occur in relation to services for older people, people with mental health conditions, people with learning disabilities and rehabilitation services. CCGs also still had the power under section 75 of the 2006 Act to enter into partnership arrangements through pooled budgets and lead commissioning and could commission health improvement services jointly with local authorities, for example, dealing with obesity or drugs and alcohol abuse. CCGs had powers to make payments to local authorities towards expenditure on community services, while in an unexpected decision they were permitted to be designated as a care trust.

CCGs had other prescribed duties to cooperate with local authorities, particularly with the new Health and Wellbeing Boards (DH, 2012c). They had to involve these boards in drawing up commissioning plans. CCGs had also to contribute jointly to joint strategic needs assessments and health and wellbeing strategies led by the Health and Wellbeing Boards (HWBs). In exercising their functions CCGs had to take account of both documents. General duties relating to integration included identifying which care pathways needed to be coordinated across health and social care and also engaging with health and social care professionals to redesign or co-produce services or pathways to deliver improved services. Cooperation could also cover planning care for services, community care assessments and mental health initiatives. The annual report of the CCG was to include comment on how it contributed to the delivery of joint health and wellbeing strategies.

In the debate on this major transition a number of possible potential benefits have been cited. Lotinga and Glasby (2012) refer to: a closer relationship between all primary care and social care promoting self-care and prevention; a focus on high-cost complex needs, particularly of frail older people; broader primary health teams, integrating with social workers; tackling long-standing boundary issues; avoiding doing things as before and moving to a more person-centred basis; and 'conversations with new players' to develop new relationships. Work has also been carried out by London local authorities to identify the main interfaces with CCGs such as hospital discharge, community health and domiciliary care and the frail elderly. The intention was to engage in better use of resources, economies of scale, and more sharing (London Councils, 2012).

A practical example of cooperation is an integrated commissioning unit set up as a joint initiative between Portsmouth City Council and Portsmouth Clinical Commissioning Group, commissioning joined-up services for vulnerable adults, children and families. The configuration of bodies involving health and social care in these sites does give an indication of how the architecture of partnership working may develop. A learning environment website was developed by NHS England so that CCGs can share good practice, for example, Sheffield CCG and its partners engaged with public and voluntary providers and communities to identify priorities and new models of care (NHS England, 2016d), while Wakefield Council and the local CCG work with provider services for those with complex needs (Care Quality Commission, 2016, p. 23).

Only a small number of sites has the configuration of one CCG and one council in a partnership and most extend to include NHS trusts. It can be noted that there are examples of very large partnerships, particularly the ambitious Inner North West London integrated care project.

NHS Commissioning Board and Monitor

From 2012 a new government centralised quango had responsibility for commissioning as part of the restructuring of the NHS. The NHS Commissioning Board (NHSCB) has specific duties for primary care, including GP contracts, as well as direct commissioning relating to pharmacy, dental, and ophthalmic services. It operates through four regional and 27 local offices. The Health and Social Care Act also imposes a duty on NHSCB in relation to integration, by commissioning in such a manner as to secure 'integration' and promote innovative ways of demonstrating how care can be made more integrated. Part of the functions of the NHSCB relates to Clinical Commissioning Groups. There are three formal responsibilities: the authorisation, oversight and performance management of CCGs; issuing commissioning guidelines and model contracts; and allocating budgets to CCGs and holding them to account. Support can be given to CCGs in other ways, including through clinical networks which bring together experts from different areas of health and social care to offer independent advice (NHS Commissioning Board, 2012). In 2013 the NHS Commissioning Board became NHS England to take on a more prominent public-facing role.

Monitor was established as the economic regulator for the NHS with responsibility to promote the efficient use of resources and quality of care. The apparent commitment to promoting competition raised issues of the importance of the duty on Monitor to also enable integration where this would make services more efficient or remove inequalities. Monitor's duty was to enable integration in contrast to the NHSCB's duty which was to secure integration. This resulted in Monitor producing an analysis of how it could use its tools and powers to best enable the delivery of integrated care. It was suggested that Monitor should not perform actions which would create barriers to integrated care. Support for integrated care could be achieved by addressing how the financial benefits of integrated care can be shared between providers and the use of alternative approaches to tariffs to enable integration of care (Monitor, 2012). From 2016 Monitor became part of NHS Improvement whose main task is to support Foundation and NHS Trusts, including working across local health and care systems. NHS Improvement aimed to work to support the required shift by encouraging joint planning and cooperation and integrated provision across primary, secondary and social care and physical and mental health (NHS Improvement, 2016).

Health and Wellbeing Boards

Health and Wellbeing Boards (HWBs) were created by the Health and Social Care Act 2012 and established in local authorities from April 2013. This initiative followed the White Paper 'NHS Equity and Excellence' which proposed that local government should take a more strategic approach in planning the integration of health and social care. The idea was expanded in the consequent policy paper Liberating the NHS: Local Democratic Legitimacy in Health proposing that local government take on the function of joining up the commissioning of local health services, social care and health improvement (DH, 2010b). The NHS Future Forum had stated that HWBs must become the crucible of health and social care integration and the Department of Health stated that HWBs could act as engines of integration (DH, 2010b). They combined political, professional, commissioning and community leadership. The eventual main role for HWBs has been described as threefold:

1. contribute to the assessment of the needs of local populations through the joint social needs assessment (JSNA) to establish the facts needed for promoting integration – the JSNA can be seen as a powerful tool for health and social care commissioning and local planning;

2. produce a health and wellbeing strategy as an overarching framework within which commissioners' plans and priorities could be developed for health and social care;

3. promote greater integration and partnership working, including joint commissioning, pooled budgets, and integrated provision.

Also proposed was that persons arranging for any health and social care services should work in an integrated manner (Hudson, 2011). There was a clear power of involvement in an oversight role over Clinical Commissioning Groups. HWBs had powers: to ensure NHS commissioning plans would follow the health and wellbeing strategies; to refer commissioning plans back to CCGs; to be consulted on how CCGs had contributed to the delivery of HWBs' strategies; and to have an ongoing dialogue with CCGs. The intention was to move to co-terminosity in boundaries between CCGs and local authorities. The legislation left open areas of discretion. HWBs could encourage persons who arrange for the provision of health and social care services to work in an integrated way, and to provide assistance, advice and support on working together (Dow, 2011). Local authorities tend to interpret the new structure as a way to promote service improvements through integration and partnerships. Staffordshire, for example, declared three aims for HWBs' activity:

1. to develop joint commissioning to support a shift to preventive and personalised care;

2. to improve the effective delivery of high-quality, safe care to deliver better health outcomes;

3. to support the development of integrated, seamless care and care closer to home to meet the needs of the population. (Ellis et al., 2013, p. 88)

The core membership of HWBs was specified in the legislation but the total membership is at the discretion of the local authority. Six categories make up the core: a nominated councillor; the directors of adult social care, children's care, and public health; a representative of Healthwatch; and representatives of the relevant CCGs; plus others. In practice this could bring together mainly local authority and CCG members but also representatives drawn from NHS trusts, voluntary bodies, the police, and other bodies. The transitional boards had a variable membership. A study of 48 HWBs found 21 had a membership of 12 or under, 23 had a membership of 13–20 and 4 had a membership of over 20 (Humphries and Galea, 2013). Most local authorities saw the leadership or chair of HWBs taken by a council member, usually the director or cabinet member for social care. However, it appeared that a fifth of HWBs had a shared leadership between the local authority and the CCG. Another model was a chair from council social care and a CCG chair as vice-chair. Local authorities also had discretion over the internal organisation of HWBs with sub-boards or a decentralised structure. Box 3.1 shows the Oxfordshire sub-structure.

Box 3.1	Structure of the HWB in Oxfordshire

Health and Wellbeing Board

Health Improvement Board   Adult Health and Social Care Board   Children and Young People's Board

Public Involvement Network

Source: Oxfordshire's Joint Health & Wellbring Strategy 2015–2019.

Decentralised structures have also been used in larger local authorities or where there are two-tier local authority areas of counties and districts. Consequently Kent and a Surrey have a structure of a central HWBs and sub-HWBs. Given the new nature of HWBs and a transitional period before 2013, there was a learning and developmental process. This focused on the interprofessional, wide-ranging, cross-cutting and holistic approaches required by integration. A tool kit produced by the NHS Confederation suggested a whole menu of operating principles to support integrated working (Box 3.2).

Box 3.2	Tool Kit for Integrated Working

The principles of integrated working included:

- building strong working relationships;
- longer-term thinking and planning;
- encouraging commitment to integrated care and working;
- clarifying roles and responsibilities;
- sharing priorities between the boards and local organisations;
- collaboration and cross-organisational leadership;
- addressing cultural change;
- constructing data sharing;
- sharing and targeting resources;
- measuring and using evidence of success;
- engaging Healthwatch to identify innovation and solutions.

Source: Adapted from NHS Confederation (2013).

There was a strong view that relationship building was important, but HWBs used a variety of modes of engagement with providers (Local Government Association/NHS Improvement, 2016). Wiltshire has providers engaged in the whole process meaning that the board has feedback on what is working and what needs adapting (Local Government Association/NHS Improvement, 2016, p. 11).

Health and wellbeing strategies became an area of discretion and differences in practice as the exercise began. Many local authorities had an existing foundation of partnerships; for example, Oxfordshire County Council already had partnerships covering better mental health, carers strategy, an urgent care programme, and a dementia plan. The Oxfordshire HWB has developed a joint health and wellbeing strategy with the CCG and Healthwatch, bringing together the work of health and social care with communities and the voluntary sector Healthwatch (Oxfordshire County Council, 2014). Most HWBs make arrangements to consult users and carers, community and voluntary groups, and to communicate with the public in developing strategies. The strategies were expected to draw on evidence from the JSNA data and analysis. Local authorities did tend to draw up a few priority areas, whether client groups, conditions or topics; for example, West Sussex cited dementia, workplace health, and families and children. Some priorities were more wide-ranging, for example, relating to criminal justice or social housing, or, more specifically, for example, Hackney council deciding on assessing the need for pharmaceutical services.

While HWBs have helped integration become a mainstream activity and move away from a series of experiments in small areas (Local Government Association, 2013) it still allowed local priority to be put in place. Many HWBs reported challenges in establishing an entirely new body (Humphries et al., 2012). A number of concerns were expressed, including the danger that an emphasis on overseeing commissioning would hinder efforts to promote integrated care. Another concern was that the HWBs could become talking shops, would not implement decisions, or would become highly politicalised (Wilderspin, 2013). Possible problems and hindrances related to a lack of clarity about roles, not everyone being signed up for tasks, or inadequate budgets and a lack of leadership across organisations (Baggott, 2013). There were also fears that the commissioning system would be dominated by the NHS Commissioning Board and national agendas and that the local HWBs would have little influence. Among the many new structures it does appear necessary for HWBs to establish a clear identity and role other than as a forum for local debates but with relatively little power in practice. As research by Humphries and Galea (2013) suggests, strong working relationships are the key to influence while the financial climate and national control are the main hindrances.

On the other hand there was a clear potential for HWBs to set a direction for the NHS, local government and public health partners to plan enhanced integration and benefits to health and wellbeing. The importance of good relations was stressed for HWBs to be system leaders rather than getting bogged down in process issues (Perkins and Hunter, 2014). The Local Government Association has viewed HWBs as responsible for driving forward integration at the local level, thus local health and wellbeing strategies were providing a platform for local partners to coalesce around local priorities and multi-faceted problems (NHS Confederation/Local Government Association, 2016, p. 21). A health and wellbeing system support programme funded by the Department of Health offers support across health and social care, including for HWB leadership development, research and shared learning, and a suite of facilitating tools. HWBs are seen as the only forum in which clinical, professional, political and community leaders come together and the need to involve the local voluntary and community sectors was heavily emphasised (Baggott, 2013, p.87). Box 3.3 shows some of the possible benefits of HWBs.

Box 3.3	Potential Benefits of HWBs

These include:

- innovative links with CCGs and fresh ways of looking at working with local partners;
- greater involvement with other stakeholders, GPs, and community activists, which could release new energy, impetus and expertise;
- better local accountability through more transparent and open systems;
- achieving more partnership working with a whole-systems approach and country-wide coverage, providing new dynamism, assets and knowledge;
- a statutory body ensuring compliance;
- allowing a strong focus on prevention rather than just crisis intervention;
- able to develop a strategic focus on commissioning;
- flexibility to develop localised approaches to details of care.

Partnership NHS trusts

The formation of partnership NHS trusts to manage the delivery aspect of health and social care for specified geographical areas has been a significant model. Such trusts would provide adult social care and community health services within local authority boundaries. Thus Staffordshire and Stoke-on-Trent Partnership NHS Trust has described itself as the biggest integrated health and social care provider in the UK through access to a one-stop service and integrated care locality teams, including a strong discharge team.

Integrated Care Pioneers Programme

The main vehicle for spreading integrated practices and innovations after 2013 was the selection and launch of 14 pioneering showcase initiatives in sites across England. The Minister for Care and Support declared that the Pioneers were a starting gun for the NHS to truly take hold across the NHS (DH, 2013b). The projects, selected from some 100 applications, were to test new ways of working for others to learn from. ADASS described the launch of the integration Pioneers as a landmark day which will be remembered as one which heralds a new health and social care journey leading to more seamless services. The selection process was then repeated in 2014 and a further 11 Pioneer sites joined the programme in 2015. For those localities not selected as Pioneers it

| Table 3.1 | Integration Pioneer Sites and Composition of Bodies |

Location	Organisations involved
South Tyneside	1 CCG, 1 local council, NHS trust
Barnsley	1 CCG, 1 local council, 2 NHS trusts, Healthwatch
Greenwich	1 CCG, 1 local council, 2 NHS trusts, 1 voluntary body
Cheshire	3 CCGs, 2 local councils
London WELC	3 CCGs, 3 local councils, 3 NHS trusts
Islington	1 CCG and 1 local council
NW London	8 CCGs, 7 local councils, 9 NHS trusts

was hoped that all areas could benefit from the experience. The 25 Pioneers represented urban and rural areas and large and small geographical areas across England (Table 3.1).

The configuration involved in a sample of Pioneer sites gives an indication of the bodies involved and the differences in composition. The usual configuration involves a CCG, a local council and an NHS trust, normally between one and three of each. Only a small number of sites have a configuration of one CCG and one council and North West London is unique in having a multi-member partnership. In a few examples another type of body, usually a voluntary organisation, may be involved.

There was quite a variety in the topics of programmes, but there was a strong focus on new integrated services; services for the frail elderly and those with long-term conditions; a whole-systems approach to health; support to live independently; or a mix of initiatives through a site. Figure 3.1 provides a brief summary of the core aims of Pioneer programmes. The 25 sites chosen represented a diverse selection of health and care economies. Pioneer funding was not extensive but additional finance, advice and support was available from central government.

The approach of Pioneers could cover a range of directions, including: pursuing existing local plans for transformation; a particular governance arrangement; a collection of workstreams and projects; a specific new integrated service, such as a frailty service; and an ethos or way of thinking about providing care, rather than a plan. The most frequent initiatives used had a focus on older people with multiple long-term conditions, frail older people, high service users, or people at high risk of hospital admission. A few were prioritising mental health problems and people with learning difficulties (Erens et al., 2016). Few Pioneer sites involved services such as housing, education, or policing. Pioneers were using a combination of integrated practices as listed below (Box 3.4) although few of these appear innovative in themselves.

As it was the intention that the whole country could benefit from the lessons of the Integrated Care Pioneers Programme a detailed evaluation process was arranged to help build the evidence on what works best in delivering quality integrated care in different contexts. The Policy Innovation Research Unit took a largely qualitative approach to its analysis. The evaluation of the first set of pioneers identified: the value of the badge, signifying national recognition for innovation and progressing integrated care; pioneers as enablers of transformation; promotion of new governance arrangements; and introduction of new integrated services as a way of thinking or representing aspirations (Erens, 2016). The main challenges that the first group of pioneers faced were: information sharing; different priorities: workforce issues; lack of extra funds; and tensions over leadership. This suggested continuing barriers to the ambition for person-centred coordinated care. The second evaluation identified a trend that with ambitions not realised some pioneers had scaled back their activities in this area and focused instead on older people with complex needs.

Box 3.4   **Pioneers' Integrated Practices**

Risk stratification	Care planning
Case management	Improved access, e.g. single point of access
Increased support for self-care	Telehealth and telecare
Hospital discharge planning	GP networks of services
Multidisciplinary teams	Rapid response teams
Personal health and social care budgets	Joint commissioning
More support to carers	Community resilience and use of volunteers
Developing community assets	Funding and payment innovations

Source: Based on Erens et al. (2016).

There was considerable variation in what the pioneers had achieved and they were coming under pressure caused by the financial situation and political context, leading some to focus on cost savings and new funding mechanisms through the Better Care Fund (BCF).

It was the intention that the pioneering projects would act as exemplars and disseminate the results quickly. This could facilitate the rapid uptake of the lessons and help remove barriers to delivering better integrated care and support (SCIE, 2013b). There was an aspiration that the pioneers could drive change at a scale and pace from which the rest of the country would benefit.

| Figure 3.1 | Pioneers and Programmes | |

Location	Groups covered	Strategies/programmes
Barnsley	All client groups	Prevention and early intervention in emergencies for individuals, families and communities
Cheshire	Connecting care for all residents	Building a service delivery model of integrated care and complex needs; integrated commissioning and enabling
Cornwall	People at early stage of illness or frailty	Integrated care tasks around organisational groups, for at-risk people
Greenwich	Emergencies in community	Integrated teams to avoid hospital admissions
Islington	Long-term conditions, mental health	Personalised and integrated care and support; greater prevention and single point of contact
Kent	Older people, mental health	Redesign of integrated commissioning; community management of learning disability; promotion of independent living; integrated workforce development
Leeds	Adults and children, older people	Health and social care co-located neighbourhood teams for long-term conditions; mental health habitat project; early start for children
NW London	Older people, mental health, learning disability, children	GPs' coordination of care delivery, prevention and early intervention; NHS trusts involved
North Staffs	Cancer, end of life	New commissioning ways, bringing together community and primary care with voluntary bodies
South Devon and Torbay	Frail elderly, mental health	Community-based model for long-term conditions; gap services; community hubs with 7-day services and single-call access
Southend	Frail elderly, long-term conditions prevention focus	Single access and referral routes; multidisciplinary teams community services to avoid hospital care
South Tyneside	Older people	New approach to early help, prevention, self-care, and integrated support services
Waltham Forest/East London /City	Older people, mental health	Care navigation, GP networks, joint assessment and intervention; self-care and independent living; single point of contact
Worcester	Long-term conditions	Service integration to promote community provision to avoid hospital admissions; GP hubs

Source: Adapted from NHS England (2016d).

Government encouragement of integration

Will the new priority given by government to integration, the new promotional initiatives, and the new structural context all result in a new era of integrated care? The environment for increasing integrated practice has not been totally positive with reductions in local government expenditure on social care, for example, 4.5 per cent less expenditure on adult social care, with increasing charges and fees for domiciliary care, and 87 per cent of local authorities restricting assistance to those whose care needs are defined as substantial or critical. At the same time demand for care has been increasing, particularly from people with long-term conditions. Clearly government policy was committed to a policy of advancing and improving the operation of integration. The new organisations set up after 2012, NHS England, the Clinical Commissioning Groups, Monitor, and the Health and Wellbeing Boards , all were given a duty to make it easier for health and social care to work together. Efforts were made to remove potential barriers to the expansion of integration, in particular; Monitor was keen to insist that the regulatory scheme and payment by results would not act as a barrier to driving forward more integrated care. Monitor stressed that most services aimed at providing good integrated care would not raise any competition concerns.

The NHS Improving Quality (NHSIQ) body came into existence in 2013 to work to improve the overall quality of care. NHSIQ declared a policy of supporting local areas to deliver integrated care and support. It expressed a belief in moving from episodic care to a more holistic approach to health and care support and a commitment to join partner organisations to tackle barriers and enable and encourage locally led, integrated services to follow. NHSIQ was later replaced by a Sustainable Improvement Team as part of NHS England and has as one of its domains long-term conditions and integrated care.

A further initiative was the establishment of a National Collaboration for Integrated Care and Support, as a network of national health and social care organisations. Twelve national partners came together to promote integrated care and support. These professional and representative bodies are described in Box 3.5

The partners signed up for a shared commitment on supporting integration. The aim of this initiative (see Box 3.6) was described as 'sending a clear signal to the entire health and social care system that integrated care and support is a critical issue and we are committed to supporting integration in the years ahead' (National Collaboration for Integrated Care and Support, 2013). Members were signing up for a single agreed vision of person-centred coordinated care and support as the key to improving conditions. They were also committed to a programme of initiatives to address barriers, encourage local innovations through pioneer projects, and establish an Integrated Care and Support Exchange. On a practical level the national partners sought to: rapidly build new strategic partnerships; lead the large-scale transformation of the system; tackle cultural and organisational barriers to improved care; mobilise people across the system; engage patients and the public; test radical options; and inform and influence change at the national level. NHSIQ was created in 2013 for a period to work

Box 3.5	National Collaboration for Integrated Care and Support Partners, 2013

Association of Directors of Adult Social Services
Association of Directors of Children's Services
Care Quality Commission
Department of Health
Monitor
NHS England
NHS Improving Quality
Health Education England
National Institute for Health and Care Excellence
National Voices
Public Health
Social Care Institute for Excellence
Think Local Act Personal

Source: National Collaboration for Integrated Care and Support (2013).

across the system and with commissioners, providers and the independent sector, with the intended aim to improve health and ensure that care was integrated, coordinated and in the right place, and to promote increased capacity, capability and knowledge (Ham et al., 2016).

Box 3.6	Aims of the National Collaboration for Integrated Care and Support

- Improving the outcomes and experiences of individuals and communities
- Taking the individual's viewpoint on fragmented care
- Dealing with the consequences of fragmented care and support
- Monitoring early indications of the positive impact of the new approaches to integrated care
- Moving resources out of hospitals into primary, community and social care
- Considering what integrated care and support looks like from an individual perspective

Source: NHS England (2013).

The Local Government Association (LGA) has developed a Care and Health Improvement Programme (CHIP). The LGA has accepted that it is essential to make integration work, noting that it is not an easy task or a panacea for financial challenges; it requires navigating complexities in accountability, leadership, and financial flows (Local Government Association, 2016c). The CHIP is designed to support local government to make sense of the increasingly complex health and care landscape. The support is geared towards helping local government and partners understand and address the blocks and drivers to integration. There has also been a focus on redesigning systems and services to invest more to prevent or intervene before health and social care needs escalate. The CHIP provides a suite of diagnosis, guidance, tools, and resources and stresses the importance of leadership. It is recognised that integration presents particularly difficult challenges of accountability, integrated commissioning, and shifting investment on to preventative and community-based provision (Local Government Association, 2015, p. 6). The LGA states it will work with new care pilots and test integrated models and share lessons. During 2015–16 LGA advisers engaged directly with over 70 per cent of councils (Local Government Association, 2016d).

Better Care Fund

The government commitment to developing integration in England as a priority did require financial support and upfront investment. The Better Care Fund (BCF) was created in the 2013 Spending Round, described as an integration transformation fund (Bennett and Humphries, 2014). The fund of £3.8billion was a single pooled budget for health and social care to work more closely together. This pooling did not draw on new or additional money, but half came from CCG allocations in addition to funds from NHS money transferred to social care, plus carers' breaks funds, reablement funds and capital grant funds. It was clear that the introduction of the BCF meant a substantial shift of activity and resources from hospitals to the community (Bennett and Humphries, 2014, p. 1). It was the government's aim that the BCF would be an enduring part of the health and care system. Taking money for the BCF from NHS services was seen widely as putting additional pressures on health provision even though overall financial savings were envisaged. An original intention was that the budget would be used to support adult social care services that have a health benefit. The implementation of the BCF would bring together health and social care and would be a locally led initiative but with national oversight by departments (National Audit Office, 2014).

The BCF was to be spent on a plan agreed between the local authorities and the CCGs, signed off by both parties and the local HWBs. Guidance was given on the details required including: data sharing between health and social care; joint approaches to assessments and care planning, public and user involvement, and agreement on the impact on acute services (Bennett and Humphries, 2014, p. 2). Also prescribed were indicators for measuring performance and an incentive pay-for-performance part of the BCF was introduced. The BCF was to commence in 2015 and all 151 HWBs submitted valid plans. Some local councils and CCGs chose to commit an extra £1.7billion of their planned spending on adult social care and out-of-hospital services to the pooled fund. Operating in a still challenging financial environment in May 2014 NHS England concluded that the estimate of gains was over-optimistic and would not make the expected £1billion savings for the NHS (NAO, 2014, p. 8). The National Audit Office also concluded that the quality of the early planning and preparations did not appear to match the scale of ambition. Alterations to the scheme followed, and the number of indicators on which payment for performance was linked was reduced from six to one, only retaining reducing total emergency admissions. Changes were also made to the forms of governance and programme management, including extra funding. Evidence on the cost-effectiveness of initiatives to promote integration would be developed by the Department of Health. The BCF has continued as one of the most ambitious programmes across the NHS and local government to date (Local Government Association, 2016c). The operation of the fund has been criticised and the House of Commons Public Accounts Committee 2017 found the BCF had failed to achieve any of the objectives for saving money, reducing emergency admissions or delaying discharges. The PAC report called the fund a complicated ruse to transfer money from health to local government in order to plug gaps in adult social care funding. The PAC also drew attention to issues of increased bureaucracy, lack of accountability for performance, and limited engagement with local government. For 2016–17 the specific issues of the BCF changed to focus on support for carers and advocacy. Better care support has been developed for the future through a programme of guidance, a Better Care Exchange, and new regional better care managers to coordinate and commission support regionally.

NICE: Standards for integration

The National Institute for Health and Care Excellence, usually referred to as NICE, was given responsibilities in the Health and Social Care Act to develop quality standards for social care as well as health. Since 2012 NICE has been developing integrated health and social care standards to drive quality improvement. NICE developed a programme of work on standards in topical areas, for some of which no guidance existed, including the transition between health and social care services and older people in residential settings as well as domiciliary care. In 2015 in social care guidance, NICE called for health and social care to be integrated so that better, more person-centred care could be provided for the growing number of older people with social care needs and multiple long-term conditions (NICE, 2015). The guideline provides a framework for offering appropriate and person-centred care including: people having a single named care coordinator; a care plan updated regularly; community-based multidisciplinary support for people using services and their carers; and having more choice and control over care and support. This guidance is aimed at commissioners, health and social care practitioners, care providers, users and their carers. NICE health and social care quality standards will apply in England only and it is for the UK devolved administrations to decide on their policies.

Vanguard sites, new care models

In 2015 NHS England announced the first Vanguard sites to take the lead in transforming care by developing local health and care services bringing together GP services, home care, mental health, community nursing, and hospitals.

The main aim was to improve health through developing new models of care and, in all, 50 sites were established. Of the five types of Vanguard set up (Box 3.7), three were more or less exclusively health in coverage while the other two types implied a degree of collaboration between health and social care. The oversight partnership did not include local authorities but did include the Care Quality Commission.

Box 3.7	Types and Numbers of Vanguard Sites

1. Enhanced health in care homes   6
2. Multispeciality community provider   14
3. Integrated primary and acute care systems   9
4. Urgent and emergency Vanguards   8
5. Acute care collaborations   13

Source: NHS England (2016c).

The first two types do clearly have an integration dimension, the enhanced health in care homes aimed at offering older people better, joined-up health care and rehabilitation services. In practice the schemes did involve local authorities and CCGs as well as NHS trusts, GPS and voluntary bodies. The Gateshead Project had a focus on delivering integrated community bed and home-based care services providing holistic care across the traditional boundaries. It was the intention to develop a sustainable model through co-commissioning and co-provision of services. Other projects focused on: enhancing the skills and training of care home staff; tackling social isolation; and enabling technologies with telehealth and telecare. The enhanced models had links with social care and created multidisciplinary teams to promote independence and the quality of care. The main focus of the second category was on moving specialist care out of hospitals into the community. The West Wakefield Health and Wellbeing Initiative is aimed at those most at risk of becoming ill through extending primary care access, pop-up primary care and social prescribing.

Multispeciality community provider Vanguards tend to be very wide-ranging and include numbers of GP practices, hospital trusts, CCGs, a local authority, voluntary bodies and perhaps an ambulance trust or a health and wellbeing board. Often there is an emphasis on the position of GPs with integrated GP led provision, or mergers or partnerships of a number of GP practices. Also popular is a focus on creating a single point of access for community outside-of-hospital services or facilitating all medical and social needs to be met in one place. Care coordination and care navigation support is popular as are more usual rapid response teams and extensive care teams for the frail elderly. An example of a multispeciality community provider includes an urgent care service, an ambulatory care service, long-term condition management, GP complex care service and extended primary care services.

City/region devolution and integration

City devolution has been a movement in England to decentralise powers to city areas through joining up the operations of local authorities. The Labour government's Local Democracy, Economic Development and Construction Act 2009 empowered some local authorities to develop combined city authorities (CCAs). By 2011 Manchester and Leeds had become the government's first areas to move ahead with planning. Under the Coalition what was termed the devolution of powers continued with separate city deals negotiated with a range of cities who applied (Smith and Wistrich, 2014) although the powers involved related mainly to transport, infrastructure and economic development. The aftermath of the Scottish referendum and the decision to increase devolved powers for Scotland led to government attention turning to further developments in city devolution. In 2014 George Osborne, the Chancellor of the Exchequer, made his Northern Powerhouse Speech, announcing his intention to have a discussion about a serious devolution of powers and budgets for any city willing to move to a new model of city government and have directly elected mayors. This was followed by the Cities and Local Government Devolution Act, providing the legislative framework to enable devolved powers for cities with elected mayors.

A city devolution deal between the Treasury and Greater Manchester was signed in 2014 and was extended in 2015 to take control of £6.2billion of health and social care budgets. The memorandum of understanding is between the Greater Manchester Combined Authority of ten boroughs, the UK government, 12 CCGs, and NHS England. This was described by the head of NHS England as the greatest integration and devolution of care funding since the creation of the NHS (McKenna and Dunn, 2015, p. 8). The deal covered the entire system: acute and primary care, social care, community and mental health services, public health, and possibly health education. Established was a Greater Manchester Health and Social Care Partnership Board, with two sub-groups, a joint commissioning board and an overarching provider federation (Sandford, 2015). The intention was that the system would be implemented with the minimum of institutional change and the arrangements would remain part of the national NHS and social care system. Greater Manchester had a track record of collaboration and thus Manchester has taken the lead with the most substantial deal. It was recognised that a number of key issues would have to be tackled including coordinating the collaboration of 500 GP practices, bringing together the health and social care workforces and the operation of the accountability of different organisations (Westminster Health Forum, 2016). Five priorities for system transformation were agreed, including transforming community-based care and support. An early review noted the financial challenge in directing the flow of monies and investing in prevention and community-based approaches. This review did note the real positive breakthrough with joint commissioning and the providers forum (Local Government Association, 2015). Four future challenges were identified: subsidiarity and operation at the right level; making the financial case for prevention; enthusing the public; and shifting the provider landscape.

In 2015 38 bids were made for devolved powers and of these around half contained some form of devolution over health and social care. Of the deals concluded, Cornwall's included an invitation to the council, the CCG and partners to work with the UK government and NHS England to move progressively towards integration of health and social care. Cornwall was seeking support to develop a devolved, ring-fenced, place-based health and social budget with a minimum five-year settlement, totalling around £2billion. NHS England has laid down overarching guidance and information there on models of devolution of health and social care. There is a focus on integrated commissioning with four possible models specified: a seat at the table for commissioning decisions; co-commissioning or joint decision making; delegated commissioning arrangements; or fully devolved commissioning involving a transfer of functions. This document also sets out assessment criteria (Box 3.8).

Box 3.8	Assessment Criteria Framework for City Devolution of Health and Social Care

- Governance, accountability, and assurance
- Financial flows, where budgets should sit, how risk sharing might work
- Workforce implications and organisations' impact
- Patient/public participation and consultation
- Impact on other organisations
- Impact of new policy announcements/broader policy direction of travel

Source: NHS England (2016b).

This form of integration in England is at an early stage and has to be part of an overall devolution deal which raises issues about the capacity of local areas to deliver. Core themes of joining up public services and increasing innovation and experimentation open opportunities for health and social care bids and ideally there may be minimal organisational change. The evidence for the whole project remains patchy and contested (Randall and Casebourne, 2015). They identify four challenges as: a negotiation process which is opaque; an extremely compressed timeline; weak centre-local relations which put sustainable devolution at risk; and a question of who leads the devolution agenda. Other issues have been raised about health and social care in terms of the relationship with regulators and the powers of NHS England. There is a general issue as to the appropriateness of the term devolution as this system is not devolution as it is defined for Scotland, Wales and Northern Ireland. In reality it may be better described as a form of the extended health and social care partnerships as they have existed in England,

Integrated personal commissioning

In 2015 a further initiative was launched, the Integrated Personal Commissioning (IPC) Programme, as a partnership between NHS England and the Local Government Association. This programme aims to enable people to blend and control the resources available to them to commission their own health and social care through personalised care planning and personal budgets, building on learning from personal budgets in social care. Each of the nine demonstration sites is working with one of four types of cohort: children and young people with complex needs; people with multiple long-term conditions; people with learning disabilities with high support needs; and people with significant mental health needs. IPC is to be delivered by enhanced multidisciplinary teams, usually located in general practice. The IPC model is characterised by five key shifts in people's experience of care, as shown in Box 3.9 (NHS England, 2015).

Box 3.9	**Five Key Shifts of Integrated Personal Commissioning**

- Proactive coordination of care
- Building community capacity and peer support
- Personalised care and support planning through conversations
- Choice and control over resources available to people
- Personalised commissioned options, contracting out and payments

Source: NHS England (2015).

Sustainability and transformation plans

The Improving Quality team moved in 2015 to NHS England as a new Sustainable Improvement Team (NHS England, 2016a) and was involved in a new initiative in 2016 known as Sustainability and Transformation plans (STPs). These are localised plans to improve health and social care across England with the country divided into 44 'footprint' areas. In each area there is a collaboration between all the statutory bodies involved in health and social care, in practice mainly NHS trusts, CCGs, and local councils. The overall aim is to improve care and also financial sustainability through building capacity for transformational change, testing of improvement initiatives, and use of the latest knowledge and best practice. This initiative is not wholly focused on integration and the key areas of work cover: capability and capacity; primary care; acute care and seven-day services; living longer lives; plus long-term conditions and integrated care. In some areas, sustainability and transformational planning can be used to set out a business case for city devolution (NHS England, 2016a, p. 11). The possibility of this planning process leading to major reconfiguration of hospitals has been raised but the process has no formal powers. The plans produced have had a strong focus on delivering more health care in the community. The future impact on integration was stressed by the public accounts committee (2017) which suggested that in future in England integration would be delivered through the mechanism of the Sustainability and Transformation footprint planning process.

Conclusions

The period since 2012 has seen four major processes in England. The restructuring of health care has had consequences for the relationship with social care and progress with integration. This arose with the creation of Clinical Commissioning Groups given a key role in commissioning integrated services, with new Health and Wellbeing Boards located in local government and the developing work of the Care Quality Commission. CCGs represented a national uniform system with a strong local foundation for joint commissioning for health and social care. A key test for the new structure was identified as their ability to lead the health care system in England (Lotinga and Glasby, 2012, p. 179). The second process was the focus on experimental initiatives embracing integrated practices, including pioneer projects, the Vanguard initiative, city devolution followed by the more controversial Sustainability and Transformation Plans. However, no uniform model for adaptation in England for integration has emerged and diverse partnership schemes remain the dominant model. The third process related to financial and funding issues. The Better Care Fund based on pooled budgets has increased resources but there have been major pressures on local government funding and expenditure, leading to estimates of a £2.6million funding shortfall for adult social care by 2020. The other significant process has been the further emergence of a wide range of reports, research and analysis of how greater integration can improve services.

4 Integration in Scotland

Introduction

In 1998 the new Scotland Act gave the Scottish government and Parliament control over health and social care, although the services had been administered in Scotland previously operated through the Scotland Office. The health system was based geographically on NHS boards but operated on a principle of collaboration and partnership and not on an internal market (Steel, 2013). Local government was responsible for adult social care and children's care. Health care was predominantly provided by the public sector with a small private sector, but independent social care and support by private and third sectors increased sharply as in England. By 2012 some 88 per cent of care homes and 51 per cent of domiciliary hours were in the independent sector (Audit Scotland, 2012). The allocation of funding for health and social care was determined by the Scottish administration but from the overall allocation to Scotland from the UK Treasury. This was calculated through the Barnett Formula, as for Wales and Northern Ireland, reflecting mainly changes in population and changes in the UK government expenditure. Broadly one-third of the total devolved budget went to health and social care in local councils' expenditure, increased in real terms by 46 per cent between 2002–03 and 2010–11 (Steel, 2013, p. 30). It has been argued that the integration of health and social care was a key policy aim of Scotland's newly devolved government (Woods, 2001). The aims of integration within health and between health and social care remained objectives of government in Scotland (Steel, 2013, p. 31). Integration became a key element in the development of health policy and also a priority for implementation and delivery. This was clearly demonstrated in the Scottish Executive's paper *Partnerships for Care – Scotland's White Paper (Scottish Executive, 2003).*

Policy development and Joint Future

Integrated care became a core component of the main policy and strategy documents for health and social care. Integrated care was a particularly prominent aspect of *Building a Health Service Fit for the Future* (Kerr Review) (Scottish Executive, 2005a) and in *Delivering for Health* (Scottish Executive, 2005b), where an objective was described as high quality services promoted by the integration of services. *Better Health, Better Care: Action Plan* (Scottish Government,

2007) reaffirmed the commitment to strengthening collaboration and integrated approaches to service improvement with a national plan. *Improving the Health and Wellbeing of People with Long-Term Conditions in Scotland* (Scottish Government, 2009) was a further national action plan which set out an approach reflecting NHS Scotland's integrated system (Steel and Cylus, 2012, p. 96). These general policy commitments occurred alongside action to implement integration. Joint Future was developed as a strategy to improve the structures and processes associated with joint working, laying the foundations for integrated health and social care to be housed together (Hutchison, 2015). This was originally aimed at developing care for older people and the strategy was progressed through the establishment of health and social care partnerships (McTavish and Mackie, 2003). The Community Care and Health (Scotland) Act (2002) helped to break down some of the barriers to collaboration by conferring powers similar to England to transfer powers to facilitate lead commissioning and to create pooled budgets. Thus Joint Future partnerships between health boards and local authority social work departments were given a strong lead from the centre, aligning budgets, sharing assessments and using joint management (Bruce and Forbes, 2005). Joint Future led to a new type of partnership body under the NHS Reform (Scotland) Act 2004, with an extended remit. Each NHS board had to plan and establish a community health board to link clinical and care teams and align with local authorities. This was intended to build on the success of partnerships operating between the NHS and local authorities up to that point and had a strong focus on organisational development (Taylor, 2015). The original guidelines had proposed community health boards as sub-committees of the NHS boards delivering mainly primary and community health although discretion was given to the details of the form of partnership. This resulted in alternative integrated models; health only partnerships; partial integration with other services, for example, mental health; or integrated health and social care services with joint management arrangements between NHS boards and local councils. The essence was partnership working at local and national levels in Scotland rather than more formal integration (Forbes and Evans, 2009). A joint improvement strategy was also developed to work with partnerships through providing practical support and additional capacity (Hendry, 2010, p. 45). Community partnerships were viewed as essential to achieve the shift in care and a key building block and led to further government action to promote better collaboration and change more uniformly across the whole system. The established configuration consisted of 29 community health partnerships and seven community health and social care boards operating with joint accountability to NHS boards and local authorities.

Establishment of health and social care partnerships

Major reviews of the operation of community health partnerships (CHPs) found both positive and negative aspects. A study of community health partnerships (Scottish Government, 2010) found good progress in shifting the balance of care to more home provision, redesign of long-term care provision and some achievements in linking health and social care. Some of the main challenges centred on engaging effectively with GPs, lack of clarity about roles, duplication and resources. Audit Scotland (2011) also reviewed the effectiveness of community health partnerships, finding the role, responsibilities and accountability arrangements for CHPs were not always clear, that CHPs' development plans and local authority plans did not always set out a joint vision, and there were different performance reporting arrangements. Petch (2011) identified problems of duplication, lack of coordination, unclear governance arrangements, limited joint funding and variation in services.

Among the key recommendations, Audit Scotland concluded that the Scottish government should work with NHS boards and councils to undertake a fundamental review of the various partnership arrangements for health and social care in Scotland to ensure that they are efficient and effective and add value. The Audit Scotland report was one factor contributing to the government's decision to consult on proposals to replace CHPs with health and social care partnerships to secure greater joined-up integrated services. The separate and sometimes disjointed systems of health and social care were seen as no longer meeting the needs of people with multiple long-term conditions. The declared objectives were to ensure that

- health and social care services are firmly integrated around the needs of individuals, their carers and other family members,
- they are characterised by strong and consistent clinical care and professional leadership,
- the providers of services are held to account jointly and effectively for improved delivery, and
- services are underpinned by flexible, sustainable financial mechanisms and increased investment in community provision.

(Scottish Government, 2012a)

The Scottish government's view was supported by local government, NHS Scotland and the third sector. Also influential was an inquiry into the integration of health and social care by the Health and Sport Committee of the Scottish Parliament. This inquiry focused on two main questions: identifying the challenges in better integrating health and social services and detailing what the Scottish government proposals needed to address to overcome the barriers to integration (Scottish Parliament Health and Sport Committee, 2012, p. 3). The Committee agreed that the Scottish government's plan for integration should avoid being driven by structures and structural change with no requirement for wholesale transfer of staff, that there should be a clear line of accountability to rest with one individual for each health and social care partnership, and that there should be closer engagement with GPs, and strong national leadership. The declared outcome by the Scottish government (2013a) was an intention to legislate to require health boards and local authorities to integrate health and social services for all adults. It was not the aim of the Scottish government to create new statutory organisations separate from the NHS and local government which were seen as creating further barriers to integration. It was the intention to legislate for the principle that health boards and local authorities would have joint and equal responsibility for partnerships and have equal voting power on health and social care partnerships. This legislation was seen as addressing a number of difficulties faced by existing partners in pursuing better outcomes (Scottish Government, 2012a, p. 7). This heralded the first attempt in the UK to place a statutory duty on the NHS and local councils to integrate health and social care services (Audit Scotland, 2015b). Local planning arrangements were viewed as central to the success of the proposals.

Support for integration

Three particular strategies have given support to the development of integrated care: the strategy on managed clinical networks, an Integrated Resource Framework, and Reshaping Care for Older People. Managed clinical networks (MCNs) have been seen as an enduring feature of the health care system in Scotland for the last 15 years (Steel, 2013, p. 36). They are constituted of linked groups of health professionals from primary, secondary and tertiary care working in a coordinated manner across boundaries. This leads to connections to plan delivery. Some 130 MCNs are in existence, some national and some local, and they cover conditions such as diabetes, stroke, respiratory diseases, and palliative care. MCNs involve work across boundaries, creating pathways, and, although mainly focused on health, there were some partnership structures involving local authorities relating to mental health and learning disability (Scottish Government, 2012b). MCNs provided a model for promoting collaborative working across care sectors and usually incorporated primary physicians, nurses, professions allied to medicine, but were more focused on dealing with more complex needs where a whole system approach is valuable. Hendry (2010) identified small wins for the strategy particularly through the development of workforce learning and practice and engagement with fellow practitioners in sharing experience. There has been some evidence of achievements in the areas of stroke and older people's care.

An Integrated Resource Framework (IRF) was jointly developed from 2008 by the Scottish government, NHS Scotland and the Convention of Scottish Local Authorities to enable the partners to have a better understanding about the costs and quality of decision-making and of their combined resources. The framework improved the ability of local authorities and boards to plan and realign resources to support shifts in clinical and care activity (Steel, 2013, p. 38). Rather than focus on money the IRF sought to enable clinicians, care professionals and managers to reflect on outcomes when committing resources (Taylor, 2015, p. 4). The explicit mapping of information allows and facilitates resources to flow between partners. Ferguson and Lavalette (2013) noted evidence of a drive for efficiency and coordination of joint working also producing shifts in the balance of care towards personalisation and self-directed support.

The Reshaping Care for Older People's programme was launched by the Scottish government for the period 2011 to 2021 (Scottish Government, 2010). This programme included the future funding of long-term care; building capacity in the community and realising co-production; providing person-centred integrated care and support at home. Many of the objectives were linked to the objectives of integration, to increase avoidable hospital admissions, to take preventative action, and to implement a whole systems approach (Hendry, 2010, p. 49). A multi-agency improvement network was also established to share learning, spread improvements, and support collaboration and local partnerships to improve person-centred outcomes (Joint Improvement Team, 2013). The Scottish government also introduced a change fund to encourage closer collaboration between NHS boards, councils and the voluntary sector. The change fund was a key element to rebalance care, support and service provision in order to support older people to stay in their own homes. The fund was distributed to each of the 32 partnerships on receipt of plans. From 2012/13, 29 per cent of funds from carers support was now aimed at preventative and anticipatory services.

A wider policy context in Scotland was created through the introduction of free personal care, under which personal care services were delivered by local authorities to people aged over 65. This policy has been as part of increasing emphasis and support for care in the community (Bell et al., 2007). It also encouraged a whole system approach with both health and personal social care free at the point of delivery (Dickinson and Glasby, 2006).

Vision for integration

Despite some good examples of partnership working, community health partnerships struggled to deliver shifts in the balance of care and were seen as lacking traction on the dominance of service provision in acute hospitals (Taylor, 2015, p. 5). The main vision statement for integration was to be expressed most clearly in 2013 by the Scottish government but there had been earlier contributions. The Christie Commission on the delivery of pubic services in Scotland emphasised the importance of joined-up services at a local level (Christie, 2011). The Royal College of Nursing (RCN) had published a vision in a document, 'Principles for Delivering the Integration of Care' (RCN, 2012). These were set out under four themes and related principles:

– ensuring local integrated plans are integrated, in partnership with a shared vision to improve outcomes
– committing to processes that sustain collaboration and respectful relationships
– securing the quality and safety of integrated care
– setting national principles and oversight for integrated care, with an inclusive approach.

In 2013 the Scottish government set out a 2020 vision for health and social care with integration as a core element, described as follows:

Box 4.1	2020 Vision for Health and Social Care

- a healthcare system where we have integrated health and social care, with a focus on prevention
- a move from care in hospitals and care homes to more community based settings
- care provided to the highest standards of quality and safety
- a focus on people getting back into their home or community environment as soon as possible.

Integrated arrangements would be led by clinicians and social work professionals.

Source: Scottish Government (2013b).

Achieving the 2020 Vision was seen as requiring major changes in the way that services are delivered and a significant shift in resources into community based services (Audit Scotland, 2014, p. 35). The role of integrated authorities was seen as critical to meeting the 2020 Vision. Setting out priorities for improvement and long-term ambitions for the health service integration appears as one of six priorities alongside health inequalities, early years, safe care, primary care, and person–centred care (Audit Scotland, 2015b, p. 43).

Integrated Authorities

Legislation in the form of the Public Bodies (Joint Working) (Scotland) Act 2014 set out the legal framework for integrating adult health and social care services. The introduction of the legislation reflected a response to the limited evidence from the existing arrangements of a shift to more community based services and a policy to provide seamless, joined-up quality health and social care services (Burgess, 2012, p. 4). The Act created new partnerships, known as Integrated Authorities, with statutory responsibilities to coordinate local health and social care services. The Integrated Authorities would oversee budgets totalling around two-thirds of Scotland's spending on health and social care. It was estimated that there could be savings generated of £138–£157 million per annum

Box 4.2	Structure for Delivering Integrated Health and Social Care

Bodies	Number
Local councils	32
NHS boards	14
Integration authorities	31

(Audit Scotland, 2015a, p. 25). Integrated Authorities are expected to coordinate health and social care and commission and direct NHS boards and councils to deliver services in line with a local strategic plan.

Councils and NHS boards are required to integrate the governance, planning and resourcing of adult social care services and adult primary care and community health services and some hospital services. There are other areas of discretion for Integrated Authorities, for example, to decide where children's social care or housing services fell within the new arrangements. As Integrated Authorities have been planned it appears most will oversee more than the statutory minimum services and the scope of responsibilities will vary (Audit Scotland, 2015a, p. 20). The Act requires each Integrated Authority to establish at least two localities, to provide an organisational basis for local leadership and planning (Burgess, 2016, p. 11). Integration Authorities can follow one of two models: the body corporate model in which NHS boards delegate health and social care functions to an integration joint board or the lead agency model in which they can delegate functions to each other. All areas are planning to follow the body corporate model apart from one area, Highland (Audit Scotland, 2015a, p. 14). NHS boards and councils delegate budgets to the integrated joint board. This would produce an integrated budget in each integrated partnership to support the delivery of integrated functions. Although Integrated Authorities will lead the planning of integrated services they are not independent of councils and NHS boards. Governance arrangements are specified and for integrated joint boards, members of the board are a mix of voting and non-voting members, but councils and NHS boards are each required to nominate three voting members. while a chief officer for a body corporate must be appointed as a single point of management (Bessos, 2015). Audit Scotland (2015a) in reviewing progress in planning for integrated authorities expressed concern about building good governance, the complexity over accountability for service delivery, and difficulties for councils and NHS boards finding agreement over budgets for the Integration Authorities, as well as disagreement over performance measurement systems and the development of the localities focus. It was also noted that there was a need for planning to show how an integrated workforce will be developed. NHS Scotland published core integration indicators to allow national benchmarking (Burgess, 2016, p. 13). There would be locality planning arrangements at sub-partnership level.

The aim of the Public Bodies (Joint Working) legislation was described as threefold (Robson, 2013):

1. to improve the quality and consistency of care for patients, carers, service users and families;
2. to improve seamless joined-up care that enables people to stay in their own homes; and
3. to ensure resources are used effectively to deliver services for a growing population with longer-term, complex needs.

The Act put in place a set of integrated planning principles for services.

Box 4.3	**Integrated Planning Principles**

Services provided in a way which

- is integrated from the point of view of service users;
- takes account of the particular needs of different service users;
- takes account of the particular characteristics and circumstances of different service users;
- respects the rights and dignity of service users;
- protects and improves the safety of service users;
- improves the quality of the service;
- is planned and led locally in a way which is engaged with the community, including users and carers;
- best anticipates needs and prevents them arising;
- makes the best use of the available facilities and resources.

Source: Public Bodies (Joint Working) (Scotland) Act 2014.

In the integrated joint board system, which most bodies have accepted, an integration scheme has to be drawn up dealing with such matters as: engagement of stakeholders; care governance arrangements; workforce and organisational development; data sharing; financial management; dispute resolution; local arrangements for operational delivery; liability arrangements; and complaints handling (Audit Scotland, 2015a).

The supporting note for the legislation in integration specifies social care services provided by local authorities must be integrated, as they relate to adults.

Box 4.4	**Social Services to be Integrated 2015**

Social work services for adults and older people
    Services for adults with physical disabilities and learning disabilities

Mental health services – drug and alcohol services
Adult protection and drug abuse – carers' support
Care home services – adult placement services
Health improvement – housing support and adaption
Day services – respite provision
Occupational auxiliary services – reablement services

Each health board must delegate all its functions as they relate to adult primary and community health services, along with a proportion of hospital sector provision.

The Act puts in place several outcomes for improvement assessing the impact on people of health and social care services. Integration authorities are expected to publish an annual performance report on progress and a core suite of indicators has been suggested, some outcome indicators based on service feedback and some from health system data collected for other reasons. Some indicators appear more related to general health performance. Petch (2014) has drawn attention to the dangers of a focus on treating outputs and performance measures as a replacement for delivering positive experiences for the individual. The Scottish government guidance highlights the importance of greater effective relationships with community planning partnerships and integrated authorities have been added to the statutory list and are expected to work together (Audit Scotland, 2016, p. 13).

The 31 Integrated Authorities became operational in April 2016, responsible for a budget of over £8 billion. Reviewing initial progress Audit Scotland (2015b, p. 5) warned that they would not be able to make a major impact facing rises with agreeing budgets, complex governance arrangements and workforce planning. Audit Scotland suggested a need to set targets and timescales and to begin to strategically shift resources towards a community based approach to health.

Assessment of progress

There have been relatively few major studies of the success or achievements of integration initiatives to date. A national outcomes framework has existed from 2008 comprising 16 performance measures across six themes of user satisfaction, faster access, support for carers, quality of care planning, identifying those at risk, and moving services closer to users. This was widely used or adapted by community health partnerships (Steel, 2013, p. 45). Two main measures used to assess integration have been reducing the rate of emergency bed days in acute specialities for older people and speeding up discharge of patients from hospitals, but progress has not been extensive. Ball et al. (2010) found significant improvement in relation to reductions in waiting time for assessment for expressed concern that objectives such as delayed discharges and number of emergency admissions were not highly prioritised. There has also been little evidence of an actual transfer of resources transferred from acute care (Steel, 2013, p. 49). The Scottish government has set targets of substantial savings to be generated from reductions in hospital admissions, limiting delays in discharge, and reducing inefficiencies, as integrated authorities develop (Audit Scotland, 2015b, p. 25). The achievements of integration tend to be assessed as part of national health and wellbeing outcomes which are fairly general in nature or as part of the NHS targets and standards, known as HEAT: health improvement, efficiency, access, and treatment (Audit Scotland, 2015a, p. 18). If one community partnership was making a significant impact in an area whilst stagnating in another then developing interventions based on sharing best practice could be considered (Ball et al., 2010, p. 405).

Concern has been expressed at two particular issues. A need for workforce development and planning has been identified as critical for the success for integration. It has been reported that few Integrated Authorities had developed a long-term strategy for a suitably skilled workforce (Audit Scotland, 2015a). A second topic of concern was the involvement of GPs in contributing actively towards the success of integrated services. GPs as key drivers of expenditure were perceived to have a pivotal role in the successful establishment of integrated budgets (Hutchison, 2015, p. 133). The Royal College of Nursing had carried out a study of nursing practitioners' experience of working in integrated teams. This study found in practice a high degree of mutual respect between professions, helped by formal development sessions, despite original scepticism. It helped that small elements of job roles could be shared and use made of opportunities for shadowing, while use of language was also important (Mathieson, 2011). Relationships between senior managers could be difficult, and social workers were found to work in a more bureaucratic or hierarchical way than nurses who had more autonomy on the job. The process of assessment has moved to a stronger emphasis on outcomes based approaches, but requiring paying more attention to the views of persons impacted by the services, focusing on the changes made by services, the impact on people's lives and independence and the experience as users (Institute for Research and Innovation in Social Services, 2013). The Scottish government has set out 23 core integration indicators, as a combination of the views of adults using services and quantitative data from a range of sources (Audit Scotland, 2015b, p. 33). Discretion has been used as regards the scope of integration with nine councils having integrated children's social work services, and 16 councils integrated criminal justice services (Audit Scotland, 2016, p. 40). The substructure of localities within these partnerships has meant differences developing with each evolving at a different pace. Difficulties in agreeing budgets, attributing adult services expenditure and uncertainty about long-term funding have hindered comprehensive strategic plans (Audit Scotland, 2015a, p. 31).

Integration activities

A number of activities have figured prominently within the main focus of integrated activities.

Long-term conditions

Long-term conditions have been a major area for the development of integrated activities. One in four people has some long-term condition and two-thirds of people over 75 have a long-term condition. A long-term conditions collaboration strategy 2008–2011 has taken an integrated approach to long-term conditions (Steel, 2013, p. 39). Integrated Authorities provide a way of managing such conditions. Integrated day services and teams have been developed to support older adults with complex support needs, including mental health problems.

The support teams consist of a manager, nurses, social care workers, and clinical support staff dealing with referrals from social workers, GPs, and mental health practitioners. Also developed have been community based learning disabilities teams.

Intermediate care and reablement

One of the aims of integrated services is to prevent unnecessary admissions to acute hospitals or long-term care residential care, and to promote independent living. Intermediate care is the bridge between independent living, another major objective of integration, and hospital discharge. Intermediate care has been described as at the frontier of integrated working whether between hospital and community or between health and social care agencies (Institute for Research and Innovation in Social Services, 2013, p. 2). It would be difficult for intermediate care to function without the relevant services coming together. Attempts have been made to link intermediate care more closely to mainstream services. A demonstration project was created in Fife to enhance knowledge and access in a capability framework with improved training to counter limited understanding of integrated services (Mitchell et al., 2011). There are also examples of discharge and reablement teams who work with referrals from multidisciplinary teams based in hospitals. Reablement services based on home care have developed, for example, in City of Edinburgh Council seeking to maximise user independence and reduce the level of support. Health and social care teams ensure that a full spectrum of needs can be considered holistically. Each reablement team consists of a term coordinator, care workers, occupational therapists, housing support officer and administrative support. The integrated approach has ensured a high standard of services for the transition to long-term provision of care at home.

Self-directed support

The self-directed support strategy in Scotland has since 2013 required local councils to give people a choice of the delivery methods for their social care. They can opt for direct payments or can be facilitated to give local councils directions on their care. The strategy has implications for integrated services as people need a combination of health and social care support (Payne, 2012). It is also the case that NHS boards can use funds to assist with direct payments. Where a package of supports includes jointly commissioned services with health, local councils are encouraged to work with their NHS partners to provide a jointly funded budget, covering health and social care (Robson, 2013). Another strategy being developed is the rapid response strategy with rapid response teams to avoid emergency admissions, and the aim of usually enabling the person to remain at home. A further development has been through integrated addiction services teams with a composition of mental health nurses, social workers, addiction workers, and support workers, taking referrals from GPs, and staff in social work, accident and emergency and criminal justice.

Conclusions

The theme of integration has become a key and consistent topic of analysis and debate in Scotland and a priority for action and implementation. The integration of health and social care has been described as the most radical reform in health care in Scotland since the foundation of the NHS (Burgess, 2016, p. 3). It has, however, been pointed out that there are often gaps between the policy rhetoric and practical implementation (Robertson, 2011, p. 31). As in the other countries of the UK integration has been promoted by government departments, senior health and social care professional bodies and organisations, local authorities, academics and user organisations. In Scotland there has been a degree of organisational stability in the NHS in the last 10 years which has encouraged local implementation to follow national strategies. It is part of the national outcome or target for living longer, healthier lives that value and quality are achieved through the integration of health and social care provision. A factor valuable for Scotland has been the decision to introduce a uniform system of integration throughout Scotland with only some local discretion. This means that the system of the new Integrated Authorities will apply across Scotland and thus produce a less disjointed structure than in England. The system is short of full structural integration. Integrated Authorities are not independent of councils and, regardless of integration, councils retain statutory responsibilities in relation to social work services. Few Integrated Authorities oversee acute services in their areas. Scotland's health and social care system has a tradition of an emphasis on collaboration, not competition. There is also in Scotland a strong commitment to localism and the localised structure of integration authorities. This is backed by an equal commitment to co-production and participation in the partnership work. A strong commitment to performance management and tracking performance has been developed through the National Performance Framework strategy which is based on measuring outcomes and indicators. Audit Scotland has also subjected the performance on integration to continuous critical scrutiny by parliamentary committee.

The imposition of a new uniform system was facilitated by the relatively small size of Scotland and the small group of senior managers involved and by a central support team for local partnerships. The size and viability of the programme of organisational change were more manageable as it was built on existing partnership schemes. Potential barriers to successful integration remain, in that major resources are required to initiate new structures and strategies, for training and staffing. At the same time there are consequences of the continuing search for efficiencies and the need to meet existing targets, while the integration of health and social care has been seen as making governance and accountability arrangements more complex (Audit Scotland, 2016, p. 5).

The willingness and ability of staff to collaborate and work together as partners remain significant factors to achieving integration. Scotland's experience with managed clinical networks has helped consolidate multidisciplinary teams and integrated initiatives including co-location of staff. It has, however, been noted that the dominance and influence of the medical model over the social model can be as great in Scotland as in the rest of the UK (Robertson, 2011, p. 35) and local councils are wary of acute care domination. The research to date in Scotland, largely on community health and social care partnerships as noted, shows progress in building relationships with primary care willing to move to an inter-disciplinary model. Whilst there were some small-scale examples of good practice, problems remain with differences in organisational cultures accountability and financial management and the cluttered landscape of partnerships (Steel, 2013, p. 35). Audit Scotland concluded that sufficient progress has not been made towards change in the balance of care to more home and community based settings (Audit Scotland, 2015b). It has proved difficult to shift money away from acute care. Levels of GP engagement in the integrated partnerships remain short of what is required for a fully integrated service. Overall Scotland has been working in a focused manner towards an ambitious programme of activity to promote integration and to a significant degree has placed a reliance on structural change to achieve transformation. However, there is not yet evidence of a major shift in ways of working (Kaehne et al., 2017).

5 Integration in Wales

Introduction

With the establishment of devolution in 1999 health and social care policy became one other responsibility of the Welsh Assembly Government. Health and health services and social services had the status in the then Welsh form of devolution as fields for executive action. Powers increased after the Government of Wales Act 2006 which allowed legislative competence over 20 specified subjects including health and social welfare which covered the social services, and the care of children and older people. Local government was also a specified subject. These powers involved a complex legislative system of measures requiring Westminster approval. In 2011 after a referendum the Welsh Government assumed full responsibility for primary legislation within the 20 fields including health and social care. The services are both operated and managed by the Health and Social Care Department of the Welsh Government. The devolved services were funded through the Barnett formula, as in Scotland and Northern Ireland, and with similar discretion over the allocation of devolved expenditure to health and social care. Wales has a tradition of a relatively small private sector and modest charges for community services. The Welsh Government had taken action to restrict health expenditure (Roberts and Charlesworth, 2014), less protected than in England, but has protected and promoted expenditure on social services. Between 2005–06 and 2013–14 expenditure by Welsh councils on social care services for people over 65 increased by 23 per cent (Audit Office, 2015). At the same time the numbers receiving care reduced and it was more focused on people with complex needs. The promotion and pattern of greater integration have progressed somewhat slowly and through rather general or localised approaches but with integration prominent in government strategies for health and social care.

Structures

A structural division between health and social care has been long-standing in Wales. Local government reorganisations had not altered this position. Major reorganisation in the mid-1990s led to 22 united local authorities in Wales with social work and social care continuing as a core important local function but in some relatively small authorities. Health services were delivered by 14 NHS Trusts which provided secondary health care and community services and 22 local health boards which acted as commissioning agencies for health provision. Concern at the number of local health boards and at the effectiveness of the provider–commissioner divide led to a reorganisation that created seven area local health boards and three specialist boards, with both commissioning and provider functions. The provider–commissioner divide was abolished but not the health–social care structural divide. Local health boards are required to work with public services through joint local service boards. They are not statutory bodies but seen as an expression of engaged public service leadership locally (Longley, 2013, p. 60). They can agree the strategic priorities for multi-agency working and ensure arrangements are in place to deliver joint working as appropriate. Their membership and role are not restricted to health and social care. Collaboration was also encouraged in a structural form through locality networks made up of clusters of GP practices working in partnership with other providers. Such networks mainly facilitated the parts of the NHS to work together. A number of wide-ranging initiatives were undertaken at local level through partnerships. *Improving Social Care in Wales* (2013) provided guidance to help local authorities address social services collaboration with other local authorities. Local health boards and local authorities could form a health and social care partnership to include voluntary bodies and user organisations.

Local Service Boards were replaced by Public Service Boards under the Well-being of Future Generations (Wales) Act (2015). Public Service Boards could coordinate and provide integrated plans for health and social care in each local authority area. The 2015 Act requires local authorities and NHS bodies to enter formal partnership agreements, including pooled budgets, for improving the outcomes for patients in health and social care. The Williams Commission on public service governance and delivery reported on how public services are governed and delivered. It proposed that significant structural change is urgently needed in local government to mitigate the risks of small-scale operations. This led to the conclusion that the 22 local authorities must be merged into larger units instead (Williams, 2014, p. 29). A reduction to eight or nine was suggested with social care functions, to increase scale and capacity and to enhance co-terminosity, although it was suggested that existing local authorities should be merged rather than boundaries completely redrawn. Following the election in 2015 the Welsh government moved to the view that restructuring should not proceed immediately but local councils should get on with formulating the delivery of services to local communities and with the job of integrating health and social care. At the end of 2016 a new approach was announced, retaining the existing 22 local councils but with enhanced systematic and mandatory regional working, probably based around city regions and a health board footprint including social services (Welsh Government, 2017).

The devolved administration at its inception had a strong commitment to support for the NHS, a rejection of internal markets, private providers support for local government continuing with major functions and for localist influence (Greer, 2004). The gap between health and social care policy in Wales and England began to widen with the Welsh emphasis on public health and tackling health inequalities (Longley, 2013, p. 58). In Wales there was also a strong emphasis on promoting collaboration between the different parts of the public services leading to the Making the Connections strategy (Welsh Assembly Government, 2004). In this context policy on integration developed through policies and frameworks with the Welsh government setting overarching principles to be implemented locally. The development of health policy up to 2007, while mainly addressing the causes of ill-health, hospitals and structures, placed a focus on holistic approaches and preventative action. The Welsh Assembly Government began to encourage greater collaboration between health and social services provision. *Designed for Life* (2005) proposed a recasting of all elements of health and social care to ensure high quality care. Following *Designed for Life* there was some rebalancing of services towards the community with provision in intermediate care, crisis teams and integrated teams. The National Service Framework for Older People (Welsh Assembly Government, 2006) included at its core multi-agency working and multidiscipline teams, single budgets and joint priorities. It was argued that there was limited evidence that meaningful progress was being made. Phillips (2008) suggested that the main factors preventing progress were target overload set for health and social care agencies; the fragmentation of budget centres; delays in planning hospital discharge; and budgetary and organisational obstacles to intermediate care. A major strategy for social services, *Fulfilled Lives, Supported Communities*, was published (Welsh Assembly Government, 2007) to operate over the next 10 years.

While models of integrated care delivery were developing in Wales local authority social service leaders had expressed concern at building partnership working, as they were imposed top-down and were often cumbersome and slow moving. But the need for a whole systems approach between social care, local government and health was widely acknowledged. A 2007 strategy for social services proposed to build on the close connection in local government with other services but social services were still mainly seen as a strong, distinct, coherent and accountable function of local government (Welsh Assembly Government, 2007). The creation of fully integrated health bodies saw attempts to take advantage of the new structures. Welsh health bodies and local authorities had a power to establish joint funding mechanisms but few chose to make much use of this power and the Welsh government originally did not force the pace on this issue (Longley et al., 2013, p. 67). There was a growing commitment to provide partners with a seamless approach to assessment, care management, planning, and delivery using local agreements; to tackle the barriers to good partnership working; and to explore better performance management. In contrast to the general treatment in existing policy and legislation of health and social care as two separate entities, a greater focus emerged on coordinated or integrated care, especially as good social care could reduce the need for health interventions, important due to the increasing older people's population (Welsh Local Government Association and NHS Confederation, 2013). *Setting the Direction* (Welsh Government, 2010) was a strategy document aimed at diverting people away from hospital where possible. It pushed for close alignment between health and social services to work seamlessly together and for coordinated preventative care services. This policy direction was subsequently repeated in another strategy document, *Strategy for Health* (Welsh Assembly Government, 2011a), which set a vision for the NHS in Wales until 2016, stating an intention to develop a simplified, integrated strategy for local areas to tackle health inequalities, improve services and early prevention. An independent report on social services in Wales commissioned by the Minister, *From Vision to Action*, had a major focus on integration. It was established to consider how the Assembly government could effect a step change in collaboration between social services and other services and also ensure integrated social services capable of meeting the needs of adults, older people, young people and children (Independent Commission on Social Services, 2010). While it noted existing partnerships had not led to joined-up services, it rejected the solution of a merger of health with adult social care and stated it vital that adults' and children's social services remain united. The independent report agreed that collaboration needed to be addressed more forcibly to rationalise the cost and complexity of the large number of strategic partnerships.

Developments in 2011 marked an increase in action taken to better integrate services across health and social services. *Sustainable Social Services for Wales: A Framework for Action* set out the basis for strategic improvement framework. Fundamental changes were proposed with the Welsh government stating that it would prioritise integrated services, in particular for families with complex needs and frail older people (Welsh Assembly Government, 2011b). The intention was to achieve a more holistic approach to improvement and ensure maximising the resources available and facilitate local delivery with an outcome focused approach. The advisory Bevan Commission in 2011, in making recommendations for a big picture view of health care, had emphasised the importance of working across the health and social care system to alter its fragmented and uncoordinated state, and to identify barriers to improvement and better practice. The aim was to ensure that social care linked up completely with health services, working more closely together and ideally integrating social care and health services to create a seamless service for Wales (Bevan Commission, 2011). These developments did mean that social service teams were working closely with health colleagues to deliver coordinated care and remove duplication. In some areas joint community teams were established to respond urgently to a social or health care crisis to reduce unplanned admissions to hospital.

One of the first new strategies developed was a framework to deliver sustainable health and social care. The main concern of the framework was to bring an end to fragmented care and set out how the Welsh government ambition for truly integrated health and social care services for older people was to be implemented (Welsh Government, 2011c, p. 2). The framework sought to establish integrated working as the normal way of working as well as a way of measuring progress. The ambitious aims for the integrated approach included creating fully integrated referral pathways and addressing all the needs of the service user. The Sustainable Social Services for Wales strategy produced in 2013 also had as a core element a three-year plan for improvement. Local authorities and local health boards would be expected to produce assessment of needs of people who needed care and support and information from users would be key measures in the framework (Welsh Government, 2011c). Ministers asked that each local health board and local government partnerships had to develop an agreed statement of intent for integration of health and social services. The Welsh vision did not specifically embrace structural change but rather changing the balance of care to the community and partnership relationships in planning, resource use, service delivery and performance assessment (Welsh Government, 2014) and ensuring effective multi/professional and multi-agency cooperation. Flexibility was seen as necessary to work across professional and organisational boundaries. A National Commission Board was led by the Association of Directors of Social Services to steer coordination between health and social care services. A number of integrated pilot studies were launched for older people, those with chronic conditions and for children with complex care needs (Kaehne et al., 2017, p. 90).

Social Services and Wellbeing Act 2014

Some of the range of changes required in sustainable social services would necessitate legislation and a Social Services Bill was prepared to provide a legal framework for social services. A major principle was to support the delivery of services in an integrated way to people of all ages, including a unified assessment process. Improved integration of assessment and service delivery would be directed at people who had more intense needs and required intervention from a number of agencies and professionals. The Bill was to be amended and published as the Social Services and Well-being (Wales) Bill which had distinctive features to strengthen collaboration and provide a framework for integration. The provisions of the Bill went further than the local service boards' commitment to a plan (Longley et al., 2013, p. 66) in requiring local authorities to promote the integration of care and support with health and health-related provision, with a view to improving wellbeing, prevention and raising quality. The framework was sufficiently flexible to enable the Welsh ministers to prescribe new integrated ways of working in particular areas or across services (Welsh Government, 2013, p. 17). Partnership arrangements can be prescribed through regulations between local authorities and local health boards. This Bill was seen as creating opportunities to shape integration in a way which had not been done since devolution (Mitchell, 2013). Local authorities had to exercise their social service functions to ensure integration with health provision, if it would promote the wellbeing of adults, children or carers; contribute to preventing or slowing down care needs; and/or improve the quality of care or support. Mitchell (2013, p. 165) notes that while a local authority could make requests for cooperation from NHS bodies, they were not entitled to make specific requests for the cooperation of a local authority. The Bill still maintained a division of responsibility between the NHS and local government.

The new legislation provided a statutory framework for integration. The new duties did not affect the existing partnership arrangements, if they were in place, and local councils and local health boards remained able to enter into formal partnership under previous provisions (Mitchell, 2013, p. 168). At the same time the new Act created a new power for Welsh ministers to make regulations to enforce formal partnership arrangements. Parts of the Act also included new duties on local authorities to promote the development of new models of delivery through social enterprises, cooperatives, user-led and third sector services, as well as promoting the availability of preventative services (Welsh Government, 2013, p. 8). The Bill was seen as providing the Welsh government with the opportunity to shape the integration of social services and health and set the tone for the relationship between health and social services. Local authorities were given the lead responsibility for developing joint approaches and partner organisations had a duty to cooperate with local authorities when requested (Welsh Local Government Association and NHS Confederation, 2013, p. 23). Partnership and integrated services could be developed in response to thorough analyses of provision and pooled budgets. The Welsh government ensured that more resources were available for social services by not protecting totally the NHS budget. It was accepted that there would be extra costs associated with integration and up-front funding would be required. It was also accepted that work was required to understand both the barriers to achieving good quality health and social care, and also users' experience of health and social care.

The Social Services and Wellbeing (Wales) Act 2014 came into operation in April 2016 with collaboration as one of the four key principles described as stronger partnership working across all organisations, to better support people. A second principle, early intervention, is closely related to integration. This is described as promoting the use of preventative approaches within the community to address people's needs before they become critical (ADASS Cymru, 2016). A strong national structure has been set up to ensure full implementation of the Act across Wales. The Welsh Government is responsible for the legislative framework and also for regulations, codes of practice and statutory guidance, with scrutiny by the Welsh Assembly. A £14million package of support has been given to help with local implementation to support more integrated working, promoting people's independence, and encouraging a focus on preventative and early intervention (ADASS Cymru, 2015). Funding is available for the Care Council for Wales to develop a national learning and development strategy and also regional training plans. The Care Council has developed a one-stop shop or learning hub for the Act. There are six regional implementation projects to implement the Act and three national partners have come together – the Welsh Local Government Association, the Association of Directors of Social Services and the Welsh NHS Confederation – to provide leadership and project management capacity and develop new services and facilitate the sharing of best practice. The Association of Directors of Social Services has an integration policy group which had adopted a number of priorities: children and young people and community mental health teams; adults of working age with mental health issues or learning disabilities; older people needing extra care and housing support; and collaboration with GPs (ADASS Cymru, 2015). Garthwaite (2013) gave advice to local authorities that in collaborating with local health bodies they should develop a shared vision and also a degree of open-mindedness and good governance structures and further advice to avoid power battles and have good reporting back mechanisms. The holistic approach in the new legislation required general agreement to maximise the resources available and to aim for overall improvement in services and outcomes.

The Welsh experience of integration

The Welsh experience has been concentrated to date on older people and chronic conditions and has taken rather different forms throughout Wales. Some of the main trends and characteristics are considered below under a number of headings.

Chronic conditions

A Welsh Integrated Chronic Conditions Management Model was developed in 2007, based upon early assessment and appropriate treatment within the community. This led to early integrated initiatives based on the introduction of a core model of care coordination, integrated teams with community service delivery and GP clusters and locality working. At this stage local authorities and local health boards were required to work together as part of multidisciplinary assessment and the provision and delivery of long-term care was commissioned in a joint working approach by both sectors (Longley et al., 2013, p. 49). The approach to chronic conditions work involved an increasing recognition of using resources in a more joined-up way. The approach did depend on localised initiatives and pilot programmes. One such initiative, referred to as the Hywel Dda Integrated Care Model, linked a health board with three county councils under an integrated senior management structure. It sought to improve services for people with chronic conditions by developing joint health and social services provision for people in Carmarthenshire (Longley et al., 2013, p. 69). This project was based on population risk stratification, care coordination, joint design of services to deliver care, integrated health records, improved communication, and integrated community response teams. Closely related was the Ceredigion Community Services Integration Programme to deliver integrated community based health and social care to people with long-term conditions and physical disabilities. This ambitious programme aimed at a single point of access, targeted interventions, planned care and support, and quality assurance with the goal of preventing admission to hospital, improving discharge from hospital and improving community services (Welsh Local Government Association and NHS Confederation, 2013, p. 44). Other specific projects were aimed at supporting people with dementia who have complex needs which involved crisis intervention services and reablement services as well as medical care. There is evidence of collaboration between local authorities and health agencies in commissioning services but a number of problems were identified including the lack of availability of care home provision with nursing care. There was also a growing disconnect between the aspirations for more home based care and long-term financial plans. It was reported that there were good working relationships between health and social care with regard to services for people with complex needs arising from dementia, with innovative approaches to managing risk (Care and Social Services Inspectorate Wales, 2014).

Care for older people

Older people's care needs often overlap with the category of chronic conditions but many of the integrated initiatives in Wales have had a focus on older people. The Welsh government published a Framework for Delivering Integrated Health and Social Care (Welsh Government, 2013) catering for older people with complex needs. This document set out how the Welsh Government ambition for truly integrated health and social care services for older people is to be implemented. Partners across Wales were expected to move rapidly on making this model the norm, building on existing good practice. This model for older people was to provide community based, fully coordinated services to support older people and give them more control over their lives. Attention was to be paid to preventative interventions: linking services in community settings; creating fully integrated referral pathways to enable users to easily cross organisational boundaries; capturing once all the needs of the service user; integrating a whole set of services; and enabling service users to take part in their care plan with a named single point of contact (Welsh Government, 2013c, p. 4). Local councils and Local Health Boards were asked to plan a year on year increase in shared budgets and resources to target a proportion of resources relating to older people. Policy in Wales has led to a number of innovative projects. The Pembrokeshire Care Closer to Home initiative comprised four community resource teams and dealt with mainly frail older people, typically with dementia and multiple co-morbidities such as cancer. The project is delivered through an integrated management structure of health and social care teams. The four teams consisted of social workers, district nurses, occupational therapists, physiotherapists, specialist nurses and care workers. A joint head of community health and social services from the council and health board holds managerial and organisational accountability for the services in this project. The teams have developed since 2010 and continue to be improved in governance and organisational structure (Thiel et al., 2013). As part of the project three community teams are also based in the emergency department of the district general hospital, covering a joint discharge team, a multi-agency support team and an acute response team to provide specialist care for patients in their own homes.

A special project for frail older people, the Gwent Frailty Programme, has attracted some attention. This project started in 2011 involving the Aneurin Bevan Health Board and six local councils in south-east Wales. The project had the aim of developing an integrative perspective of frailty (Barber and Wallace, 2012). Community resource teams as frailty teams were set up in six sites, consisting of community geriatricians, social workers, nurses, physiotherapists, occupational therapists, and support workers. The project was described as the largest single exploration of integrated care delivery in Wales (Longley et al., 2013, p. 68). Pooled budgets were used as well as invest-to-save money.

This initiative operated with an emphasis on preventative work, to reduce hospital stays and encourage alternatives to emergency hospital admissions. Approaches covered the need for both rapid response emergency care and long-term care. While encouraging integrated staff engagement, the project did face problems with the promotion of staff undertaking tasks which crossed traditional boundaries in dealing with medication, for example, taking blood pressure (Barber and Wallace, 2012, p. 312). The Gwent frailty model was a large-scale scheme, had a streamlined approach to service delivery but local authorities had an impact on differences in delivery. Another invest-to-save was the Wyn campaign, covering Cardiff and the Vale of Glamorgan, aiming to provide wrap-around services for frail older people, including in-reach support to care homes to prevent hospital admission and targeted step-up responses for frail older people (Longley et al., 2013, p. 69).

Intermediate care and reablement

Intermediate care services have traditionally been at the interface between hospital and return to the community but as a key element in integrated approaches the services have widened in scope to cover strategies to support older people to remain in their own home and avoid unnecessary hospital admissions or inappropriate admission to residential care. An Intermediate Care Fund was established in 2014 supplying £70million in 2014–16 and has supported a range of activities. A basis of the Intermediate Care Fund is to support collaboration between social services, health and housing. In Cardiff and the Vale a 'smart house' was created to provide an opportunity for older people and their family to see and trial what support can be provided in the home environment, working with health and social care practitioners at the point of admission and discharge. The fund supports the involvement of the voluntary and independent sectors and innovating work had included a voluntary sector broker service. Other projects aim to improve practice for people with dementia and with strokes. In mid Wales additional flexible intermediate care beds, intermediate care flats and dementia 'move-on' flats are provided. The Wrexham Intermediate Care Project aimed to speed up discharge and educate health professionals as to the value of the service. The Wales Audit Office (2015, p. 12) did find that the short-term nature of the intermediate care funding and weaknesses in its allocation, evaluation and reporting processes made it difficult to judge the effectiveness of funding in transforming services.

Reablement services are aimed at providing short-term support either to enable people to readjust to living independently at home or as a response to maintain people in their home rather than move to institutional care. Bridgend offers a community integrated reablement service, which brings together over 70 health and social care staff to help people get back on their feet and maintain their independence following an illness, accident or other event. The Intermediate Care Fund has been used to increase provision with additional occupational therapists added to support independent living skills, appropriate facilities, assistive technology and access to therapy services (Welsh Local Government

Association, 2013, p. 22). Associated with the development of reablement schemes has been the development of rapid or acute integrated community response services, which provide crisis intervention support to avoid untimely admissions to hospital and residential care. In North Wales such a health and social care support service is available on a 24/7 basis and delivered by generic support workers. A Framework of Services for Older People also suggested further measures to assist in avoiding inappropriate hospital admission from home to hospital including a transition service in residential settings prior to returning home, a volunteer welcome home service, and rapid response adaptations by a Care and Repair Cymru organisation, to support safe discharge. These services have required the building up of new integrated team structures and more integrated referral and assessment processes.

Bridgend Integrated Health and Social Services involved a local council and a local health board in promoting independent living, reducing emergency admissions and reducing delays in transfers of care (Carnes Chichlowska et al., 2013, p. 65). Bridgend had used a bottom-up approach to service redesign. Cwm Taf Primary and Community Services was based on a priority to integrate services and locality management and the greatest progress had been made within the area of reablement. In another initiative problems were encountered in overcoming issues with separate IT systems and limited referrals from GPs (Carnes Chichlowska et al., 2013, p. 71).

Mental health services

Partnership working had a predominant position in the mental health sector in the period after devolution through community based provision, at times with the voluntary sector, and using the new powers of Flexibilities in strategies for mental health services. However, overall it appeared problematic to implement joint working arrangements (Jones et al., 2004), mainly because of different cultures, lack of communication, and health and social care working to their own agendas. A Wales Measure in 2010 had set a stronger direction towards an expansion in primary care mental health services and a new mental health strategy for Wales was developed to cover the whole life course services. A new delivery plan 'Together for Mental Health' was produced to be implemented 2016–19, but it was criticised for not promoting closer connections with social services, given the new Social Services and Wellbeing Act, which was seen as having joined-up working and integration at its heart (Association of Directors of Adult Social Services, Cymru, 2016). It is argued that mental health services should not be seen in isolation and local authorities are key partners in supporting the delivery of mental health services. Attention has also been drawn towards the issue of transitions between Child and Adolescent Mental Health Services (CAMHS) and adult services as well as between adult services and services for older people, and the move away from the application of strict eligibility criteria for mental health services. A more whole system approach has been advocated through developments like multidisciplinary teams closely working with groups of GP practices.

Learning disabilities

Progress has been reported on the transformation of learning disability services in Wales, where local councils have a lead role. Modernisation has included supported living, day services work opportunities and short-term care. Alternative delivery models have also been developed, including social enterprises.

GPs' role

As has been the case throughout the UK there have been issues over the involvement of GPs with integrated services, and GP involvement in meetings and teams has been slow with a lack of incentives, a burden on existing workloads and operational challenges. The main and first responsibility for the public's health care rests with GPs. There are variations in practice but the Bevan Commission (2011, p. 9) saw a need for GPs to strengthen links with social care and move towards joint working and co-terminosity. In 2010 the Welsh Government paper *Setting the Direction* set out the concept of GP cluster networks, which would work collaboratively together and with other partners (British Medical Association, 2016). Although 64 cluster networks came into existence, as determined by individual health boards, they had a major focus on health coordination between community and secondary care. With integrated projects set up it still appeared there was a lack of confidence in the system. The ways of integrated working may not have provided a good relationship with GPs. It still appeared that collaboration between GPs and social workers working together lagged behind England, and the Association of Directors of Social Services in Wales was keen to develop a stronger mutual understanding with the Royal College of GPs. Collaboration has been launched between the two representative bodies to strengthen the relationship between the workforces in primary care and social care and to reconcile the two different cultures and bridge the gap that currently exists. The new Social Services and Wellbeing Act was seen as providing a move away from the dominance of the medical model (Association of Directors of Social Services, Cymru, 2016).

Other promotional factors

Funding

A package of special funding support has been made available to help implement the new Social Services and Wellbeing Act with its focus on integration. This funding is in part to support embedding integration and training and education. Social care in general has benefitted from the policy of not ring-fencing health expenditure with the aim of promoting community based care and less dependency on acute care. Despite this, social services are a local government responsibility and are not able to escape the impact of reductions in financing stemming from the UK government's austerity measures or from local government financial restrictions.

Leadership and training

Research has shown the pivotal role of key individuals in shaping the outcomes of those working in the environment of partnerships, networks and consortia. Social care in Wales had seen the role of older people's strategy coordinators able to influence joint working. Williams (2011) has identified the importance in Wales of 'boundary spanners' in cutting across organisational boundaries, promoting coordination and reducing duplication. It is seen as necessary to identify and teach the skills and challenges of working across sectors to deliver a single service model.

Williams (2012) sees the integration of health and social care as an exercise in learning and knowledge management, because it involves the collision of diverse stakeholders searching for new ways of working. Leaders are also pivotal in ensuring that organisations and systems learn from each other. In Wales the Health and Wellbeing Best Practice and Innovation Board (2013) has taken forward such ideas into training and creating an environment for the leadership culture and climate needed to promote integration.

Collaboration with other services

Social care and health services can enter into relationships with other services and bodies to deliver more joined-up responses and better services. Older people can have needs that are best met at times by different types of services (Wales Audit Office, 2015, p. 45). Housing is the clearest example and in Wales may mean internal local council collaboration or cooperation with housing associations. Housing for older and vulnerable people is significant in ensuring a good standard of living. Wales has followed England in promoting Extra Care Schemes, such as the Plas Telford scheme with apartments and an extensive range of communal facilities. Studies in Wales have indicated some of the complexities in delivering seamless patient-centred care across organisational boundaries. Thomas (2015) found in a study of a housing association and a nursing home that the public bodies' approach was often limited in thinking and action to public sector integration. Other research indicated the difficulties that occupational therapists experienced in Wales in developing integrated occupational therapy services across health and social care for frail adults and found collaboration required dogged determination (Kelly, 2015). Problems also arise in promoting integration if the contract relationship predominates. A study of 12 months of pioneering collaboration between a health board, five local authorities, and nine registered social landlords identified inherent systematic barriers and factors both cultural and professional that had an impact on the collaboration (Edmunds and Kilbride, 2015). Also influential, however, was the context of increasing demand on public services and financial austerity and the history of housing being on the margins of discussion when considering the integration of health and social care services. Evans (2014) reported many examples of effective partnership across social care and housing departments where local authority and registered social landlords were working with health and social care professionals. Cooperation aimed at finding solutions to avoid an institutional outcome, through extra care or supported accommodation. This approach helped reduce separate assessments, avoided duplication, saved professional time, reduced waiting times and provided more tailored responses.

Initiatives have been introduced to improve relationships, including one to set up one point of access for services to be commissioned from third sector organisations to support health and social care needs (Dickinson and Neal, 2011). The new Social Services and Wellbeing Act increases the role of the voluntary sector in participating in policy formulation and policy implementation. There have been warnings against care silos operating if the voluntary sector took over a whole area. A single IT system has also been seen as a prerequisite for effective integrated care, and consideration in Wales has been given to an integrated platform for use between the local health boards and councils (Carnes Chichlowska et al., 2013, p. 12). Local authorities have a statutory duty to offer a direct payments arrangement to all individuals potentially eligible to receive it. The use of direct payments has been growing across Wales with some councils having significant growth in recent years. This scheme helps people mould their own solutions to care and support and has an impact on integrated provision. The integrated family support service has engaged with direct payments. The role of unpaid carers is important in providing care and support and reducing pressures on statutory services. It has been regarded as essential in Wales to support carers to take an integrated health and social care approach. Legislation in Wales has also assisted carers to assess and support their own needs to maintain and improve their own wellbeing, through an integrated approach to information, advice and practical support. Integrated commissioning is part of partnership working and in the case of home care is seen as having an important dimension in involving the private and voluntary sectors in commissioning services that have elements of integration. New forms of services may be very amenable to integrated approaches, such as social enterprises and user-led support, although this may be difficult to achieve. The development and use of common templates for jointly assessing, recording and monitoring needs has been a further area of progress. A unified assessment process (UAP) is in operation as a single mechanism for assessment to bring the contribution of professionals together to develop a coherent care plan, thus avoiding serial assessments from a range of agencies.

The Social Services and Wellbeing Act creates a right to needs assessment information. An innovative feature of the 2014 Social Services and Wellbeing Act is a provision that each local authority with the assistance of their local health board partners must make available information and advice relating to care and support in their area, to be known as the Information, Advice and Assistance service. This will serve as a first point of entry and allow people to begin to discuss their care and support needs, present options and may actively assist people in accessing services.

Assessments of integrated care

Difficulties in isolating and quantifying the impact that different services have in supporting people to live independently and also the lack of data for non-health and social care services have been noted (Wales Audit Office, 2015, p. 53).

Progress with integration can be assessed in terms of evidence of general achievement but also noting the availability and depth of evidence as well as comments on the lack of progress and barriers to progress. Longley et al. (2013, p. 71) reported a certain unease that progress has not been as rapid or far-reaching as was hoped. It has also been argued that statements in policies and legislation have remained largely aspirational (Kaehne et al., 2017, p. 91). There is some evidence that the levels of unplanned admissions and emergency readmissions have reduced. Progress was reported on the effectiveness of integrated care in reducing levels of delayed transfers of care but after 2008 the figures were disappointing (Longley et al., 2013, p. 70). It has been suggested that there is little data across Wales with which to systematically track progress over time and between settings (Longley et al., 2023, p. 69). There is also little evidence of a whole-scale transformation from acute to community care or of calculations of what funding model or financial support is necessary to promote more integration, prevention, and personalisation (Welsh Local Government Association and NHS Confederation, 2013, p. 18). Welsh Government social research has reported that the current working models of effective integrated care in Wales are a bottom-up approach to delivering care (Carnes Chichlowska et al., 2013). Some evidence of achievement is to be found in particular local initiatives. The project involving Pembroke County Council and Hywel Dda Health Board reported that an outcome directly attributable to integration was a drop in waiting times for assessment plus the uptake of emergency plans (Thiel et al., 2013, p. 21). There were still concerns at the lack of benchmarking and evaluation practices across Wales to measure the benefits and costs of delivering integrated care (Carnes Chichlowska et al., 2013, p. 13). Even the new legislation there appeared to be a lack of agreed indicators of what constitutes successful integration and how to routinely evidence progress (Kaehne et al., 2017, p. 91).

By 2006 the interface with health was provoking much debate but with an acceptance of the need to take a whole-systems approach and have joint needs assessments. It was reported, however, that there were scant signs that the move to look after fewer people in acute care with improved community health and social care was being achieved (Social Services Improvement Agency, 2017). Writing before the new legislation, Longley et al. (2013) concluded that integration remained difficult because of cultural differences, lack of mutual understanding or the dominance of performance measures belonging to one sector. It was suggested that common IT platforms between agencies needed to be adopted as staff from different agencies did not have full access to patients' full records. Different agencies did not always have the same objectives or performance arrangements. Strong evidence was identified in Wales of the value of leadership, the coordination of a large number of service providers involved in integration and the need for sufficient resources to be allocated to integrated care as it was not a cheap option (Longley et al., 2013, p. 73). Successful integration was also seen as based on the views and experience of patients and carers to enable partnership working. This was seen as a sporadic occurrence with little investment for patients' needs. It was also noted that typically it took five years or more to deliver its objectives and at this time in some parts of Wales there was a noted reluctance to embrace integrated working, nervousness about the ability to deliver or worries about possible reductions in an agency's own resources (Longley et al., 2013, p. 75). The top-down approach in implementing integration in three counties of West Wales was seen as delaying and inhibiting the scale and pace of integration through frontline services (Carnes Chichlowska et al., 2013, p. 78). Responses in integrated care provision did differ between locations and availability of types of care. Difficulties remained over disputes between the NHS and social services regarding financial responsibilities, and even bureaucratic battles over the lines between health and social care. Some concern has been expressed at the possible development of a separate 'integrated care service' in its own right (Carnes Chichlowska et al., 2013, p. 57). In 2015 on the eve of the introduction of the Social Services and Wellbeing Act the Association of Directors of Social Services identified the top priority issues to address as integrated children's and young people's mental health services across Wales; adults of working age with learning disabilities; and older people focusing on extra care and other housing support. Despite difficulties at the national level, local initiatives have been delivering services in different ways across Wales to make integration happen with the major focus on care for older people.

Conclusions

The integration of health and social care is an important policy objective for the Welsh Government. The ageing population and growth of numbers of people with long-term chronic conditions have encouraged a long-term policy of shifting services out of acute hospitals and nursing homes. As we have seen, the new Social Services and Wellbeing legislation gives a picture of how the devolved administration will drive the integration of health and social care. This groundbreaking piece of legislation requires health and social care to work together. However, the local government system in Wales remains separate from the NHS with different funding, delivery systems and accountability mechanisms. This does leave a structural weakness in that there are seven local health boards working with 22 local authorities. The Williams Commission (2014) in proposing local government reform argued that mergers of local authorities should not occur between local authorities in separate health board boundaries as this would undermine the integration of health and social care. The governance of integration in Wales is a less radical departure from the English system than the more thorough-going structural differences in Scotland and Northern Ireland. The health boards in Wales are integrated structurally for all health services and this means that they are large organisations with resources to underpin relationships with local councils. The evolution of integration in Wales has not followed an explicit theory of what has been tested, or a template or prescriptive guidance. Bevan (2013, p. 3) suggests that integrated care should mean: coordination; no big gaps in care; shared and accurate information; and shared decision-making. Joint working is seen as mainly valuable in managing chronic diseases, innovations in meeting mental health needs and with programmes to allow people to live independently and avoid unplanned admissions to hospital. The need for cultural change in both health and social care often receives comments but a different concluding note is struck by Greenwell and Green (2015) who focus on how hard and messy it is to deliver truly joined-up care and support. Work had continued on increasing an understanding of the essential requirements for successful integration. Mutual understanding and respect are seen as critical in breaking down organisational and professional barriers. There is some evidence in Wales that integration initiatives through a bottom-up process are more effective than initiatives by a top-down process. There is a view that detailed barriers to integration have largely been unnoticed among the wider noise of policy statements (Kaehne et al., 2017, p. 9). Cuts in local government expenditure, cuts in services and the overall atmosphere of austerity policies (Jordan and Drakeford, 2012) have presented problems for innovation. The separation of health and social care has left parts of the health and social care system underfunded. The impact of austerity requires councils to make difficult decisions to balance budgets and councils struggle to maintain expenditure on services that support the independence of older people (Wales Audit Office, 2015). This has not overall stopped the emergence of community service models such as intermediate care, rapid response teams and reablement strategies.

6 Integration in Northern Ireland

Introduction

Northern Ireland has had a model of structural integration of health and social services (social care) since 1972. It also has lengthy experience of devolution going back to 1921, although interrupted by a period of direct rule from Westminster from 1972 to 1999. Health and social care were confirmed as devolved matters in the new devolution legislation of 1998. Northern Ireland has chosen to follow closely the principles of the NHS and maintain parity with the rest of the UK in standards of health and social care provision. Thus, much of the framework of policies and strategies has been similar to Great Britain in terms of community care, purchaser–provider division, and GP fund holding, but this has not prevented some significant differences in administration and some policies. The long-standing commitment to structural integration has developed as one of the most comprehensive structured integrated systems for health and social services in Europe (McCoy, 1993).

Historical context

The original decision on structural integration owed more to a requirement to reorganise local government than to any thought-out, evidenced-based strategy on integration. A radical restructuring of local administration in Northern Ireland was first mooted in a 1969 parliamentary Green Paper, *The Administrative Structure of Health and Personal Social Services in Northern Ireland* (Government of Northern Ireland, 1969). A review body reported in June 1970, and in 1972 the shape of the new structure was outlined in a report by appointed management consultants. The rationale behind the restructuring was declared as being 'the improvement of the provision of health and social services to the community in Northern Ireland through establishing an integrated approach to the delivery of hospital and specialist services, local authority health and welfare services' (Government of Northern Ireland, 1969). The changes would, it was hoped, provide a more rational and comprehensive structure in which to decide priorities, develop policies and 'work together toward a common goal of meeting the total needs of individuals, families and communities for health and social services' (Government of Northern Ireland, 1969). These dramatic changes took place against a backdrop of social and political unrest. It has been contended that, rather than as a means of delivering more efficient and effective services, structural changes were introduced as a reaction to the political turmoil and were an attempt to exert control and stability by removing power from discredited elected representatives and placing it in the hands of appointed bodies (Birrell and Murie, 1980).

The proposed integration under a structure of four area health and social services boards received 'remarkably little discussion' in the Green Paper apart from brief references to the need for cooperation and joint planning (Heenan and Birrell, 2011, p. 55). The Permanent Secretary of the Department of Health and Social Services, speaking in 1971, identified some of the main advantages of the new system as making possible comprehensive planning at every level; encompassing the totality of medical and social care; reducing the number of boards; increasing understanding between all the professions; and ensuring public participation (DHSS, 1972). The proposals received a cautious welcome from the social work profession, which had no objection to the removal of social work from local government but had some concern at the departure from the Seebohm proposals in England at the time for comprehensive social work departments in local government.

Development of integrated structure

During the period of direct rule from 1972 to 98, to reform and the development of policy and strategy in health and social services was limited in scope and vision. The default position was to copy English policy changes, and the UK government appeared content to keep this unique system of governance ticking over. Stability was the key priority, and social and public policy reform was generally sidestepped by Direct Rule politicians. To some onlookers this may appear rather surprising. Direct Rule health ministers were in a somewhat unusual position in that they were not directly accountable to the local electorate and could have taken clinically necessary but politically unpopular decisions. The absence of local political accountability, and as the 'democratic deficit', could have made Northern Ireland's health service a fertile ground for innovation and modernisation. Perhaps unsurprisingly, it was quickly apparent that Direct Rule ministers were unwilling to make politically contentious decisions.

Northern Ireland, it appeared, already had sufficient political controversy without adding health and social care reform to the mix. Importantly, Direct Rule was also largely viewed as a short-term stopgap with a devolved administration just around the corner, so it was considered best to leave the more controversial decisions to local politicians and pointless to embark on long-term projects. Consequently, health and social care in Northern Ireland largely stagnated under the period of Direct Rule, and there were few, if any, attempts to pursue distinctive policy approaches based on the needs of the local population. The lack of distinctive innovation with regard to social policy-making is clearly reflected in a number of key areas.

Initially Health and Social Service Boards, organised on a geographical basis with a district substructure, were established. Seventeen districts were created as subdivisions of four Health and Social Services Boards. Following a review in 1978 the Department of Health and Social Services was introduced to enable integrated services to be more effectively planned and managed. This meant the introduction of a new substructure based around the concept of a unit of management, which could be, for example, an acute hospital, a community unit, or a psychiatric hospital. In effect this marked a move away from fully integrated districts to specialist units of management. Further change was introduced in the 1990s with the emergence of the community care agenda and the purchaser–provider split. Northern Ireland operates under the vision and principles set out in *People First* (1990) which includes enabling individuals to remain in their own home or in homely settings in the community.

People First (DHSS, 1990) was the Northern Ireland equivalent of the guidelines for community care published in Britain as the White Paper *Caring for People*. As a result the role of the four Boards evolved into two purchaser–provider levels. Health and Community Trusts and Hospital Trusts were established as legal entities separate from the Boards.

The Board–Trust division reflected a purchaser–provider split, though still within an integrated structure. Four commissioning Health and Social Services Boards regulated integrated health and social services which were delivered by 18 Trusts. Eleven of these Trusts were Community Health and Social Services Trusts, some including hospitals, and seven were hospital trusts largely based around acute hospitals. Trusts were independent entities with their own budgets. Health and social care services were commissioned within nine programmes of care, which were underpinned by an integrated approach.

A central theme in the *Caring for People* strategy was the need for stronger links between health authorities and local authority social service departments in Great Britain, but the Northern Ireland equivalent paper *People First* (DHSS, 1990) stated that Northern Ireland already enjoyed the advantage of an integrated organisational structure embracing both health and social care and it was therefore not necessary to introduce formal arrangements for joint working and planning. It was expected that general managers would ensure that the caring professions worked closely together at all operational levels. A framework for setting standards, delivering services and improving monitoring covered six areas of improvement of services, fair access, effectiveness in delivery, efficiency, user involvement, and outcomes. The six areas all referred to health and social care but there was little comment on integration processes (DHSS, 2001). The first major strategy document after the establishment of devolution, *Developing Better Services* (DHSSPS, 2002), had a focus on hospital provision and other than a brief mention of partnership working made no comment on integration. The operation of integration was not assisted by research or discussion and some observations were rather dismissive of any achievements. Hudson and Henwood (2002) argue that much of the integration between health and social care was more apparent than real and structural integration did not guarantee well-coordinated practice on the ground. Field and Peck (2003) stated that evidence showed that far from creating seamless joined-up services, community care suffered from the same difficulties as in mainland Britain. Some limited evidence of achievements had been produced. Anderson (1998) found some fragmented evidence for improvements in hospital discharge, while Richards (2000) argued that services were more person-centred and Dornan (1998) noted that teams from more than one profession had the ability to meet all needs within the same structure. A formal independent review of health care (Appleby, 2005) noted that the success of the integrated system varied across trusts and, while there had been some innovative practices, the transition between home and hospital was not as seamless as one might expect. Appleby suggested that Northern Ireland appeared to be many years behind England in terms of achieving the aim of providing social services in the community to avoid hospitalisation.

The major Review of Public Administration (RPA) set up at the time devolution in 1999 proceeded slowly and dealt with health and social care separately from education, other quangos and local government. The review was to state that the integrated system of health and personal social services was one of the strengths of the system and any change to the structures should not work against the integrated services approach First and Deputy First Minister (2005). A specific review of spending and the health system in 2010 suggested that more efficient services required greater integration and consolidation of primary, community and social care (McKinsey and Company Review, 2010). This McKinsey report prescribed a different service provision landscape, with primary care centres as hubs for integrated health and social care. It argued that, given that health and social care are integrated, people have reason to expect an efficient joined-up service. A follow-up to the Appleby report (2011) focused on funding needs, and made little comment on integration other than a recommendation that the integration of health and social services should be re-examined with an initial first stage being the implications of ring-fencing of funding of social services from the acute sector. A European Observatory study of the Northern Ireland health sector (O'Neill et al., 2012) simply noted that health and social care is financed within an integrated system, but in most other respects social provision is similar to the rest of the UK.

The publication of the 20-year strategic framework for primary care *Caring for People beyond Tomorrow* (2005) acknowledged that demographic trends and lifestyle factors would have a dramatic impact on the demand for primary care services. This increased demand would require extensive development of community-based alternatives to hospital admission. In order to ensure that the health and social care system was fit for the future it recommended:

- more responsive and accessible primary care services with an increasing range and number of services available in the community;
- an increased number of multidisciplinary partnerships;
- enhanced engagement with service users;
- improved service delivery through the use of new technologies.

At the heart of this framework was integrated working which envisaged a new role for GPs in the development of population-based primary care teams. In 2010 clinically led pilot projects known as Primary Care Partnerships (PCPs) were established to promote new approaches to commissioning care. These PCPs were voluntary alliances of health and social care professionals and community and voluntary groups to inform the commissioning of services.

Fifteen PCPs were set up addressing a diverse range of issues including mental health, dermatology and medicines management. The key objective of these pilots was to enhance integration and coordination between services and identify alternative pathways. Despite their modest achievements PCPs formed the foundation of service developments under Transforming Your Care (Figure 6.1) (Thompson, 2016).

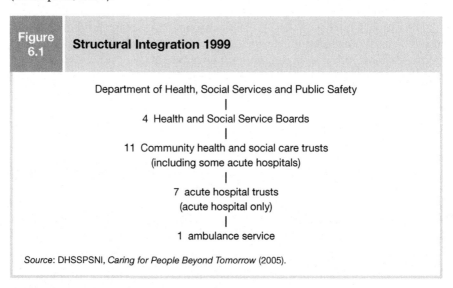

| Figure 6.1 | **Structural Integration 1999** |

Department of Health, Social Services and Public Safety
|
4 Health and Social Service Boards
|
11 Community health and social care trusts
(including some acute hospitals)
|
7 acute hospital trusts
(acute hospital only)
|
1 ambulance service

Source: DHSSPSNI, *Caring for People Beyond Tomorrow* (2005).

| Box 6.1 | **Characteristics of Integrated Trusts** |

–   single employer
–   single finance system and overall budget
–   single overall strategy
–   integrated management
–   operates through programmes of care
–   integrated inspection body

Reorganisation of health and social care

A reorganisation of health and social care was subsumed within the implementation of the Review of Public Administration taking place after the restoration of devolution in 2007 and led to a short review of the existing proposal for health administration.

The Health and Social Care (Reform) Act (Northern Ireland) 2009 was introduced following the RPA to reduce the number of bodies involved in the administration, commissioning and delivery of health and social services. As Northern Ireland had structural integration of health and social care since the early 1970s, this further major restructuring aimed to maximise economies of scale and improve outcomes. This Act created a single large commissioning body, the Health and Social Care Board, and five large Health and Social Care Trusts (HSC Trusts) responsible for the delivery of primary, secondary and community health care. Co-terminous with the new trusts were five local commissioning groups which would advise the Health and Social Care Board.

The Health and Social Care Board (HSCB) sits between the Department and the Trusts and is responsible for commissioning services, managing resources and performance improvement. The board is also directly responsible for managing contracts for family health services provided by GPs, dentists, opticians and community pharmacists. These are all services not provided by HSC Trusts. The five local commissioning groups cover the same geographical area as the HSC Trusts. The five HSC Trusts provide health and social care across Northern Ireland on a geographical basis. A sixth trust, the Ambulance Service, serves that particular function and operates on a regional basis. While the HSCB commissions services, it is the trusts that actually provide them 'on the ground' (Figure 6.2). Each trust manages its own staff and services, and controls its own budget. The average population per trust was 359,878.

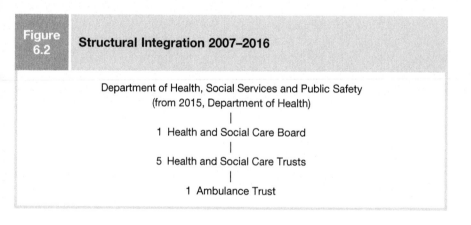

Figure 6.2   Structural Integration 2007–2016

Department of Health, Social Services and Public Safety
(from 2015, Department of Health)
|
1 Health and Social Care Board
|
5 Health and Social Care Trusts
|
1 Ambulance Trust

Transforming your care and its impact

In 2011, Edwin Poots, Minister for Health, Social Services and Public Safety in Northern Ireland, launched a review of health and social care services, which was to undertake a strategic assessment of the system and bring forward recommendations for the future shape of services with an implementation plan. *Transforming Your Care: A Review of Health and Social Care in Northern Ireland* (the Compton Review; TYC) was published in December 2011 (Department of Health, Social Services and Public Safety, 2011b). Described as the biggest shake-up of health care in the region's history, it concluded that doing nothing was not an option, as the current and future pressures on the health and social care system provided an unassailable case for change. The review engaged with over 3,000 members of the public, clinicians, voluntary groups, and took cognizance of national and international evidence. It identified a clear mismatch between the needs of the population for proactive, integrated and preventive care for chronic conditions, and a health care system where the majority of resources are targeted at specialised, episodic care for acute conditions. The report set out a vision for the future of health and social care in Northern Ireland which ensured safe, sustainable, effective services for all. It envisaged a new enhanced model of integrated care underpinned by a number of principles including:

Box 6.2	Principles of Transforming Your Care

- modelling care around the service user
- providing the right care at the right time
- building on integrated care through population planning
- tackling health inequalities
- focusing on prevention
- promoting the personalisation agenda
- ensuring value for money.

Source: DHSSPS (2011).

Box 6.3	TYC Included 99 Recommendations; Key Drivers for Change

- care provided as close to home as possible
- resources moved from hospitals and invested in community health and social care
- development of 17 Integrated Care Partnerships (ICPs) led by GPs
- quality and outcomes the key factors shaping services
- focus on empowerment and prevention.

Source: DHSSPS (2011).

TYC set out integrated care and working together as one of the key principles. This was justified in terms of a need for improvement, expressed as: 'Different parts of the health and social care system should be better integrated to improve the quality of experience for patients and clients, safety and outcomes' (Department of Health, Social Services and Public Safety, 2011b, p. 40). There was little analysis or evaluation of the failings of existing integration, but there were implied criticisms in comments such as 'the professionals providing health and social care services will be required to work together in a much more integrated way to plan and deliver consistently high quality care' (Department of Health, Social Services and Public Safety, 2011b, p. 7). There was much concern at the slow implementation of new integrated services for learning disability (Department of Health, Social Services and Public Safety, 2011b, p. 94). It highlighted the over-reliance on hospitals and noted the need to deliver care closer to home. Evidence for this included a bed utilisation audit of 2011 which showed that, on the day in question, up to 42 per cent of the inpatients reviewed should not have been seen.

A 2012 report from the Patient and Client Council, representing service users supported the view that care should be provided as close to home as possible, with a shift in resources from hospital to community enabling this transition. There is support for the concept of 'home as the hub of care'. However, the report suggested that it is evident that many people do not have full confidence in community-based services. Across a number of projects people have voiced concern about the quality, planning and delivery of community care, particularly for the most vulnerable in society. The Care at Home report into domiciliary care for older people (Patient and Client Council, 2012) provides a good example of this dilemma. While most people said they would prefer to receive care at home where possible, many raised concerns about the inconsistent delivery and quality of home care. Age NI reported that evidence gathered through their discussions with older people suggested that the current model of social care is based on outdated ways of working, which results in poor value for money and does not always meet the outcomes that those in receipt of care expect (Age NI, 2013).

Following extensive consultation, the Department published *Transforming Your Care: Vision to Action*. This document set out how TYC objectives would be achieved. Five strategic factors were identified as enablers for reform: finance; infrastructure; procurement; technology; and the workforce. Whilst there has been widespread support for the vision articulated in TYC, there has been frustration about a lack of clarity around the plan and a timetable for implementation. Progress was slow and uneven.

A number of documents have called for support for integration but in general terms. *A Strategy for Social Work* (DHSSPS, 2012), discussing improvements to social work services, called for the promotion of effective partnerships and the strengthening of integrated working in practice and service delivery in multidisciplinary ways. It also called for social workers to be equipped with the knowledge and skills to deliver effective services. A formal discussion document was published by the Department entitled *Who cares? The future of adult care and support in Northern Ireland* (DHSSPS, 2013) but this was a limited analysis of policy including the financing of residential care and surprisingly made no mention of integrated care or structures. A report in 2014 into dealing with adverse health incidents broadened into wider comments on the health and social care structures with comments made on governance, noting less cooperative working than might be expected, and suggested that better regulation was needed and that there should be a timetable for implementation of TYC. The existing commissioning-provider system was criticised and a simpler redesigned system urged (Donaldson, 2014). This was to lead to a later decision after further analysis that the commissioning body, The Health and Care Board, and its functions would be absorbed into the Department and the five HSC Trusts. The Donaldson report was also to propose setting up an expert panel to review the configuration of health and social care services.

In 2017 a Northern Ireland Audit Office report noted that TYC had provided a shared vision for the reform of health and social care, one which all stakeholders could unite behind. Whilst acknowledging the complexity of health service reform exacerbated by financial pressures, it noted that the pace of change had not been as rapid as was originally envisaged. Also whilst change had not been on the intended scale, progress had been achieved. Individual initiatives such as Acute Care at Home, Respiratory Care Service and Reablement are identified as good practice. However, scaling-up these programmes has proven particularly challenging (NIAO, 2017).

Integrated Care Partnerships

A recommendation from the *Transforming Your Care* report led to a new initiative to establish 17 Integrated Care Partnerships (ICPs) to better promote integration. An ICP was described as a collaborative network rather than an organisation they did not have a statutory basis but operated within the five trusts (DHSSPS, 2012). The proposal did appear somewhat unusual given the existing structural integration. The ICPs were to respond innovatively to care needs and coordinate integrated care pathways through the health and social care system from an individual perspective. The ICPs used risk stratification to identify people at the greatest risk of developing a chronic condition and prioritise early intervention and prevention of hospital admissions. Initially all ICPs were to focus on five clinical priority areas: frail elderly, respiratory disease, diabetes, stroke, and end of life care. It can be noted that these priorities were mainly disease defined (Birrell and Heenan, 2014), with people's needs defined in terms of health attributes and management of illness. ICPs have no specific budgets and can be viewed as having the potential to be networks of provider bodies. Concern about the contribution of ICPs also related to the governance structure of a type of appointed type quango board with 12 or 13 members but the inclusion of only one social work representative attracted criticism. Originally the ICPs were to be led by GPs, and, although later changed, the view has been expressed that one of the objectives of the scheme is to engage GPs more in integration and collaboration (Birrell and Heenan, 2014, p. 215).The initiative has had a focus on localised projects and may have some positive impact in raising the profile of integration and fostering links with the voluntary sector.

The initial focus has been project orientated and intended to assist those with long-term conditions. The main projects have covered the four main prescribed areas, through community respiratory teams, stroke rehabilitation, end of life care, and diabetes prevention through for example, foot care teams. In the category of frail older people the dominant initiative has been acute care at home or enhanced care at home. These offer a wrap-around short-term intensive care to help people manage their conditions and are led by a consultant geriatrician and can include nurses, physiotherapists and social care staff. Over three years £12million has been spent on ICP projects but problems have been noted in obtaining commissioners' approval and also with the short-term nature of funding (Health and Social Care Board, 2016). While this initiative may combat some of the difficulties that have been encountered to date in reaping the full benefits of the system, the projects have mainly reflected health agendas rather than health and social care integration. ICPs have been created with limited powers, are not widely known even among practitioners and have an unclear relationship with the existing system of structurally integrated health and social care. The activities of ICPs can be described filling gaps within the existing system of integration.

Research on integration in Northern Ireland

A striking aspect of integration in Northern Ireland is the lack of rigorous evaluation and assessment, despite the fact that closer integration has been a key policy objective of successive British governments for decades. In Great Britain a range of methods and initiatives to facilitate closer working, including partnerships, have been introduced, piloted, and subject evaluation. Yet scant attention has been paid to the system in Northern Ireland. Heenan and Birrell (2006, 2009) highlighted this anomaly and noted the following:

> Despite the uniqueness of the structure, it has received surprisingly little attention from policy analysts and academics. On the rare occasion where work on the integration of health and social services has referred to Northern Ireland, comments have tended to be somewhat dismissive of any beneficial achievements, without any substantial evidence to support this view. (Heenan and Birrell, 2006, p. 49)

Policy documents from DHSSPS and sessions of the Northern Ireland Assembly Health Committee have paid little attention to the potential of integration. Among politicians, policy-makers and academics there continues to be a lack of understanding of the unique structures in Northern Ireland and the possibilities that they present. The challenge of achieving a holistic system of care across the spectrum of needs is an international one and this model of health care could provide important insights, but it requires robust evaluation and assessment. Despite the continuing support for integrated approaches, there is surprisingly little interest in reviewing the unique model.

Heenan and Birrell (2006, 2009, 2012) have published a number of small-scale reviews of the integrated system and highlighted the benefits and limitations of the system in Northern Ireland. The operation of the integrated structure has delivered benefits through programmes of care and integrated care teams. Reduced delays in hospital discharge have also been identified in some trusts as a key advantage of this integrated system. It is, however, difficult to assess the extent to which the integrated system has directly achieved better value for money or has made tangible differences to service users.

Following the RPA and full integration of the seven hospital trusts into five HSC Trusts, Heenan and Birrell (2009) suggested that any achievement of the promised potential of full structural integration in Northern Ireland would require:

Box 6.4 **Enhancing Integration**

- a higher profile for social care in the modernisation initiative
- joint initial training for health and social care professionals to reinforce a culture of integration
- a focus on evaluating outcomes for service users
- a renewed debate on the value of social models of care
- the composition of new bodies to reflect a more equal status between health and social care
- a systematic programme of detailed research and evaluation of integrated working to provide a robust evidence base.

Source: Based on Heenan and Birrell (2009).

Existing small-scale research projects suggest that structural integration is not a panacea for the fragmentation that bedevils health and social care. Whilst it has the potential to address some of the issues associated with two separate services, over 45 years of integration in Northern Ireland demonstrates that achieving a seamless system requires vision, leadership, financial incentives and a whole system approach.

Operation of integration

Programmes of care

Programmes of care are the mechanisms through which resources are allocated, divisions in health and social care organised, policy decisions made, and to which activities and financial data are assigned and which provide a management framework. Programmes of care follow a similar pattern in all trusts and the overall list and percentage of expenditure is given in Table 6.1.

The degree of integration varies between programmes, with the elderly, mental health and learning disability the most integrated and childcare the least (Heenan, 2013, p. 18). The Programmes of Care to a significant degree do not represent boundaries between health and social care and do not represent any earmarking of funding between health and social care. Overall the resources for Programmes of Care are all within the one budget.

Table 6.1	Programmes of Care by Percentage Expenditure	

	% expenditure 2012	% expenditure 2015
Acute	38	43
Elderly	19	21.7
Families and childcare	6	7
Health promotion	3	2
Learning disability	7	7
Child health	4	4.5
Mental health	7.5	7.7
Disability	2.8	3.3
Primary and community	3.5	3.6

Source: Health and Social Care Board (2012/2015).

Integrated commissioning

Integrated commissioning has usually meant that the separate parts of the health and social care system come together to decide what services are needed and to plan and design services in an integrated way, and determine resource allocation and procurement. Northern Ireland's experience is with structurally integrated bodies commissioning care so it is not necessary for different organisations to join together or enter into partnership arrangements or for budgets to be pooled. The responsibility for commissioning has rested with a pan Northern Ireland body, the Health and Social Board, advised by five local commissioning groups. In practice the five delivery trusts had the power to commission adult social care services, especially domiciliary services. A number of shortcomings with integrated commissioning have been identified (Gray and Birrell, 2016). These included the lack of narratives in commissions documents concerning integration including those produced by local commissioning groups; the lack of specification of integrated services; and the separation of funding between health and social care. While programmes for care should have provided a basis for integration, in practice the programmes were largely deconstructed, separating health and social care into distinct constituent parts, for example, for older people and mental health. A further criticism related to the small representation of social work and social care interests on the membership of the commissioning bodies. In 2015 a review of commissioning led to the Department announcing major changes to the structures with the abolition of the main commissioning body and also the local commissioning groups and a move away from the separation of commissioning and instead trust led planning for local services. It was acknowledged that work would need to continue to better integrate services and that the new processes for commissioning must be built on the principle of integration (DHSSPS, 2015).

Integrated teams

Historically, even under the integrated system social workers tended to be based in social work teams consisting solely of social workers. It is in more recent years that integrated multidisciplinary teams have been developed bringing together a range of professional workers to provide an integrated service. In a survey in 2014 of 400 social workers, 75 per cent reported that they worked in integrated multidisciplinary teams (Northern Ireland Association of Social Workers, 2014, p. 11). The same survey noted that many social workers felt that other team members were not aware of the contribution that social workers made in holistic plans of care. There has been recognition that social workers had to be equipped to work in teams dealing with service delivery, including working with users and communities, at team level with other disciplines, and with other agencies and sectors (DHSSPS, 2012). Social workers also saw themselves as playing an important role in assessing need, identifying unmet need and acting as gatekeepers. The integrated teams also, as required, were involved closely in comprehensive packages of care including aspects of children's services. In new developments multidisciplinary teams have been set up to work in rapid response teams involving social workers with health staff (Heenan, 2013, p. 19) although it has been the case that some reablement teams did not include social workers. Officially designated integrated care teams working with older people consist mainly of social workers and district nurses.

Multi-professional management

Integrated teams are managed by a member of the team who is responsible for the operational supervision of all team members. The team manager can come from any profession within the team. Thus, for example, a social worker could occupy the position of team leader of a multi-professional team. An advantage of this system is that there is a wider pool of potential managerial talent. The move to integrated team structures has in practice resulted in fewer frontline managers from the social work profession, for the reason that there has been a lack of applications from social workers for posts at the level of team leader (Northern Ireland Association of Social Workers, 2012, p. 12). Formally management positions are open to a range of professions and in principle this means regarding all professions equally.

Views of social workers

Social workers must work at a team level with other disciplines and they have embraced integrated multidisciplinary teams and the move away from professional line management structures, accepting the breakup of a professional management structure to enable more effective collaboration and working with health related professions. However, it has been acknowledged that the changes to these models of integration, designed to deliver better inter-professional working, have had consequences in diminishing a social work identity (Northern Ireland Association of Social Workers, 2012). Employer Trusts are expected to ensure professional governance arrangements. A structure has been maintained to deliver unbroken lines of professional social work accountability, access to professional supervision and support for continuous professional development (CPD).The Department has recognised that employers have a responsibility to ensure all professions including social work have a right; to support to practise effectively, to have access to professional supervision and to deliver work to professional standards (DHSSPS, 2012, p. 13). There has been some questioning of the view that integration would increase understanding between professions and the importance of purely medical professional perspectives would decrease. Some issues remain concerning the acceptance of social work and its unique contribution and also the dominance on occasions of the medical model of care services in integrated teams (Northern Ireland Association of Social Workers, 2012, p. 11). On the other hand inter-professional relations are largely good and cordial, with the growth of an integrated mindset among many staff.

Hospital discharge

In the integrated structure in Northern Ireland the one Trust is responsible for the operation of the hospital and the discharge of patients but also responsible for the arrangement of post discharge care in the community. It therefore should be easier to arrange and act promptly in hospital discharge and, importantly, to move more resources into hospital discharge when necessary. Social workers or discharge staff based in hospitals have the same employer as hospital staff or social care staff in the community which can ease communication, exchange of data and speedy and flexible responses. The structure also makes it simple to locate social workers in A&E departments. There can be conflicting views on what constitutes success in hospital discharge or the benchmark for assessing delayed discharge. The limited evidence in Northern Ireland has shown that in 2009 there were conflicting reports between Trusts on problems with hospital discharge (Heenan and Birrell, 2009, p. 7). One Trust reported that it had reduced the number of delayed discharges and others noted that integration had improved the flow of patients through hospitals. A target was set that 90 per cent of patients with ongoing complex care needs would be discharged from an acute setting within 48 hours of being declared medically fit and no complex discharge would take longer than seven days (Heenan, 2013, p. 16). Comparisons with Great Britain are difficult because of different ways of calculating the complete patient journey. The integrated structure should also have helped the closure of institutions for people with mental illness or severe learning disabilities but in practice there were significant delays, particularly in running down institutional facilities for those with learning disabilities.

Reablement and intermediate care

Community rehabilitation has been established for some time with the aim of reducing the length of time in hospital. McKinsey (2010, p. 11) noted that an enhanced intermediate care service had reduced 'bed blocking' (beds being taken up by people waiting to be discharged) and reduced the length of stay. The development of new forms of intermediate services appeared to be well accommodated by the integrated structure. Thus homecare reablement, based on short-term intervention, to either rehabilitate people or prevent hospital admissions, has been adopted. Reablement teams normally operate on an integrated basis but surprisingly some have been set up without social work representation. Another important development has been rapid response and access teams. Rapid access for GPs and A&E involves a multidisciplinary team making an assessment. One such initiative reported that of 300 people seen, 221 were discharged with 79 admitted to hospital, thus for 74 per cent of service users hospital admission was avoided on the day of the assessment and for 59 per cent acute admission was avoided after 30 days (Heenan, 2013, p. 19). Teams have been developed in trusts consisting of acute care at home multidisciplinary teams of professionals led by a consultant geriatrician. The focus is on helping older people to manage conditions such as chest infections, urinary tract infections, cellulitis and dehydration with the aim of avoiding hospital. The service provides rapid assessment, diagnosis and treatment as an alternative to in-patient care.

Mental health services

Integrated mental health teams have operated and mental health is an important area linking psychiatric care with ready access to social care in the community. Research by Reilly et al. (2007) found factors mainly associated with the greater integrated approach were in the provision of special services, outreach activities, and shared policies. This research indicated that in these respects Northern Ireland had advantages over comparable areas of England. Integrated management systems were seen as beneficial in the area of old age psychiatry. Children's and young people's mental health services teams are well placed to coordinate with family services, community paediatric services and the voluntary sector. A related research project found some evidence that Northern Ireland provides more coordinated care for older people (Challis et al., 2006). This research found that Northern Ireland Trusts were able to more easily access and share information covering health and social care aspects of users' conditions when compared to England. The research also found that the Trusts in Northern Ireland all provided services to older people through specialists teams compared to 36 per cent in England. There was not such a significant difference in terms of community based integrated services.

Other operational aspects

Supported housing has benefitted from close cooperation between the integrated Trusts and the public housing body in providing housing related support services for vulnerable people. Housing adaptations are managed by the Northern Ireland

Housing Executive, while the Trusts provide these services for the private sector. One-stop shops have developed as an obvious feature facilitated by structural integration and in practice have assisted access to social care services.

Planned changes

In 2016 an expert panel chaired by Professor Bengoa (DH, 2016) called for a transformation of care from the acute to the community sector. The report suggested that the benefits of the strong foundation of integration had not been fully realised. The Bengoa report (2016, p. 22) advocated more locally based systems, more emphasis on the experience of users, and the creation of new generic roles between health and social care workers. The Minister of Health published a plan and consultation on the reconfiguration of health and social care services (DHSSPS, 2016). This was largely a continuation of the *Transforming Your Care* agenda of a model of what was called person-centred care. It was suggested that this would be underpinned by a more holistic approach to health and social care with more collaboration. There was no particular commitment to the use of integrated structures and both this plan and the Bengoa report appeared to take the view that structures were unimportant. The more radical recommendations of Bengoa on generic roles, co-production and localism were ignored. The most significant proposal was for fully integrated multidisciplinary teams to be embedded in general practice, although the detailed notion of placing a single social worker in a GP practice seems an old-fashioned approach to integration.

Conclusions

Northern Ireland has an almost unique model of structural integration but there has been a consensus that the full potential of this has not been realised. Some elements of integration have become well established and accepted by staff to the extent that incentives to integrated working are not normally seen to be required, but at the same time the full requirements of integrated working may be overlooked. Despite some 45 years of the experience of integrated working there are still issues about the dominance of health and fears that social care values and priorities may be neglected, as has been obvious even in recent government reports. Despite a number of reviews, health and social care remains marked by an over-reliance on acute and institutional care. The dominant position of health care means that it remains difficult to divert resources from acute care into community care. However, the integrated structure with one funding source and a unified employing body makes it easier to make links between services. Changing to a focus on integration, with prevention, participation, self-management and well-resourced community and mental health care, remains aspirational. The Northern Ireland model of structural integration does significantly include acute hospitals and while this has presented difficulties there is widespread acceptance and participation by the acute sector. Not all the problems with inter-professional working have been settled, in particular in relation to initial training and GP involvement. As indicated, it is difficult to assess clearly the effectiveness of integration given the lack of research, especially since the comprehensive structure was set up in 2009. There is evidence of achievements through integrated teams, multidisciplinary management, leadership, programmes of care planning, commissioning and unified assessment. Overall it can be argued that Northern Ireland does provide some evidence that comprehensive structural integration can operate, embed an acceptance of integrated values, and facilitate integrated working, even without strong legislative underpinning.

7 Achievements of Integration

Introduction

Identification of the achievements of integration of health and social care requires examination of a range of material which has focused on the outcomes of integrated projects and working. The evidence, which is now considerable, consists of policy and project evaluations, reviews, research projects, pilot studies, and case studies, and can be categorised as follows:

Box 7.1   **Main Sources**

- Overall academic reviews
  A number of reviews of evidence on the achievements have been published including Cameron and Lart (2003), Cameron et al. (2014, an updated version) and Petch (2011).

- Specific academic reviews
  Some academic reviews address findings for specific groups, for example, disabled people (Gridley et al., 2014) and people with chronic conditions (Goodwin et al., 2013). Other academic evaluations have been more locally based or council area based.

- Evaluations of pilot initiatives
  A number of major pilot studies on integration have been launched including a national evaluation of the Department of Health Integrated Care Pilots (Rand Europe, Ernst and Young, 2012) and the Pioneers Project launched in 2013.

- Evaluations by statutory and related bodies
  This includes government reports on strategies and policies, as well as reports by the National Audit Office and Parliamentary Committees or representative bodies, for example, the Local Government Association (2013b).

- Case studies form the largest category of research material and tend to be based in a locality, dealing either with a single integrated programme or an activity within a local council area or with a range of integrated activities within a local authority. Sources include a series of case studies published by Skills for Health/Skills for Care (2014). Caution should be exercised in extrapolating general lessons for good practice or making wide-ranging claims from specific case studies.

The discussion of achievements and benefits is considered under seven headings:

1. clinical outcomes including less use of hospitals and less delayed discharge
2. operational rational achievements including access, integrated teams; unified assessment, integrated commissioning, one-stop shops and GP involvement, and care pathways
3. community care including reablement, intermediate care, and rapid response teams
4. cost-effectiveness
5. patient experience and staff experience
6. care for groups including mental illness, physical disability, learning disability, elderly and frail elderly, and people with chronic illnesses
7. wider impacts including training, housing, children's services.

Limitations of the findings

Much of the early evidence on the achievements of integration tended towards two main conclusions: firstly, that much of the early evidence concentrated on the processes of intervention rather than the outcomes and, secondly, that there was a dearth of research evidence to support the notion that joint working between health and social services was effective (Cameron et al., 2000). This cautious approach by researchers was to continue. A research study carried out in 2000–02 compared two integrated teams for older people with traditional non-integrated teams. The authors concluded that the research had not produced evidence which suggested that integrated primary health and social care teams are more clinically effective (Brown et al., 2003). However, it was noted that the systems may not have had time to develop into full integration. Overviews of the studies of integration continued to suggest limitations with the research. Dowling et al. (2004) in a literature search found a lack of firm and consistent evidence that positive outcomes or benefits to users were being achieved. Rummery (2009) found the evidence base incomplete and Glasby and Dickinson (2008) stated that the notion that partnership working should improve services for users remains largely unproven. Some such comments were more specific and Rosen and Ham (2008) noted that the impact of integration on hospital admissions and costs of care is under-evaluated, with only weak evidence available.

Gleave et al. (2010), in noting that the published evidence was far from comprehensive, found the financial benefits were particularly not well documented. Some wider perspectives on the lack of clear evidence also appeared. It was suggested that the lack of evidence of outcomes is an expression of the complexity of integration rather than the lack of impact (Glasby and Dickinson, 2009). Attention was also drawn to a lack of clarity of purpose or consensus in integrated projects and different expectations in judging success and demonstrating the benefits of integration (Williams and Sullivan, 2010). Continuing caution on overall achievements was also reported by statutory bodies. The Audit

Commission (2011b) reported that progress on joint working between the NHS and local councils still remained patchy across health and social care and evidence on the impact of interventions on an integrated basis was not always clear.

Evidence from the integrated care pilot studies in 2012 showed that integration between health and social care was extremely difficult to achieve, particularly in producing a seamless service (RAND, 2012) . On the basis of this and other evidence Priest (2012) suggested that success can really only be judged on a case by case basis and the pilot studies had demonstrated how the different groups involved in integration, for example staff and patients and users, can develop different views on success. The evaluation of integrated care projects did show a number of benefits: better coordination following hospital discharge; staff enthusiasm for pilots' future impact; staff belief that patient care had improved; reductions in cost; and a range of local service improvements. However, Priest (2012, p. 8) accepted that there remained significant gaps in the evidence base, particularly about long-term impacts, but pointed out that certain groups were most likely to benefit from integration; frail older people, people with multiple chronic and mental health illnesses and people with disabilities. In examining the mixed results of the integrated pilots Goodwin (2012) identified a common shortcoming: that the emphasis is on doing the integration and the care experience gets lost in the process. Overall, the pilots highlighted the measuring of user experience as a major factor assessing achievement.

Recent analysis of research on outcomes still tends to the view that there is a paucity of robust systematic research. There is a general view that not enough has been done to assess the results of better integrated care and there is not enough focus on the outcomes for users during the care process (UK Government, 2013). Cameron et al. (2014) undertook a further review of research related to joint working in the field of adult health and social care services in the UK. Overall they found the evidence base still weak on effectiveness. Gridley et al. (2014), following a review of studies, argue for an urgent need for more rigorous evaluation of models of integrated care for disabled adults and older people with complex needs. Cameron et al. (2014, p. 230) do acknowledge a greater emphasis on evaluating outcomes but note that studies largely report small-scale evaluations of local initiatives and few studies are comparative in design between 'usual care' and 'integrated care'. Although it is suggested that recent developments have achieved benefits for organisations as well as users, some research and evaluations demonstrate that joint working can lead to improvements in health and wellbeing and reduce inappropriate admissions to acute or residential care and that intermediate care can save costs. This finding largely accords with another survey of existing evidence by the Local Government Association with limited evidence on the effectiveness of integrated care related interventions. They note a reliance for evidence primarily on case studies and qualitative data rather than quantitative data (Local Government Association, 2013b). Attention is drawn to an important consideration in reviewing research on achievements by Bardsley et al. (2013), which is the need to recognise that it takes time to implement large-scale changes. Thus the limited reporting of success in achievements of community based care interventions may reflect the setting of unrealistic short timetables for judging results. However, a subsequent National Audit Office Report (2017) still found that Departments in England had not yet established a robust evidence base to show that integration leads to better outcomes and whether any success is both sustainable and attributable to integration (National Audit Office, 2017). This report again suggested that the rate of progress to integration can be relatively slow with some areas realising success after two decades of working. Evaluations of a number of case studies have cautioned against generalising their findings and stress that outcomes are influenced by specifics. Coupe (2013) warned that it should not be assumed that community services have the spare capacity to support a shift from institutional care. GPs' working practices and levels of flexibility vary widely and this will impact on their ability to implement change.

Clinical outcomes

One of the major anticipated achievements is keeping people out of hospital unnecessarily. It has been suggested that there is some evidence of reductions in patient admissions and the length of stay (RAND, 2012). Torbay is often quoted as demonstrating the benefits of integration and statistics showed a reduction in the number of occupied beds from 750 in 1998–99 to 502 in 2009–10 and the lowest emergency bed usage in the region (Thistlewaite, 2011). The benefits of integrated care management were also demonstrated in three areas of Wales which had a shared care model of working between primary, secondary and social care and reported that for people with multiple chronic illnesses total emergency admissions for the three areas reduced by 32 per cent, 13 per cent and 10 per cent (National Audit Office, 2013). It has also been reported that in Greenwich, one of the Pioneer sites, over 2,000 patient admissions were avoided due to the work of integrated teams (DH, 2014). An integrated care pilot project in Norfolk showed fewer patients had unplanned admissions to hospital. A further study showed outpatients attendance and elective admissions were significantly reduced, by 22 per cent and 21 per cent respectively (Goodwin et al., 2012). There was also some evidence of reductions in re-admissions and an increased time between discharge and re-admission. A study of evaluations highlighted well-integrated and shared care models had the potential to reduce hospitalisation (Trivedi et al., 2013), although there may not be sufficient evidence to justify the view that integrated working is the key to keeping people out of hospital. Actual emergency admissions to hospitals in England had increased between 2014 and 2016 (National Audit Office, 2017, p. 4).

Reducing delays in the discharge of patients from hospital or, as it is popularly known, reducing 'bed blocking' has come to epitomise the measure of success in integrated and partnership working. The problem of delayed discharge has become a major issue in the operation of efficient and effective services and hospital admissions. Delays rose for a number of reasons including communication problems between health and social care, the availability of community based facilities and services to permit discharge and the alignment of hospital and community care. Delays occured in meeting patients and families and pre-discharge visits, and, in, communication and joint working between community based services (Beech et al., 2013, p. 602). Achieving reductions in delayed discharges can reduce inappropriate continuing hospitalisations and waste of resources and secure financial savings. A number of studies have shown achievements in discharges, with evidence from the Torbay integrated project that delayed discharges were close to zero. Organisational practices can vary between integrated discharge teams and Goodwin et al. (2013) report on the success of community resources teams in reducing delays in hospital discharges. While there is evidence of reduced overall numbers of delayed discharges through integrated working, there remains scope for improvement. The integrated discharge in Torbay used discharge coordinators in the acute hospital setting on a seven-day basis, supported by the local authority discharge team for more complex cases. The discharge staff worked closely with ward staff, staff managing patient flows and community teams to ensure efficient discharge. Reductions in social care expenditure between 2014 and 2016 have prevented major progress and delayed transfers in England increased by 185,000 (National Audit Office, 2017, p. 4).

Operational achievements

Access – Ease of access through integrated services should mean that both health and social care can be accessed through a single call or approach so that people may only have to tell their story once rather than face repetition, confusion and duplication. Such access may be identified as 'one-stop shop' where there is only one simple entry point to services and the needs of users can be addressed quickly and dealt with by an integrated team or the user directed to the necessary services. Generally better and faster access comes through easier communication and quicker responsiveness. Physical co-location in one building can enhance access to care and degrees of integration. One-stop shops have developed as a model of integrated delivery working across organisational and sectoral boundaries. The role of integrated provision in achieving greater accessibility and quicker responses was identified by Dowling et al. (2004). Evidence, however, by Hardwick (2013) suggests that the organisation may not be as important as the values and attitudes of staff.

Integrated teams – The creation of integrated teams has been a major achievement in operational practice. An essential feature is the multi-disciplinary basis of integrated teams which involves mutual understanding, a shared commitment to a culture of integration and acceptance of new roles. Integrated teams tend to be built around themes of specific users. It has been suggested that teams form the largest category of models of joint working (Cameron et al., 2014, p. 6). An area of major development has been in mental health with community mental health teams formed from staff from both health and social services. Gridley et al. (2014) report that evaluations of multidisciplinary teams for young adults found continuity of care with improved coordination and access to support. A study of eight integrated health and social care teams in Salford, supporting older people and vulnerable adults with the teams aligned with GP practice based commissioning clusters, found largely successful working (Syson and Bond, 2010). Shared practice and knowledge transfer helped to deliver improved interventions. A review of 19 studies described as using an integrated team model showed many leading to improved health and functional ability, reduced caregiver burden, increased satisfaction and quality of care (Trivedi et al., 2013, p. 119). Somewhat overlooked has been the development of integrated teams in hospital emergency departments. While the professions involved differed and team leadership varied, approximately one-third of emergency departments had an embedded team and demonstrated the benefit of the close involvement of social care services (Bywaters et al., 2011). An associated achievement of integrated teams is flexible working with it easier for staff to work and move between settings. In some areas flexible working has been developed more radically, with the acceptance of crossover and exchange in traditional roles, for example, having social workers taking bloods. However, the major benefit of team working is probably the ease of exchange of information and communication.

Unified assessment – Integrated practice has led to the setting up of single and unified assessment processes, which span existing institutional and professional separation. Unified assessment can apply to all adult service users but is mainly found for all types of assessment between local authorities and primary health providers (Abendstern et al., 2011). A single assessment process has been promoted since the National Service Framework for Older People (DH, 2001) which proposed a standardised assessment across four approaches: contact, overview, specialist, and comprehensive. When applied fully the unified assessment of needs for individuals can achieve effective joint working; reduce duplications in assessment; produce appropriate and comprehensive interventions; take into account complex patterns of need; and encourage more creative and innovative approaches. A successful process requires the use of standardised tools, guidance and training on multidisciplinary involvement, proportionate scale and depth of assessment, appropriate IT and record systems, and involvement of users. The overall performance on unified assessment remains patchy with obstacles identified including IT systems, limited practitioner involvement, and the belief that care coordination is a social care responsibility (Seddon et al., 2010). Difficulties can also arise from the professions involved taking different approaches. It has been reported that most difficulties arise with the involvement of the acute sector and the need to involve more clinicians and GPs (Abendstern, 2011, p. 474). There is still some way to go to fully develop unified assessment.

Also developing have been statutory requirements in England for area joint strategic needs assessment by local authorities and health bodies. Ellins and Glasby (2011) found examples of good practice and success stories in more systematic joint working although they also found a tendency for it to happen less frequently on a day-to-day basis. Respondents in the study felt that joint strategic needs assessment had the capacity to raise the profile of the importance of integrated working. Locally sensitive and responsive assessments may help improve the extent to which integration improves outcomes. The state of play with regard to Joint Strategic Needs Assessment (JSNA) was summarised (Harding and Kane,

2011) as a lack of consistent, structured approaches and an absence of clear specifications. Most JSNAs do now aim to support decision-makers with quality insight rather than simply data and wider partners are recognised as a key to filling data gaps. In England there is a growing awareness that JSNA must lead strategic discussions in the Health and Wellbeing Boards. What appears needed to achieve effective JSNA is genuine joint ownership and better public engagement.

Integrated Commissioning – Integrated commissioning was originally not so systematic and achievements described were not so spectacular (Hudson, 2010). The importance of integrated commissioning was promoted by policy changes, advocating bringing care closer to home rather than in expensive hospitals or residential care, and also by budget reductions. Most integrated commissioning involved local authorities and Primary Care Trusts, until the latter were abolished. This relationship had produced some local success in delivering better services and support through joint approaches (Hudson, 2010). The actual process of decision-making may rest with a negotiating forum, a partnership board, a special merged board or a small leadership board. Care priority setting has been seen as a key component of joint commissioning (Williams et al., 2010). However, differences in approaches do exist over such issues as a focus on preventative action, promoting productivity, and reducing health inequalities (Dickinson and Glasby, 2013). Joint commissioning has become well established, usually driven by a number of key objectives and outcomes, particularly greater efficiency, empowerment of users, better services, dealing with complex needs, and joined-up negotiated decisions. Outcomes based commissioning has come to the fore, requiring the overall strategic direction to be defined, attention to be paid to the goals of health and social care services, and the commissioning partnership to focus on exactly what they want the provider to achieve (Petch, 2011, p. 41). The main bodies involved in joint commissioning have now moved to local authorities and Clinical Commissioning Groups (CCGs), with the abolition of PCTs. CCGs largely represent GPs and GPs had not been major players in local authority/PCT joint working and commissioning (Lotinga and Glasby, 2012). The new relationships could promote more integrated commissioning related to community health services and more GP practice based joint working. Still left uncertain is which model of joint commissioning is best to achieve improved health and social care outcomes. A study by Addicott (2011) identified two distinct frameworks through which CCGs were arranging integrated service delivery: a prime contract model in which a single organisation takes the responsibility for the management of other providers and an alliance contract that sees a set of separate providers enter into a single agreement to deliver services. Addicott examines five projects, including integrated services for older people in Cambridgeshire and Peterborough, personalised support services in Lambeth for mental health rehabilitation, and older people's services in Salford. Four areas are identified for achieving success in commissioning which will improve outcomes and greater integration: engaging with local providers, users and the local communities; building good relationships and inter-organisational trust; flexibility in payment methods and shifting budgets; and building governance and organisational modes (Addicott, 2014, p. 52).

Cost-effectiveness

There have often been assertions that there is a lack of economic evaluations, which makes it difficult to draw conclusions. Major difficulties arise over the variation in the organisational environment, the financial structure and with the diversity of approaches to integrated services (Cameron et al., 2015, p. 229). It is also difficult to compare integrated services with the traditional, usual and standard modes of provision. The calculation of benefits is also confounded by the difficulties measuring each element of the cost and defining the scope of the costs (Monitor, 2012, p. 12). Recent work has still tended to find a lack of robust evidence on cost-effectiveness and problems related to attribution although Goodwin et al. (2013, p. 19) found that notwithstanding these problems care coordination did produce improvements in services without adding to the overall system costs. Bardsley et al. (2013) found methodological difficulties in relating integration to changes in hospital use and costs.

The increasingly difficult financial times for adult social care led to more expectations of integrated care as one means of securing greater efficiency, through a renewed emphasis on community based services. In Great Britain local councils had a strong interest in improving value for money and the health and social care interface became an increasingly important area. An Adult Commission study showed 35 per cent of councils referred to partnership working aimed at achieving efficiencies (Audit Commission, 2011a). A further Audit Commission report (2011b, p. 6), while noting that improving joint working across the boundary between health and social care has the potential to make savings, considered it was still the case that relatively few examples existed where it was possible to demonstrate that integrated working had achieved efficiencies. This Audit Commission report found that a joint commissioning project in Essex had resulted in the council and a Primary Care Trust identifying approximately £30million of efficiency savings.

The Local Government Association (2014) in a survey of cost-effectiveness in a number of studies and research projects identified some significant evidence of cost savings. This included Northumberland with savings of approximately £5million through their integrated care model. Richmond's Integrated Reablement Service saved £2.1million over three years. A Dementia project in 2012 based on a whole-systems approach reported savings of £2.1million. A value case commissioned by the Local Government Association on integrated care in Greenwich found in the first 12 months an immediate productivity saving on health services alone, the social care budget was reduced by £900,000, and shared management arrangements reduced the numbers of managers in health and social care. While the evidence base on integrated approaches showed greater efficiencies and financial savings in some projects but not others, it does appear that the evidence was only assessed over short time periods.

There is also growing evidence that home care reablement is cost-effective because it leads to savings in both health and home care services (Wilde and Glendinning, 2012). A study of the cost-effectiveness of reablement demonstrated that following reablement people's needs for social care services were reduced by 60 per cent compared to conventional home care and the research has concluded that reablement is more likely to be cost-effective than not (Francis et al., 2011). There is also some innovative work in training care workers in some aspects of medical care, for example, blood pressure and urinalysis which reduced A&E attendances, ambulance attendances and GP contacts at a residential home (Skills for Health/Skills for Care, 2014).

The National Audit Office has reported still no compelling evidence to show that integration in England leads to sustainable financial savings, although it does draw attention to the lack of comparable cost data across different care settings (National Audit Office, 2017, p. 7).

Rehabilitation and prevention

Reablement – Reablement, as a strategy, was introduced as part of a greater investment in rehabilitation and prevention. It was based on a short period of intensive intervention to re-establish an individual's capacity and confidence to perform basic personal care and domestic tasks. The period of intervention is normally six weeks but does include intensive supervision and constant assessment. Reablement has been seen as a more dynamic and flexible process compared with traditional home care services and is linked with access to a range of services and shared understanding (Rabiee and Glendinning, 2011). Most reablement teams bring together social care and health. Although some are based in social care, usually occupational therapists have a key role.

Research evidence shows that reablement is significantly associated with better health related quality of life and social care related outcomes compared with conventional home care, and improves independence and prolongs people's ability to live at home (Francis et al., 2011, p. 3). Some people showed lasting benefits and, in particular, the people who used the services welcomed the improved independence and confidence that reablement provides.

Managers and frontline staff welcomed the opportunity it provides to work flexibly and responsively with people (Francis et al., 2011, p. 5). It has tended to be effective with people who have falls, are disabled for other reasons, or are recovering from illness and injuries. The strategy has also assisted families and carers in balancing care, work and other responsibilities. Well-established tools have been used to monitor improvements and assess the effectiveness of reablement, including the Adult Social Care Outcomes Toolkit (ASCOT) and the East Midland Reablement Evaluation Toolkit (SCIE, 2012b). Leeds Adult Services Reablement reported 70 per cent of users who completed a repackage did not require any further intervention and were enabled to live independently at home (Skills for Health/Skills for Care, 2014). It has to be noted that reablement is likely to achieve more for or be directed towards temporarily disabled service users and thus those with more complex and long-term conditions may not derive the same benefits from the intervention (Wilde and Glendinning, 2012, p. 589). For 2015–16, statistics showed 83 per cent of older people still at home

91 days after receiving reablement or rehabilitation services, exceeding the target (National Audit Office, 2017, p. 4.).

Intermediate Care – Intermediate care developed to bridge the gap between hospital and community care and promote faster recovery from illness. It was targeted at mainly older people who would otherwise face longer hospitalisation or residential care. Intermediate care did involve the use of a facility usually in a residential setting where some nursing care could continue. It was recognised that the creation of a successful system depended on the establishment of robust collaborative arrangements with intermediate care, not the responsibility of only one professional group (Lymbery, 2006, p. 1127). Thus development of intermediate care was seen as explicitly intended to dissolve the barriers between health and social care services (Moore et al., 2007). Its development involved multidisciplinary teams as a major feature with access for users to a range of professions. A study of a Community Integrated Intermediate Care Service found it brought together from an NHS Trust and local authority over 70 staff, occupational therapists, physiotherapists, nurses, health visitors, social workers, support workers, and other therapists (Williams, 2012). Services did develop in a joined-up way with strong relationships between professions. The outcome of collaboration in this area did expedite hospital discharge, reduce admissions to long-term care, reduce dependency and increase independence. A further study did identify benefits in terms of being responsive, patient-centred, flexible and holistic, but the scheme had not fulfilled its full capacity with insufficient funding for intermediate care (Regen et al., 2008). Williams (2012, p. 557) in the study of the service found the course of the integrated service was driven more by aspiration and principles than by adherence to a preconceived model of delivery, and voluntary bodies could have a major role. The change in focus to reablement was to reduce the priority given to intermediate care, and also part of innovations in this area was the development of integrated rapid response services.

Rapid response and access teams – Rapid response teams developed from intermediate care services with a specific context of responding to a health and social care crisis. The aim was to rapidly assess, treat and/or support an individual to avoid unnecessary and costly hospital admissions. Such crises almost always involved both health and social care dimensions and therefore required an integrated response. Rapid response teams had a multi-professional membership, partnership arrangements between health and social care, and aligned budgets. The team would consist of nurses, physiotherapists, occupational therapists, social workers, health care assistants, administrative staff, and perhaps a support planner (NHS Evidence, 2011). The integrated health and social care team had usually one dedicated manager. Response teams operated mainly through primary care referrals and usually in the setting of either the person's home or a hospital emergency department or a clinical consultation. The object of a rapid response approach lies in the area of preventative action and this is a distinguishing feature from reablement and intermediate care. This also makes it easier to judge the achievements of rapid response strategies. Small-scale studies of rapid response teams have an important role in supporting people to remain in their own homes (Cameron et al., 2012). One study of rapid assessment support found that only four of all the people using the service were admitted to an acute hospital (Brooks, 2002). In another study of Thurrock Rapid Response Assessment Service 88 per cent of people seen avoided the need for a GP call and 66 per cent avoided residential care and only 3 per cent required admission to hospital (Skills for Health/Skills for Care, 2014). In this largely new area of integrated working there can be differences of terminology between rapid response teams, rapid assessment teams, and rapid access teams.

User and staff satisfaction

Assessments of the impact of integrated working on the experiences of service users have been limited (Cameron et al., 2012), whether because of omission, small research samples or lack of attention by users to who provided a service. It has been argued that successful integration care as experienced by the individual is not well defined (National Voices, 2013) .This endorses a view following the Integrated Care Pilots in England that the experience of patients and service users must be captured and acted upon as, to date, patients have not appeared to share the sense of improvement (RAND Europe et al., 2012).

It has been suggested that successful integrated care is primarily about patient experience (Redding, 2013, p. 317). Where accessible evidence exists, integration is associated with increased user involvement, choice and control (Cameron et al., 2013, p. 14) and particularly with satisfaction with timely initial assessment, partnership relationships, improved communication, navigating complex systems, and maintaining people's independence in the community. Carpenter et al. (2004) found a statistically significant advantage in terms of users' satisfaction with integration as an approach, with users less limited in their choice of care, better informed about services, and more positive about being supported in independent living. Research by Petch et al. (2013) explored the outcomes important to service users of health and social care partnerships. Good outcomes were identified as quality of life outcomes such as safety from falling, safety in the home, freedom from abuse and stigma, but also changes with less social isolation and more contact with services and the identification of good outcomes with good support and continuity of resources. The evaluation of the 16 national pilots had found that patients did not share the same sense of improvement as staff. One explanation has been given as the fact that integration was driven by professionals rather than users (Monitor, 2012, p. 27). One of the few studies on the views of staff shows a distinction between positive attitudes to general achievements, such as making a difference to people's lives, and more practical achievements such as freeing up more time for professionals (Lotinga and Glasby, 2012). Overall it appears more work is necessary to make the service user perspective a central or organising principle for integrated care (Redding, 2013, p. 323).

Integration and service groups

Discussion of success in outcomes of integrated working as already indicated has had a strong focus on provision for older people. This is related to a core element in the relationship between acute care hospital care and domiciliary care, both in preventing older people having to enter acute care or residential care and also ensuring rapid discharge with support for returning to live at home. However, much attention has been paid to other defined categories of users of integrated services, which may include older people, particularly those with long-term and multiple conditions, those with a mental illness or learning disability and particularly dementia, and those with a physical disability.

Long-term and complex needs – The definition of complex needs can be broad and reviews of the evidence may not suggest a specific model of integration but there has been evidence of the value of multidisciplinary specialist teams, interprofessional training, intensive case management, and dedicated or expert key workers (NIHR School for Social Research, 2008). Taking a joint approach between health and social care can be seen as necessary to identify service users and patients with very complex and long-term needs. A fully joined-up approach and close working has been seen as not only crucial but also long overdue (Lotinga and Glasby, 2012, p. 177). The Partnership for Older People Projects in 29 pilot sites had the aim of developing services to prevent or delay the need for higher intensity or institutional care. The national evaluation found projects providing services to individuals with complex needs to be particularly successful (DH, 2010). Integrated provision leading to an experience of continuity of care has been seen as important for older people with multiple health problems (Cornwell et al., 2012). In Wales three chronic care management demonstration pilots pioneered strategies to coordinate care for people with multiple chronic illness. They used a shared care model of working between primary, secondary and social care with multidisciplinary teams and one achievement was a reduction in the total number of bed days for emergency admissions by 27 per cent, 26 per cent and 17 per cent in the three areas (Goodwin et al., 2012, p. 5). Work in this area can cover a range of activities and teams including the relatively new reablement teams. A well-documented example is in Devon, described in Box 7.2.

Box 7.2	Northern Devon Stroke Service

Northern Devon Stroke Service

Stroke rehabilitation unit – early supported discharge – physical fitness programme – complex care team – review.

Further support – social care reablement, domiciliary care, night sitting – depression service – primary care – voluntary services.

Source: Local Government Association (2013b).

Patient experience surveys reveal high satisfaction with this service which patients have described as exemplary and the length of hospital stays fell by six days. Some 92 per cent of all new stroke patients discharged from hospital were supported by the early supported discharge service. The whole service was largely delivered by reorganising the use of existing staff and facilities with actual reduced costs for long-term support.

An analysis of five UK based case studies of care coordination for people with long-term and complex conditions demonstrated improvements in care experience and outcomes, but the impact on reducing costs was limited (Goodwin et al., 2012). Knowsley Integrated Recovery Service developed community services to improve the management of people with long-term conditions with a case management and workforce development approach, bringing together a spectrum of professional groups in a single system – the Knowsley Care Campus (Skills for Health/Skills for Care, 2014).

Mental health services – There has been a general view that the integration of health and social care in mental health services is complex with some reports of patchy progress but also with some documentation of significant achievement. A detailed study of mental health services integration based on specialist teams found that service users and carers regarded specialist integrated teams positively. Major positive aspects were: responsiveness to changing needs; liaison with other services and tapping into expertise; displaying sensitivity and dignity to users; and access to social activities and better support for carers (Freeman and Peck, 2006). A review of the research (Maslin-Prothero and Bennion, 2010) found mental health service users reporting that integrated team management has resulted in services that are more responsive, have reduced waiting times and have increased the levels of explanation given to users. However, a more specialist study of psychiatrists specialising in old age found in a large study of 318 consultants that structures to deliver integrated care across the interfaces between specialist old age acute and primary care and social care were poorly developed, with few of the distinguishing markers of integration with social care (Tucker et al., 2009). Some innovation based on integrated approaches has emerged, for example, a Wellness Recovery Action Plan for good mental health fitting in with personalisation and self-management principles and operated through a partnership between Hampshire County Council and Southern Healthcare Trust (Skills for Health/Skills for Care, 2014).

Dementia teams – There has been a major expansion in the use of dementia teams with some differences in focus but based on different training programmes which have been developed. However, integration has been a common factor in the organisation and operation of dementia teams. Bracknell Forest Community Dementia Support Team was created around a home first policy and improved access to personalised support. The team were trained in a programme of communication and caregiving and worked in partnership with the Acute Trust and Mental Health Trust. Their focus was on having a specialist team go in to the home and work with the person and the carers for a transition period of 12 weeks before handing over to other agencies.

Box 7.3	Impact of Bracknell Forest Community Dementia Support Team

- admissions to hospital and call outs to GPS reduced
- a marked decrease in medical problems for people with dementia
- service prevents or delays admissions into institutional care settings
- low delayed discharge rate
- financial savings estimated to be between £100,000 and £300,000 each year

Source: Skills for Health/Skills for Care (2014).

The West Sussex Integrated Dementia Crisis Service had a focus on a quick and flexible response where there was a sudden deterioration in a person's situation. The service had a focus on a person-centred approach and was based on an integrated team from the NHS, the local authority and the third sector. Underpinning the service was a strong emphasis on integrating it with the wider health and social care system.

Box 7.4	Impact of the West Sussex Integrated Dementia Care Team

- reduced hospital admissions
- supported people with dementia and their carers in the transition to long-term living arrangements
- improved hospital discharge
- contributed to cost savings

Source: Skills for Health/Skills for Care (2014).

The JackDawe service in Nottingham is a specialist multi-agency service to support and promote independent living. This title was used to counter any stigma. The service is staffed by mental health nurses, occupational therapists, home care workers and managers. The aim is to work as a multidisciplinary team and create a high degree of integration between health and social care staff. Other main aims are to help people remain at home, link with voluntary agencies and support informal carers. The project has been based on the Skills for Care New Types of Worker initiative.

Learning disability – Special services for people with a learning disability have largely been delivered by adult social care departments but the linkage with medical diagnosis and concerns about access to health services have raised issues relating to integration. Neurological conditions are a major cause of disability with long-term consequences and implications for support across service boundaries. A study of provision (Bernard et al., 2012) found some service models stood out including the work of community rehabilitation teams drawn from a range of professions. The teams were most highly valued by service users where they showed expert knowledge about neurological conditions, where support was ongoing and where provision was flexible to meet people's needs. Nurse specialists were also valued for their role in coordinating care and services within and across the health and social care system. Day services have been an area of further development and modernisation with day centres, community facilities and projects to enable people to access services close to home. Another area for innovation is end of life care. A Leicestershire Partnership NHS Trust project brought together different staff from learning disability services, generic NHS services, other specialisms and voluntary bodies and there is evidence that training and conferences have had an impact (Skills for Health/Skills for Care, 2014). Other initiatives have been filling a gap by bringing social care workers into closer working with palliative care and health staff in hospitals.

The new initiatives

In England the Department, health bodies and local authorities have responded to the limited evidence relating to the success, efficiency and achievements of integration with a series of initiatives evaluating integration, both to improve outcomes and to save money. Early evaluations of the Pioneers programme have not found evidence of major service changes. It has also not demonstrated improvements in the planned outcomes on savings. Evaluations conclude that it is too soon to identify potential improvements in the implementation process while the environment has become hostile for transformation (NHS, 2016d). The first report did find considerable variation in what different sites had achieved. Some sites had reported fewer hospital admissions over two years and reduced waiting times and referred to some evidence that Pioneers had initially coped slowly but subsequently built quickly the relationships that are necessary (NHS England, 2016, p. 49). Pioneer projects have also acted as an important catalyst for local commissioners and providers to discuss transformation. The Better Care Fund did not achieve its principal financial or service target over 2015–16, its first year, but on the other hand there was some achievement in incentivising local bodies to work together and provide integrated services as alternatives to hospital and residential care (National Audit Office, 2017, p. 11). There was less achievement to report in managing demand for health care or improved outcomes for patients. Vanguard test sites working on new care models have also not been able yet to report conclusions on achieving savings or reductions in hospital activities. Some sites have reported on new wrap-around services for individuals and a new focus on preventative support for those in the community (New Local Government Network, 2016). The Sustainability and Transformation Planning initiative has been established to work for transformation including work to integrate local care services, but the main early focus has been on plans to reduce the financial deficits of NHS Trusts (National Audit Office, 2017, p. 11). A focus on the acute hospital footprint had led to an examination of the effectiveness of a new clinical care coordinator role.

It is the Pioneer projects that have come up with some innovative practices in integration schemes in their localities and examples are presented in Box 7.5

Box 7.5	Pioneer Projects: Examples of Best Practice

Islington
- Care navigators commissioned from the voluntary sector
- Development of integrated training framework
- Integrated community ageing team
- Proactive work with care homes
- Delivering integrated digital care record
- Linking personalised health and social care budgets

Nottingham.
- Relationship between councils and CCGs
- Assisted technology strategy
- Transforming care in care homes
- System wide urgent care
- Empowering people with long-term conditions to live independently

Leeds
- Leeds care record
- Technology enabled care – mental health habitat with digital solutions

Cheshire
- Enabling people to live more independently through personalisation and assistive technology
- Integrated case management for individuals with chronic needs
- Joint approach to performance framework and workforce development
- Shared care record
- Development of integrated personalised intermediate care services

Sheffield
- Independent living solutions in commissioning
- Co-design of active support and recovery
- Community support workers project

Source: Based on NHS England (2016d).

Wider dimensions

With the voluntary sector – The voluntary sector is networked into overall provision and tends to have a more extensive role in social care, through partnership working with local authority services and health bodies or provision through commissioning. Voluntary bodies normally operate with an independent identity but will attempt to align their activity with other services and this would apply to integrationist requirements. A Life after Stroke community service provided by the third sector Stroke Association involved: family and carer support, communication support, and long-term support through the use of coordinators. The integrated role of the service was designed to follow on from the acute and active rehabilitation phase of stroke recovery, complementing the statutory health service provision by adding a longer aspect of care as well as supplementing and bridging the link to social care services (Jenkins et al., 2013). The service was highly regarded by service users as providing personal and emotional support complementing acute hospital provision and community nursing and working across health and social care boundaries. Among recent developments has been a more central role for the sector in a preventative approach for people who are visually impaired.

Housing and integration – One of the main areas of achievement in integrated care relates to enabling people to live independently in the community appropriate accommodation. Cooperation with housing bodies to provide extra care accommodation can be seen as a wider dimension of integration. Extra care housing is especially designed housing with flexible on-site care and there are several variations in forms of sheltered housing. This accommodation is mainly available for older people and is an alternative to acute provision and care homes. While in Great Britain social housing and social care have traditionally been a local government responsibility, the transfer of many social housing functions to housing associations means that cross-sectoral collaboration is necessary. A wholly integrated approach does imply the involvement of health. There has been evidence of community based housing associations working closely with hospitals and hospital discharge services. A study of integration and housing support found most people were extremely positive, especially about the quality of life, although a third of the survey participants described problems related to boundary issues where gaps, delays or confusion had arisen at the interface between organisations or professional groups (Blood, 2013).

Integration and children – In England the structural reorganisation of social care following Every Child Matters led to a separation of adult social care and children's social services within local authorities. Owing to these changes, later amendments had to be made to operationalise integrated teams and interdepartmental working to meet children's needs (Collins and McCray, 2012), particularly within the context of families and their holistic needs. The need to integrate children's and adult's social care with health arises mainly in the context of children's needs and child protection for children with long-term and complex needs. This may be children in families characterised by mental health difficulties, substance abuse, poor parenting and domestic violence. Success in the transition of children into adulthood also is an area requiring an integrative approach, especially for disabled children. Good working relationships and multidisciplinary working have been seen as an essential component for good outcomes (Devaney, 2008). Local authorities are in a position to ensure close working across internal organisational boundaries between adult, family and children's services.

Conclusions

The listing of achievements tends to come from either summative accounts in academic or government/public body studies or literature reviews or else from pilot and research studies. There has been a shift in the evaluation of success away from the original focus on the process of integrated working. The nature of the integration analysed differs between case studies, which are usually small-scale local initiatives; pilot projects as part of national initiatives; localised collaboration in relation to one service or a locality; large-scale collaboration across a range of providers and services; more structured forms of integration; studies from the separate countries of the UK; and national studies. The main achievements and benefits can be noted as reflecting mainly specific case studies or major pilots with some consensus that the impact of integration is hard to measure, that it can take time to materialise and that there are gaps in the evidence base (NHS Confederation and Local Government Association, 2016, p. 16). The dominance of case studies has been noticeable with a focus on identifying organisational processes or mechanisms. Dickenson (2014) suggests that understanding organisational processes may not be the main value of case studies, as they provide insufficient insight. They are, however, valuable in illustrating what professionals do in practice. The summary of major impacts of integrated projects by Skills for Health and Skills for Care (2014) found four key impacts: reducing avoidable hospital admissions; reablement and timely hospital discharge; smoother transitions through care; and better use of resources. The value case studies by Integrating Care and the Local Government Association (2013b) noted some difference in benefits between recipients. For users it was enhanced patient experience, seamless transition of care, improved wellbeing and peer support for users and carers. For commissioners it was delivered targets and improvement in outcomes, reduced system costs, and more care delivered at home or close to home. For staff it was greater staff satisfaction, increased staff motivation, and improving outcomes for users they work for. For the public interest it was equity of access to services, holistic and personalised approaches, and better links with voluntary groups and local support networks. A review by the National Audit Office (2017, p. 9) concluded that the existing evidence base does not support the propositions that integration saves money, reduces hospital activity, or improves patient outcomes. More planning is needed to develop understanding of how to measure progress in integration of health and social care. While doubts remain about the achievements of integration it must be noted that the actual quality of services delivered remains high. The Care Quality Commission (2017) found nine out of 10 services delivered as good or outstanding and recognised that the best care systems are those where health and social care go hand in hand.

8 Promoting Integration

There has been an extensive analysis of the factors which have been identified as contributing to the promotion of integration. Such an analysis makes use of research and evaluation studies, policy analysis and reports and work by practitioners and professional bodies. Most of the analysis in this chapter relates to practices and lessons from experience in England. Relevant work related to the rest of the UK is discussed in the chapters on the devolved administrations. While it is possible to arrange the analysis into a few general headings, the categories can overlap or do not add much clarity in specifying the details of promotional factors. Therefore the chapter is organised under a wider number of headings based on the major factors under discussion as promoting integration.

Financial support

The promotion of integration has generally meant a degree of change in administrative structures and service delivery with related training and change costs and most initiatives or pilot projects requiring substantial investment. This is accompanied by expectations that integration will produce more cost-effective services and overall financial savings. Some government assumptions of savings have been ambitious with the Better Care Funding initiative expected to secure £1billion savings (National Audit Office, 2014). Adequate financing of integrated care has been seen as a way of reducing the need for more expensive hospital provision. The delivery of funding to assist integration has to take recognition of the different financial systems for health and social care and that users often have to pay charges or are means tested for social care, in contrast to health which is free at the point of delivery. The main way of funding collaboration has been through pooled budgets between the NHS and local authorities. Pooling of budgets has the potential for more flexibility and more sustainable funding. There has been support for the argument that health and social care budgets should be used more collectively (Oldham, 2014, p. 65). Joint funding has been a major enabler of integrated care and has facilitated networks and coordination of services and better use of resources. Pooled budgets can also promote innovations, for example, in funding career breaks. The Better Care Fund meant that a major component of the UK Government's policy to achieve integration was based on financial incentives through a single pooled budget embracing a shift in spending on acute services towards integration based prevention, personalisation and self-directed care. Plans submitted by local authorities and Clinical Commissioning Groups tended to pool a higher amount than envisaged, leading to more centralised control (Humphries, 2015), although not actually composed of new money. Other funding arrangements supporting adult social care have the potential to increase resources for integration in England. The social care precept in council taxation has contributed as well as permitted increases in council tax. There has also been the development of direct payments and personal commissioning programmes, through which individuals can organise their own care.

Information sharing and communication

There was widespread support for the view that 'information is the key enabler of integration' (NHS Future Forum, 2012; Local Government Association, 2016e). The Pioneers initiative in 2015 highlighted information sharing as a key challenge along with the need for frameworks and materials to support intensive information sharing (NHS England, 2016d, p. 74). This suggests the value of sharing individuals' data including other documentation and emphasises that health and social care professionals need to understand why information should be shared, how this is beneficial, and how information should be used to promote more integrated decision-making. Access to shared information facilitates a more holistic and comprehensive approach, helps to improve the quality of services and enhances the safety of care and support. While face-to-face communication and conversations about people may be of value, electronic records are seen as the key to success meaning the sharing of information through compatible IT systems (Cameron et al., 2015, p. 10) and specifically the interoperability between NHS IT systems extended to social care (Priest, 2012, p. 20). Progress in the sharing of data between health and social care has not gone smoothly (Ham, 2009, p. 10), while the Oldham Report (Oldham, 2014, p. 10) called for more ready access to information to improve joint commissioning and evidence bases. Technological advances will enable further advances in integrated planning and working across the system with initiatives such as mapping all individuals' interaction with health and social care. IT systems can promote effective communication between the members of multidisciplinary teams (Goodwin, 2012, p. iv) and effective communication about people and tracking users' care records is a major way of enhancing joint working. Care records enable integrated care provision through the viewing of an individual's total care needs, increasing the complementary nature of care across organisations, assisting assessment and removing duplication. The shared care record has been seen as absolutely fundamental to working better together (NHS England, 2016d, p. 54). Some sites in the Pioneers initiative created an integrated care payment forum (NHS England, 2016, p. 75) to discuss payments for outcomes or standards or whole care pathway funding. In England data sharing agreements between NHS bodies and local councils are necessary (New Local Government Network, 2016, p. 44).

Advances in the use of technology can also improve communication with patients, clients and carers, mainly through providing access to information or advice increasingly on a personalised basis. It has been reported that there is a wealth of evidence from Pioneer sites in England using technology, particularly assistive technologies, to monitor people outside of traditional care settings (NHS England, 2016, p. 58). These technologies, remote patient monitoring, and video conferencing can operate to detect early deterioration, improve care at home and contact with professions. Telecare uses electronic equipment to measure vital signs at home and can alert carers. Telecare is a telephone based monitoring service that can include electronic sensors so people can live safely and independently. Northern City Delivery Telehealth offers schemes to help meet users' entire health and care needs (NHS England, 2016, p. 60). Assistive technology can also be used to promote prevention. The city of Leeds also developed telecare technology for emergency use by older people and telethon for people with chronic conditions.

Leadership and management

Effective leadership is widely referred to as a necessary requirement to initiate and deliver integrated care successively. Efficient and stable leadership is seen as essential to develop partnership arrangements (Priest, 2012, p. 13) and manage multidisciplinary teams. There is a requirement to lead staff engagement in a joint enterprise in one direction, facilitating the inclusion of senior and middle management. Professional bodies, such as the Association of Directors of Adult Social Services, have endorsed the view that strong leadership and commitment from the top help integration (ADASS/NHS Confederation, 2013). The leadership of integrated projects requires the replacement of traditional leadership approaches, needing different knowledge, skills and behaviours and an emphasis on the importance of place (Fillingham and Weir, 2014). Leadership needs to adapt to complex cross-organisational structures and deal with change, improvement, and relationships across diverse teams. Leadership to promote integration has been seen as characterised by a desire to create collective identity and ownership, sustained long-term commitment, and boundary spanning across organisation levels and professional identities (Petch et al., 2013, p. 13). Leadership has also been related to instilling a vision and Oldham (2014, p. 19) describes leadership as key to developing a persuasive vision and a shared outcome among those involved.

Leadership is multi-layered and required both within and between organisations and across professional boundaries. The NHS Future Forum (2012) noted: 'Whether at the level of commissioning or provision, the development of shared goals, culture, plans, governance, procedures and practices is a complex and difficult task, often requiring years of effort from leaders and staff.' Leadership is required to ensure that there is commitment and alignment within and between organisations. It ensures that there is clarity about aims and objectives, vision and direction of travel. It enables an understanding of broad, long-term objectives rather than a focus on individual or team successes or targets. For optimal effectiveness, initiatives spanning a number of organisations or boundaries require strong leaders with the legitimate authority to lead. Creating and communicating a shared vision of integrated care is of the utmost importance. A collective leadership culture is characterised by collaboration both within and between organisations. Health and social care is delivered by a broad range of organisations with differing values, cultures and governance. Shared leadership enables working in partnership with the best health outcomes for service users. It requires that leaders work collaboratively to achieve agreed collective objectives rather than simply focusing on their particular components (West et al., 2014). A 2012 national evaluation of the Integrated Care Schemes identified strong leadership as pivotal to their success. Strong leadership was identified as central to the success of pilots. Whilst leadership was required at all levels, the importance of clinical leadership was highlighted; GPs and other clinicians had the ability to engage with their professional peer group regarding the credibility and feasibility of the intervention, and to motivate participation.

The NHS Confederation (2016) addressed the dimension of leadership in negotiating the complex system of public and personal accountability of transcending organisational boundaries and responding to local needs. Williams (2012) has argued that the leadership role needs to focus on four main areas: promoting common purpose; developing a collaborative culture; facilitating multi-agency teamwork; and supporting team communication and skills. Williams also emphasised the value of trust in inter-agency teams building a collaborative culture, the value of knowledge as a powerful driver, and the value of encouraging teams to share leadership functions. Miller et al. (2010) suggest leadership of integration activities requires an ability to simplify complexity and to tell a coherent story, and suggest a special leadership paradigm within the complex and fragmented health and social care landscape. Attention is also drawn for leaders from a social care background to confront their historic position of having less influence than health staff. However, a rather different emphasis is suggested by Close (2010) who sees the leadership role for promoting integration as requiring bridging rather than bonding, in pursuing collaborative leadership. Health and Wellbeing Boards will aim to provide strong collective leadership direction which appears to be a significant challenge across different organisations and territories (Baggott, 2013, p. 83). While there has been strong support for a commitment to collaborative working and new leadership skills or style it has been seen as an under-researched area of practice (Fillingham and Weir, 2014, p. 31). Timmins (2015) drew attention to the view that NHS leaders had relatively little training or experience in managing systems as opposed to organisations, although that was necessary given the complexities of integrated care.

A shared vision and culture

A shared vision and shared values have been regarded as a strong integrative driving force for some time (Hudson, 2007) and described by Goodwin (2013, p. 22) as 'the development of a clear joint vision shared by all stakeholders'. This entails stressing the importance of developing support for the vision, also described as a culture of integration (Ham, 2009, p. 11), including a shared view of why integration matters. An essential starting point is a 'shared vision and commitment from a leadership coalition to create significant drive and momentum' (Local Government Association, 2016b, p. 6). Securing the commitment and understanding of staff to a vision, aims and outcomes has been identified as crucial to effective joint working. Collaboration is part of the vision or culture necessary as a key ingredient to make a success out of integration. This is a vision of a common purpose reflecting shared ownership and it has been noted that this is particularly important as full structural integration is not common (Weatherly et al., 2010). An important dimension of a clear joined-up vision is a holistic focus with an ability to see the whole picture (Miller et al., 2010). Such a holistic dimension means stepping away from a medical or social care silo and embracing a vision and culture stretching across boundaries. It helps to promote integration if the benefits and outcomes are a shared goal. It has also been suggested that a shared language is important in identifying common goals for the whole integrated system or objectives to work towards, described also as a narrative that can be used and adopted to shape services (National Collaboration for Integrated Care, 2013). A number of other considerations may promote a clear joined-up vision. All staff need to see how an overall vision is productive and that a strong narrative based on the vision should give compelling support for integration (Monitor, 2012, p. 12). The vision and narrative should apply at both national and sub-national levels and have a long-term commitment to integrated working.

In a document produced by four main bodies in England, the NHS Confederation, the Local Government Association, ADASS and the NHS Clinical Commissioners, a shared vision of integrated care is held to have as essential characteristics holistic care, co-production, commitment to change, a focus on prevention, local governance, common information and technology, and integrated workforce planning (NHS Confederation/Local Government Association, 2016). The promotion of integrated care is also seen as dependent on the acceptance of cultural change in the implementation of the vision. Petch (2012) argues that there is a need for the acknowledgement of cultural change, as seeking to retain an existing culture leads to a struggle for dominance. The drive to deliver integrated care and support should lead to the emerging of a new cultural identity, informed by a clear vision. This view is challenged somewhat by Glasby (2016) who suggests successful joint working depends on working with different professional values and cultures to avoid a lack of trust which requires meeting each other halfway. A pragmatic suggestion has been that as health and social care staff often speak different languages, the role of 'system translators', to communicate the benefits of integration, instil new ways of behaving and promote change, is significant (New Local Government Network, 2016, p. 56).

Education and training

More integrated professional training for those who work together has an important role in breaking down barriers. Team building and multidisciplinary decision-making are seen as areas for attention, whether through training or forums for professionals to understand the concept of integration and encourage changes to practice, sharing information and joint accountability (Kassianos et al., 2015). A flexible approach to in-service training with ways of utilising staff, resources and information is regarded as valuable. An integrated care workforce also requires training in areas such as unified assessment and care coordination (Goodwin, 2013, p. 5). Multidisciplinary working has to be encouraged in a context of strong traditions of specialism. The idea of communities of practice has also been mooted as a way of promoting collaborative working. Communities of practice are groups of six to 10 practitioners in frontline practice who meet regularly to identify learning for improved practice (Cornes et al., 2013). Communities of practice involve people interacting, undertaking joint tasks, and sharing insights. They are valued as acting to overcome fragmentation and isolation, encouraging face-to-face contact and building collaborative networks (Miller et al., 2016, p. 177).

Education in working together has not been developed into a major driver of integration, particularly at undergraduate level, but it has been operating at the level of local education and training boards (McCririck and Hughes, 2013). There have been developments in postgraduate training, particularly for health and social care management working across shifting boundaries, interprofessional working and facilitating integration. Williams (2011) notes the role of trained boundary spanners, operating across and within collaborative areas with particular competencies, knowledge and attributes, including managing in different forms of organisation, and dealing with multiple accountabilities. With the need to grow the social care workforce and develop new qualifications a range of skills has to be taught, including making judgements, counselling, and developing skills related to the practice of integration (Dickinson, 2014). New roles and ways of working which are relevant for integrated care can be built on the existing skills of the workforce or new boundary-spanning skills (Gilburt, 2016). Working on a basis of skill-mix or equipping individual staff to use skills which cross traditional professional boundaries is still problematic. A study of key localities with initiatives promoting integration found extensive training and team development programmes evident across all the sites including training staff in new ways of working with shared records, identifying gaps in roles, and involving staff in new care modes and evaluation (Local Government Association, 2016e, p. 4). Other programmes have been developed on a continuing educational basis for health and social care managers and commissioners (Miller et al., 2016, p. 170). A number of bodies and initiatives have been set up to produce resources, reports and guidance for use and consultation. The Better Care Exchange is a collaborative network enabling collaboration, information and knowledge sharing, and the sharing of good practice for delivering integrated care. Support is supplied also to Health and Wellbeing Boards and to Clinical Commissioning Groups (SCIE, 2016). NICE has also developed a local practice collection as a national resource, while the Integrated Care and Support Exchange (ICASE) supports local authorities, Health and Wellbeing Boards, Clinical Commissioning Groups and GPs. The National Collaboration for Integrated Care and Support also provides resources to promote integration. Local Education and Training Boards (LETBs) were set up under Health Education England (HEE) and have been given a key role in promoting a joined-up approach across health and social care (McCririck and Hughes, 2013). This has meant looking at skill-mix, including developing health care related skills in social care services linked to integrated care pathways.

Co-location

Co-location of health and social care staff has been reported to be an important, even necessary, element in the success of joint working (Cameron et al., 2015, p. 10). Co-location leads to informal contacts, easier communication and facilitated learning across professional boundaries. Priest (2012) states that the creation of co-located integrated teams is one of the most commonly cited ways to improve working together and suggests that co-location should be considered in all areas where integration is operating and seen as a key factor. Co-location in England will usually involve staff from different organisations and therefore is important in promoting working collaboratively. Co-location also has advantages in facilitating important informal contact and developing relationships. The argument has been made that integrated teams must have co-location and alternatives a weakness (Hudson, 2011, p. 7). It has also been argued that there is mixed evidence for the importance of co-location (Maslin-Prothero and Bennion, 2010). A further advantage claimed for co-location is that it can provide a single entry point to care, and help operate care pathways and holistic assessments (Weatherly et al., 2010, p. 21).

Flexible roles

A commitment to the introduction of flexibility in work roles has been supportive to promoting integration (Cameron et al., 2015, p. 10). The opportunities for this type of innovation are more likely to occur for frontline staff within multi-agency teams or in aspects of domiciliary care or intermediate care. Flexibility means that there is a willingness to bend traditional professional boundaries with skill-mix and staff substitution, for example, with social care workers allowed to take blood pressure or samples. A more open approach may arise in reactions to the changing needs of users or in rapid responses, in forms of role substitution or sharing (Goodwin, 2013, p. 13). Generic working practices are more achievable in well-established systems of integration. Flexibility in response may also be identified in developing creative and innovative integrative delivery to problems, although this assumes the freedom to take such decisions and training in risks. Adaptability is also desirable in identifying priority and in setting key performance standards for projects and services (Oliver et al., 2014, p. 55).

Person- and user-centred

An emphasis on the person-centred focus of integrated care has been seen as promoting integration through the close involvement of users or putting people at the centre and making the care system more navigable. The user focus has been seen as important in driving forward the integration agenda. Developments of individual care plans, pathways and care coordination are valuable aspects of integrated approaches. Alakeson (2013) suggests that developments at the level of the individual suggest that the individual user is best placed to integrate care, and this may be as significant as structural integration. There is broad agreement that the assessment process, care coordination and interdisciplinary process must involve providers and users. Protocols of guidance are needed for the multiple providers in relation to risk, preventative care, elective and unscheduled care. Gregory (2015) refers to the example of Trafford Clinical Commissioning Group and Trafford Council having a person-centred approach through robust shared guidelines; care protocols; consultations between professionals; technological support; and a focus on quality assessment.

Care pathways and care coordination are one major manifestation of a person-centred approach. Care coordination tends to flourish at the level of multidisciplinary care teams and at local and neighbourhood level (Goodwin et al., 2013) although there may be variations in the holistic nature of care coordination. It is also easier to promote person-centred integrated services in some areas of need, for example, dementia. Shared decision-making, close communication, organisational support, and risk-taking are identified as advantages of integrated care for dementia (Woolrych and Sixsmith, 2013). Also developing has been the idea of a single named care coordinator or care navigator who would act as a first point of contact who leads in assessment, and liaises and works with all health and social services to ensure that providers tailor person-centred services (NICE, 2015). Guidelines for a care coordinator would apply to older people with social care needs and those with multiple long-term conditions. The most radical form of user control is through personalised and individual budgets which have the potential to bring together health and social care individual budgets providing a vehicle for more holistic whole person care. Personal budgets and personalised care planning can provide opportunities for integrated care commissioning and a pilot study, an Integrated Personal Commissioning Programme, has been launched (NHS England, 2015). This operates through a partnership between NHS England and the Local Government Association and nine demonstrator sites were created to redesign models of care for people with complex needs. A caveat is that person-centred planning does not always result in person-centred outcomes.

As a general principle the importance of the engagement of users has been well established but more so in social care delivery than in healthcare (Beresford, 2016). It has been argued by Ham (2009, p. 1) that the journey to integration should start from a focus on service users. The Department of Health's Future Forum analysis (2011) saw users and carers as key drivers of integration which can contribute to building support for integration. Initiatives in promoting integration have usually sought to embrace user engagement (Goodwin et al., 2013, p. 18). Public engagement has an important role as well in explaining and justifying the priority given to integration. There is a further benefit in the general promotion of integration through participation and co-production leading to greater user and public satisfaction (Cameron, 2016, p. 9).

Legacy of joint working

A previous history of joint working has been seen as supportive of integration, enabling new initiatives to be built on an existing foundation (Cameron, 2013, p. 4). A history of successful joint working is an advantage in taking processes forward, although Weatherly et al. (2010) note that the advantage is difficult to quantify. Lotinga (2015) has also noted that local history and context are crucial in shaping the nature of local joint working initiatives. The major developments in the Manchester city region since 2016 have been based on an integrative approach in operating since 2010. It can be suggested that any movement to a degree of joint working where previously there were clear silos between health and social care will be of value in promoting integration.

GP engagement

Securing the support and active engagement of GPs in integration initiatives has been well established as a measure that would help realise the aims of joint working, cracking old boundaries, creating a groundswell of involvement, and improving the relationship between GPs and social workers (Lotinga and Glasby, 2012). The anticipated benefits are well rehearsed but there have been barriers to major engagement. The growth in the numbers of people with chronic multiple conditions has provided some imperative. Studies have suggested how GP involvement can be encouraged or improved. Problems with lack of resources or staffing in GP practices can be tackled through more collaborative arrangements between neighbouring practices (NHS Future Forum, 2011, p. 25). Successful attempts have been recorded of more joint working between GP practices and local community care staff (Tucker and Burgis, 2012). There can be better guidance at encouraging general practice to adapt more rapidly to provide a platform (Goodwin et al., 2010, p. 9). It has been suggested that more 'hard wiring' can be put in to promote joint working, with teams of social workers linked to GP clusters and using small-scale opportunities to establish integrationist activities. Mainstreaming closer relationships is viable as GPs are often keen to improve collaborative working (Mangan et al., 2014). In England CCGs and HWBs have been important structures although with integrated initiatives in promoting GP engagement.

It has been stated that the wider importance of good professional relationships should not be underplayed as part of a strategy to promote integration and create staff satisfaction (Priest, 2012, p. 14). While building relationships between colleagues is always beneficial, it is especially advantageous to build bridges between health and social care staff and related professionals and to create integrated team working and understanding (National Collaboration for Integrated Care and Support, 2013). Wistow (2011, p. 9) even describes effective personal relationships and mutual confidence as important lubricants of integration.

Evidence and research

It is a truism that a strong foundation of evidence will promote the acceptance and introduction of integrated care. Priest (2012, p. 13) notes that the most important evidence will relate to the linkage between integration and improvements in patient care. Also closely related is the identification of examples of good practice. Measuring outcomes and experiences is an essential task and use can be made of the national outcomes frameworks for both the NHS and adult social care. It has been suggested that research and evidence are more valuable and useful than central government guidance (ADASS/NHS Confederation, 2013). Analysis can also be made of existing data sets. The National Collaboration for Integrated Care and Support (2013) has urged all localities to strengthen the evidence base. The sharing of knowledge and evidence has also been seen as a key cornerstone of effective integration, in areas such as multidisciplinary case management (Morris, 2012). More research and evidence are necessary to match the priority now given to promoting integration and to make up gaps in research. The evidence that integration can improve clinical and care outcomes is stronger than evidence of improving efficiency (Bevan Commission, 2013). Areas where research is needed include the impact of independent providers on integrated approaches. Effective mechanisms are required to make research findings and their implications for practice readily available and the Social Care Institute for Excellence, the King's Fund, the National Audit Office and other organisations play a significant role. Monitor (2012, p. 11) encouraged networks to share learning, evidence and ideas. The National Audit Office (2014, p. 45) also urged the integrated care Pioneers to collect and share evidence. The importance of research and evaluation is demonstrated in the extensive work that the government has commissioned on the Pioneer and Vanguard projects.

Integrated teams

The operation of integrated teams, usually in Great Britain within a divided health and social care structure, has become one of the most high profile aspects of integration. Integrated teams have been described as the most frequently evaluated models of integrated working (Cameron, 2016, p. 8). Working in teams seems central to putting integration into effective operation and is the main vehicle for creating multidisciplinary capacity drawn from different professional groups. Williams (2012, p. 557) sees the transfer of tacit knowledge between professionals in teams as the 'key to integration'. In some service areas integrated teams are now well established, for example, community mental health teams, and there have been rapid advances in crisis intervention or rapid response teams, in hospital discharge teams and also major developments in reablement teams. It has been suggested that there is no evidence that one form of management is inherently superior but Petch (2013, p. 21) sees as the key issue a shared team ethos and relaxing into more inclusive identities. There have also been initiatives with forms of integrated commissioning teams in England

(Crossman, 2015). NICE (2015) has also begun to give detailed guidance on the nature of community based multidisciplinary support and recommend the composition of mental health teams. Integrated care teams operate on a localist basis whether on geographical administrative hubs or centred on GP practices or community health centres. Beacon (2015) suggests that the GP practices, nurses and social workers developing stronger relationships increases the capacity of integrated care teams. Other evidence suggests that effective integrated teams need a strong team ethos (Williams, 2012), while Cornwell (2012) argues for the importance of team leaders and for high status and remuneration. Evidence from Northern Ireland suggests that team leaders can and should be drawn from any of the professions making up the team (Heenan and Birrell, 2009). Although cultural factors are important in the success of integrated teams (Fillingham and Weir, 2014, p. 30), more technical factors of access and exchange of information, scale of resources and co-location are also important. Team working itself can bring benefits through reducing errors, sharing risks and greater job satisfaction, although simple labelling as a team does not automatically ensure success (Miller et al., 2016, p. 174). The most effective configuration of integrated teams and specialist initiatives may also depend on local needs while localities may decide on different priorities or innovations (National Collaboration for Integrated Care and Support, 2013, p. 8). Integrated neighbourhood teams have also developed with wider interventionist services (NLGN, 2016, p. 58). As integrated teams become well established they can provide continuity in care and practice. Some allowance, though, has to be made for the fact that organisational arrangements may not produce a totally holistic approach or eliminate all differences in professional approaches. Integrated teams provide an arrangement to construct new services, for example, a frailty service.

Commissioning integrated services

The process of commissioning services is of importance in supporting the growth and effectiveness of integrated provision. The models of integrated commissioning for health and social care can range from all services to specific groups or conditions or localities. The main model of joint commissioning in Great Britain has been between a local authority responsible for social care and a health board or trust and has encompassed joint arrangements or one body having delegated responsibility. Oliver et al (2014) argues that a single holistic commissioning plan reflects best real integration. Oldham (2014, p. 14) argues that commissioning whole person care is one of the drivers that has sufficient power to change fragmented provision. In practice commissioning in England takes place mainly between Clinical Commissioning Groups and local authorities. Recent reforms have enabled local communities to increase their focus on commissioning and ensure the kind of care and support that best meets their needs (National Collaboration for Integrated Care and Commissioning, 2013). Health and Wellbeing Boards have a key role in building alliances to support and promote integrated commissioning and to scrutinise local commissioning plans (Humphries and

Galea, 2013). Greater local control and flexibility have also been encouraged over commissioning and pooled budgets (EY, 2015). Engagement with the providers of services is a further dimension as it will often be the providers who are directly delivering the integrated services. Thus the standards for integrated services have to be made specific in contracts, even implying new types of contract (Goodwin et al., 2013, p. 10), especially with independent providers who have more limited awareness and experience of integrated principles. The commissioning bodies also have responsibility for ensuring the quality of services and the standard of outcomes. Oldham (2014, p. 23) suggests that commissioning has focused on inputs rather than collective outcomes. Independent providers can also be supported and encouraged to work and learn from each other (Local Government Association/NHS Clinical Commissioners, 2015). The lesson being developed is that successful integration is dependent on good commissioning.

Other promotional factors

A number of other factors have been mooted as having a role, if not such a significant role, in promoting integration as the factors discussed above.

Integrated decision-making and governance

This refers to the idea that there should be unified decision-making at senior management level as opposed to multidisciplinary cooperation at senior level. Following the Flexibilities legislation there was a focus in England for a period of joint senior appointments covering health and social care across trusts and local councils. This strategy has rather fallen into disuse. Attention has moved to either creating integrated structures with integrated joint posts, as in Scotland and Northern Ireland, or bringing together major decision-makers. Managing care coordination has been seen as a crucial enabler but not an easy task (Oldham, 2014, p. 36). Robust and clear governance arrangements are cited as essential enablers in integrating initiatives for undertaking joint work across organisations (Local Government Association, 2016b, p. 48). New organisational forms may have to be developed to facilitate joint action on integrated care in Great Britain. Specialist community trusts, joint boards, networks, agreements, business units are all possibilities. Enabling more localised decision-making has also been advocated to have all integrated arrangements responsive to local or devolved needs. Inter-professional collaboration needs equal influence and respect and to avoid imbalance against social care.

Frontline integration

It can be argued that integration is promoted by ensuring frontline staff are merged in an integrated ethos as far as possible, meaning, practically, that there should be contact between professionals in wards and offices on the front line (Cornwell, 2012). Also important is the integrated ethos as a way of thinking about providing care, rather than as a specific plan. There can be variation in the depth of integrated working across organisational boundaries (Petch, 2012a, p. 78). Also relevant is the degree of flexibility that can be made operative in frontline working between staff groups.

While there is considerable research, comment and guidance on factors likely to promote integration, it is important to note the practical influence of key pieces of legislation as discussed above. The Care Act 2014, which placed a statutory duty on local authorities to carry out their care and support functions, integrated these services with those provided by the NHS and provided a new legal and policy framework for integration. In Scotland and Wales new legislation has also introduced statutory requirements to promote integration and in Northern Ireland legislation in 2009 included a statutory duty to promote integration. Legislation does set a framework for the production by respective administrations of regulations, guidance, funding, strategies, research and quality assurance.

The factors that have been identified as contributing to the promotion of integration can be categorised into seven themes/groupings and are set out in Box 8.1.

Box 8.1   **Groupings of Factors Promoting Integration**

Managerial.
    Leadership
    Shared/joint appointments
    Operation of integrated teams
    Collaboration between partner organisations

Resources.
    Government funding, well resourced
    Pooled budgets and resources
    Local budgets
    Special funding initiatives, for example, Better Care Funding

Integrated commissioning, integrated working and practice.
    Inter-professional working
    Sharing information and data
    Holistic approaches
    Flexible approach to tasks
    New integrated initiatives – reablement, rapid response,
       hospital discharge, dementia

Education, training and workforce integration.
    A shared vision and narrative
    Educational courses, initial and post-qualifying
    Training in integrated working
    Facilitating exchange of good practice
    Using workforce efficiently

Research and evaluation.
    Funding and support for research projects
    Range of research organisations working in area
    Extensive process of evaluations and reports
    Monitoring of outcomes performance
    Comparative research analysis
    Dissemination of research findings

Government support.
    Legislation and regulations
    Guidance and policy strategies
    Monitoring operations
    Organisation of pilot studies

User participation.
    User and career support
    Mechanisms for user and public participation
    Principle of co-production
    Personalisation and support for integration
    Commitment to person-centred services

The discussion in this chapter does demonstrate the complexity of determining the main factors that promote integration as well as indicating the range of views and factors which can be discussed. If the six main factors identified in this analysis are listed, four are perhaps not unexpected, which are: available finance; exchange of data and shared records; leadership; and research and training. The other two may not be anticipated, which are: a vision; and user involvement.

Some commentaries have suggested that there is evidence that strong relationships are the most important factor in leading successful integration, reflecting the core requirements to overcome traditional boundaries (NHS Confederation and Local Government Association, 2016, p. 20).

Conclusions

Reaching some conclusions on the essential factors that promote integration is an exercise that requires some reference to areas of uncertainty. There is not major support for the view that full structural integration on the lines of the Northern Ireland model is necessary to promote comprehensive integration. There is stronger support for the view that structural integration alone cannot deliver effective services (Petch, 2011, p. 6) and it has been argued that organisational change alone is unlikely to be sufficient to drive greater care coordination and integration at a clinical and social care level (Goodwin et al., 2013, p. 6). A body of evidence also shows that successful integration through partnership initiatives and pilot programmes has not been easy. There can be some disagreement over whether some mechanisms actually promote integration or are a barrier to integration. (Glasby, et al 2012), for example, preserving line management for staff from different professional backgrounds. It has been noted that what works to promote integration in some areas may not work in other areas, because of variations in relationships or contexts (Ham, 2009). A review of the experience of the new pioneers to date found the focus on enablers such as information and technology, workforce, organisational forums, communication and engagement, and contractional mechanisms (NHS England, 2016, p. 25). It can be argued that no single element by itself has been shown to be effective (Morris, 2012, p. 257), the 'no single silver bullet' perspective (Wistow, 2011, p. 9).

It is possible to identify the key enablers without a clear list of priorities. It can be noted that some of the more successful examples in England have been pursuing integration for a lengthy period of time. In England there is still an ongoing process of experimentation and evaluation in identifying the most significant enabling factors.

9 Barriers to Integration

Introduction

There remain a number of problems to be faced in pursuing the objective of implementing integration seen both in limited initiatives and projects and in more comprehensive strategies and processes. Their continuing significance is demonstrated in the use of the strong language of barriers and obstacles in discussions of the issue. There is more of a consensus on the nature of the main barriers than on the more diffuse identification of enablers of integration. In some instances it can be noted that the conditions and actions that promote integration are the reverse of factors that are identified as barriers (Wilkes, 2014). In other issues examined, the barrier may be of a more complex nature. Some of the clearer examples of barriers have been integrated partnerships which had to be ended because of a breakdown in delivering the intended objectives. Other barriers have been identified and addressed but with varying degrees of success.

Professional differences

Differences in professional values and attitudes, different priorities and even different languages, supported by different structures, have combined to create a professional barrier, originally seen as so intractable as to be called the 'Berlin Wall'. Baggott (2004, p. 287) argued that it was the cultural barriers between professional groups and organisations that have caused major problems. Different approaches to service eligibility, assessment, delivery, and priorities in respect to community care are emphasised by Cestari et al. (2006). Attention has also been drawn to the lack of empathy, understanding and trust between professions, with health staff unfamiliar with social care perspectives and social care marginalised within a health paradigm (Huxley et al., 2008). Frequent references have been made to the barrier between medical and social models of care. Lack of trust between professional groups would correlate with lack of trust between the organisations involved. Given the limited nature of integrated structures and projects, health and social care professionals have a history of normally operating separately within very different administrative and management systems. Not all innovations have helped remove barriers and some, such as the widespread introduction of direct payments in adult social care, may present another 'difference' challenge. The impact of traditional professional differences is demonstrated in aspects of integrated practice. The Care Quality Commission (2016, p. 12) reported difficulties in organisations creating a culture to work together and a lack of understanding.

Even when integrated working projects are set up or integrated teams established, professional stereotyping and a rigidity of views may continue. With different views and philosophies and a lack of appreciation of professional contributions even within multi-professional teams (Cameron et al., 2015, p. 13), some groups may see their professional values and integrity as under threat. This also may affect attitudes to information sharing. Attention can be drawn particularly to the perception that social workers' status is under threat in a health dominated environment. Differences in attitudes towards risk management have also been identified as a continuing problem (Cameron et al., 2015, p. 12). Communication across professional boundaries may remain difficult within partnership and team working although there is evidence from Northern Ireland's experience that removing structural barriers can be important (Birrell and Heenan, 2012). The absence of team building and a lack of time to develop relationships can enforce barriers (Lotinga, 2015, p. 176) indicating a need for focused training. The two most common barriers were cited by Glasby and Dickinson (2014) as different language and different models of care. Priest (2012, p. 13) found that staff still considered existing different perceptions that professionals held were a barrier to implementing integration. Cameron (2016) describes different professional ideologies, working practices, definitions of care, and continuing rivalries between medical professionals, social workers, district nurses and home care staff. Staff can become socialised into a profession's way of thinking and values, and develop a loyalty to protect their particular 'turf', skills and values from others (Miller et al., 2016, p. 158). These professional tensions arise over skills and identity; status and power; communication and understanding; and incentives and performance. A consequence of the continuing prevalence of professional differences is a difficulty in accepting change required to promote integration, or resistance to new ways of working. The British Association of Social Workers (2015) emphasised the different value base of social care, covering the empowerment of users, person-centred focus, self-determination, and social justice. Ham (2009, p. 4) suggests that adaptation to new ways of working may be more of an obstacle for managers than for frontline staff. It has also been noted that social care has made greater progress in relation to personalisation, co-production and user voice than is the case with the NHS (County Councils Network, 2016, p. 30). With integrated working, cultural differences can lead to tensions between professional groups working in integrated teams and those who are not working in this manner (Hutchison, 2015, p. 133).

Equity issues

Equity in the balance of power and respect in relationships has been an issue, particularly relating to full integration and equal status between health and social care. The problem or barrier has been the likelihood of the health side and the health professions dominating, meaning that social workers are a minority voice on partnership boards compared to health professionals. Social care might be in danger of being marginalised (Weekes, 2006, p. 18) or there is a perceived status difference between professions, with a higher status given to health professions. Traditionally, even as professions working separately there was a lack of equity in power relationships (Cameron et al., 2014), mainly driven by the dominant position of the acute sector. The continuing acceleration of the integration of social care with health care has drawn attention to the issue through the introduction of legislation and developments such as the formation of multidisciplinary integrated care teams. Even structural integration may not resolve this problem, as in the integrated structure in Northern Ireland social workers still experienced a vulnerability and a lack of equal partnership (Heenan and Birrell, 2006). The composition of management boards and special bodies related to integrated working may also reflect an inequity in representation between people with backgrounds in health and social care. Other consequences may be: the medical model may dominate operational and service configurations; performance targets and outcomes may have a health bias; and there may be inequalities in allocations of budgets (Cameron et al., 2015, p. 11). The most extreme expression of this barrier is the view that attempts to integrate health and social care under a principle of equity is a mistaken endeavour (Huxley et al., 2008) and social care should adjust to being either a junior partner or one of a multiplicity of professions. The alternative view is of two equally large structures having to come together in a more egalitarian relationship.

Funding difficulties

The funding systems for health and social care have traditionally been separate and different in Great Britain. The funding mechanism for the NHS has been through the government Department out of general taxation but for social care it is through local authorities. The funding relationship with the user has also differed with health services free at the point of delivery and universally available on the basis of need whereas social care services are substantially means tested and this can be seen as an obstacle to integration (National Audit Office, 2014, p. 45) although there are differences in the constituent parts of the UK. The barriers that finance can impose have been expressed thus: 'if adult social care is not put on a sustainable foundation, integration becomes more difficult' (Local Government Association, 2015, p. 6). The main vehicle for funding integration has been through pooled budgets but this process has been subject to difficulties. There has been an underuse of joint budgets. Less than 5 per cent of combined budgets is spent through joint arrangements and pooling budgets has been seen as difficult, complex, and sometimes an impossible task (Priest, 2012, p. 20). Pooled budgets carry with them the potential for disagreement and conflict between those involved over such issues as cost shunting between health and social care contributions. Differences over spending criteria can also contribute to the undermining of the aims of joint working (Cameron et al.,

2015, p. 11). Funding pressures have been increasingly identified as a barrier to integration. This can arise over uncertainties about the financing of joint initiatives, or over a lack of financial investment in integration or insufficient funding on social care. As spending on health and social care has been under pressure and falling as a proportion of GDP, Barker (2014, p. 16) suggests there is a need to move towards a new financial settlement to strengthen integration. Combining health and social care budgets also faces a potential difficulty as social care provision has become increasingly the responsibility of the private and voluntary sectors. External providers may not be incentivised to pursue integration.

It has been argued that the Care Act (2014) created substantial new financial burdens for local authorities which are currently unfunded (Maker and Lucas, 2015, p. 47). Funding for innovations is often pump-priming and aimed at short-term pilot studies (Goodwin et al., 2012, p. 7). Integration developments have financial requirements including: setting up costs; matching spending to contracts; targeting government grants; organising pooled budgets; having to undertake disaggregation for dispersed accounting purposes and limitations on discretion and flexibility (Weatherly et al., 2010, p. 18). An initiative in England has been the introduction of the Better Care Fund, as a form of a single pooled budget for health and social care services, for local areas based on a plan agreed between the local authorities and the NHS. The Better Care Fund (BCF) will bring together existing resources, so is not new money. Thus most CCGs will have to redeploy monies from existing NHS funds which could cause financial pressures and the Better Care Fund may not ameliorate the financial pressures faced by local authorities and CCGs (Bennett and Humphries, 2014). Pioneer pilot projects have found themselves caught up in rows over the BCF pots of money as they put pressure on hospital finances without guaranteeing cost savings. The BCF has been criticised as being too heavily centralised and bureaucratic, as undermining relationships between local authorities and Clinical Commissioner Groups and an actual barrier to promoting locally led integrated care (Maker and Lucas, 2015, p. 39). While there is some pessimism regarding long-term funding for integrated care, the BCF has raised more in budget contributions than anticipated, but has still been criticised as only compensating for reductions in local government expenditure (PAC, 2017). Funding remains a core constraint in realising the full ambitions of integration.

Lack of clarity

A lack of clarity and understanding concerning policies, the roles and responsibilities and procedures has led to concerns, confusion and inappropriate referrals which can affect both managers and frontline staff (Cameron, 2016, p. 10). Frontline staff may not always understand the reasons for the introduction of integration or their roles. It has been suggested that there is a need for a commonly accepted definition of continuity of care, coordination of care, team working and partnership in response to ambiguity and confusion (El Ansari, 2011). The absence of a shared vision has also been referred to along with a lack of interest in formulating rationales. There is a need for strategic agendas to be turned into operational reality with similar aims and objectives. The need for clarity can also apply to integration supplying a much simpler pathway through the maze of health and social care delivery systems (Barker, 2014, p. 6). There continue to be issues concerning the major direction of integration, for example, the sustainability of adult social care initiatives and the implications of integration reducing the need for acute care. In a study by the County Councils Network (2016, p. 32) 85 per cent of respondents identified conflicting targets and incentives as the number one barrier to health and social care integration. If professionals can be confused over the aims of integrated processes then users and the general public are more likely to have a limited understanding of the meaning of integrated care.

Problems with information sharing

This can be presented as one of the main barriers to successful integration where there remain major difficulties in the sharing of data between different organisations. This results in incompatible IT systems, resulting in a lack of access to data. Glasby et al. (2012, p. 14) refer to IT systems as the most common barrier and one study found IT systems were most cited as a hindrance (ADASS/NHS Conference, 2013). Oldham (2014, p. 46) argues that organisations could do more to examine how information systems can be linked, while it has also been suggested that some bodies are 25 years behind in making use of modern technology, and creaky infrastructure and lack of IT investment remain clear barriers (County Councils Network, 2016). There are also some difficulties related to legal constraints on the release of an individual's information. Goodwin et al. (2012) state that the absence of a robust shared electronic patient record is a major drawback to supporting integrated responses. Beech et al. (2013) found communication between professionals, particularly across organisational boundaries, remained problematic and noted the absence of vertical integration in governance. The National Audit Office (2014, p. 45) has commented on the lack of investment in IT to improve data sharing and end separate information systems. The absence of common access to electronic care records stands as a key factor making integration more difficult. The evaluation of the North West London Integrated Programme revealed how the lack of information sharing was a barrier to progress (Wistow et al., 2015). The report on Pioneer pilots found in most cases IT has proved a barrier to progress (Erens et al., 2015). The Care Quality Commission (2016, p. 13) found it striking that health and social care professionals reported that information from assessments was not routinely shared. In general a lack of effective communication between staff in different organisations and unawareness, or lack of use, of data sharing tools create barriers. It does not appear that information governance now precludes the transfer of information for direct care but data from different systems needs to be compatible (Oldham, 2014, p. 48).

Structural divisions and complexity

The NHS and social care have continued in Great Britain to be administered by different structures with different models of governance and accountability, distinct legal frameworks and accountability systems. This underlying structural divide has continued even within operating partnership arrangements. It has been suggested that in many ways the biggest barrier to local integration is the massive disparity between a highly centralised NHS and a localised social care model (County Councils Network, 2016, p. 52) with different approaches to national and local control. In England different central government bodies have responsibility for policy and funding, the Department of Health, the Department for Communities and Local Government and NHS England. Conflicting organisational priorities can be regarded as one of the biggest barriers to achieving more integrated care in that each of the two sectors has its own internal processes and different ways of working (Priest, 2012, p. 4). Coordination becomes more difficult between multiple organisational structures which may have different geographical boundaries, while fragmentation within bodies may lead to even bigger problems (Oldham, 2014, p. 22). Integrated practice has often been promoted by ad hoc arrangements which may only add to the complex mosaic of arrangements. A significant number of respondents in surveys and research have highlighted organisational complexity as a key barrier (Glasby and Dickinson, 2014). Work remains to be done on reducing the importance of the traditional structural barrier in Great Britain between the NHS and local government. A series of contemporary reforms in structures across the whole area of health and social care for adults and children carries the risk of adding to the complexity in organising integrated services.

Adaptation to change may present barriers for those involved. This may arise in the context of developing integrated initiatives or pilot studies, where tensions may arise with boundary disputes, unrealistic expectations, reactions to the blurring of roles and orchestrating the implementation of change (Fillingham and Weir, 2014, p. 32). A different form of barrier has also arisen because of major changes in the overall structure of health service delivery and planning. The NHS in England, in particular, has undergone major changes including the abolition of Primary Care Trusts and the introduction of Clinical Commissioning Groups. Priest (2012, p. 12) described the constant changes in health structures as preventing stability and a barrier to integrated structures. Glasby and Dickinson also argue that system stability is essential to enable integration to become established. Continual reform of the NHS structures in England can cause confusion and complexity in governance and accountability and may create barriers to effective integration. Some case studies have demonstrated that any changes in governance should be driven by the functional requirements of the care delivery model (Local Government Association, 2016e, p. 48). Robust and clear governance arrangements are cited in these case study sites as an essential enabler. The increasing role of the private and voluntary sectors in social care provision can also bring challenges for determining integrated governance arrangements across health and social care.

Staffing differences and problems

Differences between professionals can still constitute barriers to the development of integration. Medical staff and social care staff can still be identified as having differences in mindsets, values and worldviews (Brand, 2012). The health workforce is highly professionalised whereas the social care workforce is only partly professionalised, and is largely low paid, has low status and has a rapid turnover of staff. The relationship between GPs and social workers has been seen as a major barrier to integration or fundamental to the success of integration. A study by Mangan et al. (2014) highlighted the poor quality of the relationship and GPs' poor knowledge of social care services but also found that GPs wanted better relationships. A further study of focus groups (Mangan et al., 2015) showed that the negative aspects of GP–social worker working outweighed the positive, based on different values, lack of knowledge of each other's roles, poor communication and a hierarchy with GPs at the top. GPs' reluctance to take on the role of care coordinator, which can be seen as necessary to promote whole person care, is a further difficulty (Hudson, 2015). Structural changes have, at least in part, been intended to increase GP engagement. The introduction of CCGs with a major role for local GPs has provided opportunities to improve collaboration with local authority social workers. The continuing limited development of senior managers and practitioners in the social care workforce produces obstacles for a balanced professional relationship. Also identified as a barrier has been rigidity in traditional roles and skills or what has been called the 'not invented here' syndrome (SCIE, 2015). An example is skilling-up staff to take on roles that community nurses would traditionally have done.

Lack of training

A lack of inter-professional training on integration remains a barrier to developing integrated approaches and practice. Undergraduate and initial training for the main groups in medical training, professions allied to medicine, sub-specialisms and social work are largely uni-disciplinary and separate with little teaching or study in common and on integrated themes. Post-qualifying training is little different but may introduce some more integrated material. Social work training also does not escape criticism in terms of excluding material relevant to integration, such as housing (Oldham, 2014, p. 26). The fault rests mainly with the various professional bodies in protecting professional status and with higher education institutions in following traditional academic boundaries which are no longer aligned with the pace and complexity of change in policies on integrated practice (Preston-Shoot, 2010, p. 32). The development of training tends to come late and is directed at those staff working directly in integrated teams but resources for continuous professional development may be stretched. For integration to work, an integrated workforce can be seen as necessary, and integrated professional training seen as necessary to remove silos.

Poor communication between health and social care agencies in general has also received much attention and criticism, and was particularly highlighted in the case of Baby P. The inquiry into the death of Baby P identified inadequacies in communication and sharing of information across agencies and poor planning and frontline practice (McKimm and Phillips, 2010, p. 143). There was a clear need to reduce the barriers inherent in university structures and use appropriate placements for inter-professional and integrated learning. An associated dimension is the large growth in size of the social care workforce and the need for appropriate levels of training related to delivering quality care. An independent inquiry argued that care was the key to the new spectrum of integrated health and care and significant improvements were needed to increase the capacity of the social care workforce across a continuum of pay, training and conditions, to tackle poor standards (Kingsmills, 2013). A government review proposed new common training standards across health and social care and noted the growing issue around the blurring of roles, not just between health and social care but between registered and non-registered staff. The Cavendish Review (2013) suggested that the support workforce in both sectors is increasingly going to need to draw on similar core knowledge and approaches and to be flexible across health and social care.

Other barriers

A series of other barriers have been suggested which are essentially the opposite side of an argument or factor identified as contributing to the promotion of integration. These have also attracted less attention than the barriers discussed above and a brief summary of the nature of these barriers is presented below.

Lack of evidence – Limited research and evidence on successful ways to bring about integration has been seen as a major barrier (National Audit Office, 2014, p. 9). There are particular gaps in data across adult care provision and in people moving between health and social care. Cameron (2016) sees the variety of different approaches making conclusive evaluations difficult. The lack of hard evidence has prevented the emergence of guidance for use. More research is needed to provide empirical evidence of processes which integrated teams use. Writing in 2015, Glasby and Miller (2015) still described the limited nature of the evidence base and the need for new research to shape policy and practice. Although much evidence is now emerging from Pioneer and Vanguard projects and case studies in England it has been argued previously that integrated care takes five years or more to deliver its objectives (Bevan Commission, 2013, p. 4). One research study has highlighted a lesson that caution must be exercised in focusing solely on the evidence of specific outcomes as this may miss the value of how professionals work together to deliver care (Institute of Public Care, 2017).

Leadership – The complexity of leadership and management within multi-agency teams has been thought to impede integrated working. Leadership in these teams is seen as challenging, with a tendency to rely on senior managers and neglect more middle management. It has been suggested that there has been a lack of insight into the dimensions needed to approach integration (Hafford-Letchfield, 2009).

Specialist models of leadership and management tools have been slow to emerge for complex structures. Much of integrated practice has been project based and these have often one or several key individuals who become central to running the initiative and consequently the loss of leadership may be crucial and produce difficulties (Miller et al., 2016, p. 200). Lessons from the North-West London project highlighted management issues in implementation and balancing tensions between collective leadership and local autonomy (Wistow et al., 2015, p. 16).

Fragmented commissioning – The lack of integrated commissioning presents a barrier to integrated services. Even with joint budgets there can be difficulties in the nature of integrated commissioning. Hospital based provision is based largely on episodic treatments (Oldham, 2014, p. 22) while social care extends from short periods of care to lengthy periods. Generally health and social care are still commissioned separately (Barker, 2014, p. 3), including key services of reablement and intermediate care. Some aspects of primary care are not commissioned at a locality level while short-term commissioning makes expenditure on prevention difficult (Ernst and Young, 2015, p. 19).

Views of service users – It has been suggested that there is still a lack of knowledge of the aims and value of integrated care (Cameron et al., 2015). There has not been a strong focus on explaining the benefits of integrated structures, practice and programmes. This has contributed a knowledge barrier to user and public support for integration and the lack of demand for the more extensive development of integrated provision.

Lack of vision – The absence of a strong vision at political, central, local government and professional levels has the potential to present a barrier to integration. There have been improvements in policy narratives, including elements of a vision, but it has been suggested that turning strategic agendas into operational reality is a problem (Cameron, 2016, p. 10). Spreading a shared vision concerning aims and objectives among frontline staff could help make practice less difficult. While producing compelling vision statements on integration is relatively straightforward, obtaining wholesale buy-in has proved much more challenging.

Legal constraints – A number of legal obligations can impose constraints on the establishment of integrated services, for example, on the nature and terms of integrated partnerships and the legal basis for sharing social care data.

Central government role – Too much central government control over the development of integration has been put forward as another possible barrier. The argument is that too much central guidance, too many rules, monitoring mechanisms, centrally imposed pilot studies have prevented more rapid progress and been a barrier to locally appropriate solutions. On the other hand it has been argued that central government's governance and oversight across new integration initiatives has been poor and uncoordinated (National Audit Office, 2017, p. 9), with the departments not systematically addressing the barriers to integration they had identified.

Limitations of Health and Wellbeing Boards – While HWBs are a new framework to promote integration, an opposing view regards the initiative as likely to prove ineffective as the boards do not hold budgets, have no delegated powers and do not commission services.

Barriers in different services – There is a view that some areas of integrated provision experience more barriers than others. Monitor (2012, p. 36) noted difficulties within mental health, children's services and chronic conditions arising from sharing information between organisations, unclear accountability, financial problems, cultural differences, and relationships with voluntary bodies. Areas with the involvement of a large number of agencies, whether within health and social care or including other services, are more prone to encounter barriers.

Conclusions

Wilkes (2014, p. 18), in a research study, found barriers in England related to five principal areas: cultural differences, financial structures, fear of loss of autonomy, insufficient upfront investigation, and lack of trust. Another study implied four main barriers to joint working as culture, underfunding, fragmented commissioning, and national regulations (Ernst and Young, 2015). The National Audit Office (2017, p. 10) identified the three main barriers as misaligned financial incentives, workforce challenges, and reticence over information sharing. Four major barriers identified by Maker and Lucas (2015, p. 31) are conflicting target incentives, short-term financing, cultural differences, and problems with data sharing.

The factors presenting barriers to the development of integration which have been identified can perhaps best be classified into three groupings: factors which can be regarded as primary and core and often complex; second-level factors, which can be identified as enabling or advancing integration but which amount to barriers when they are missing in some circumstances; and thirdly, specific barriers that in practice are not so important. The primary barriers identified were:

Box 9.1	**Primary Barriers**

- professional and cultural differences between staff and a lack of knowledge or understanding of what different professional roles bring
- insufficient financial resources and lack of investment, funding difficulties with pooled budgets and cuts, and underfunding of adult social care
- loss of equal status and autonomy between health and social care sectors
- confusing and complex organisation, structures and accountability mechanisms
- problems with information, data sharing and integrated record systems.

The second level of barriers are those enabler factors which may be lacking or poorly developed:

Box 9.2 **Second-level Barriers to Integration**

- a lack of leadership and senior leaders failing to recognise problems and difficulties and agree priorities
- limited research and evaluation and limited dissemination of good practice
- continuing issues of trust between health and social care professionals
- limited general training and staff development in multidisciplinary working, shared roles and improving staff capacities
- fragmented commissioning and underdeveloped joint commissioning
- a lack of user, carer and public support
- difficulties in moving from design to delivery
- reliance on evidence from small local projects which may not be effective.

The third category of barriers identified includes less significant but specialist factors:

Box 9.3 **Third-level Barriers to Integration**

- local barriers that exist for political reasons, or staff differences arising in different service areas
- local constraints within community organisations and the operation of partnerships
- the role of central government, whether in Whitehall or the devolved administrations, which may be too restrictive or may lack clear direction
- major structural reorganisations in health and local government, which may impact on integration.

The second category of barriers does have the implication that action can be taken and lessons adopted to remove the barriers and replace them with more enabling and promotional structures and processes, thus turning things around. The third category requires locally based solutions and again potentially the barriers can be removed. The first category may present more severe obstacles and in particular the active participation and help of staff, leaders and decision-makers may need to be sought to reduce the significance of the barriers.

While listing these remaining barriers and evaluating the differences in their significance it may be argued that more action has been taken to reduce barriers to health and social care integration, compared to other public services. Generally, in England there is successful reporting of removing at least some of the barriers that existed.

10 International Perspectives

As noted in the introduction the NHS and social care services are entering a period of unprecedented financial challenges and the need to ensure that the system is efficient and effective is greater than ever. These are not, however, just UK issues, but international priorities and universal challenges. Irrespective of how systems are financed, organised and what services are delivered, gaps and inefficiencies exist, and greater cooperation, coordination, collaboration are core objectives in health care. While the definitions used, the strategies adopted and the extent of policy change vary across the globe, the underlying desire to create services that operate more efficiently and effectively in an integrated manner is strong (Dickinson and Glasby, 2009). A common understanding of integrated care has developed in Europe but has been criticised as being too idealistic with the reality often not living up to the rhetoric (Billings, 2005). Though widely acknowledged as a positive development producing favourable outcomes, Minkman (2012) noted that implementing integrated care is a complex, difficult task. While the commitment to integrated care has developed globally, outside the UK the main focus has been delivering coordinated care for older people with chronic conditions.

In an international study of integrated health and social care for older people with complex needs, Goodwin et al. (2014) concluded that there is no single organisational model or approach that forms the blueprint for integrated care. Guidelines stressed that the fundamental objective should be a service model designed to improve care for people, not an organisational model with a predetermined design. Integrated care was described as a complex process, which has to be nurtured and supported over time. Often initiatives have had to navigate and overcome a number of barriers including existing organisational, professional and funding silos. There is broad agreement in the literature that fully integrated organisations are not an end in themselves but a means to an end.

The integration of health and social care services is usually viewed as an attempt to make the whole greater than the sum of its parts. Developing comprehensive systems of care that are efficient and effective is a key driver in the quest for seamless services. Worldwide there is a recognition that person-centred care involves designing and delivering a model where professionals work collaboratively to achieve the best outcomes. Integration has been described as a dynamic process, and there is no 'off-the-shelf' or 'one size fits all' set of integrative processes that are suitable for all contexts (Rosen et al., 2011) and this is confirmed by international comparisons.

The majority of international health care systems were not designed to provide integrated care, thus services are provided by an array of organisations spanning the multi-level public, private, occupational and voluntary sectors. Each of these organisations has its own objectives, governance, structures and client groups. Whilst attention has been paid to the nature and quality of care provided, much less attention has been paid to how these organisations interact with one another. Generally they are concerned primarily with their own governance, structures and objectives rather than with broader national objectives. As a result service users are often confronted with bewildering and disjointed parts of a health system with links or components of social services that are expected to meet their needs, but regularly fail to do so (Goldberg, 2014). Across the world, the ageing population, increasing prevalence of chronic diseases, complex co-morbidities and technological innovation require an integrated, coordinated response to improve the quality and efficiency of care. Globally, there is largely a consensus that integrated delivery systems are associated with better outcomes and consequently providing integrated, seamless care is a goal of health systems worldwide. The World Health Organization's 'Framework on Integrated People-Centred Health Services' (2016) represents a call for a fundamental shift in the way health services are funded, managed and delivered. It states comprehensive coverage will not be achieved without significant improvements in the delivery of health services. Unless a people-centred and integrated health and social care services approach is adopted, care will become increasingly fragmented, inefficient and unsustainable.

With the lack of comprehensive integrated systems of health and social care, international approaches vary between initiatives ranging from relatively small, localised pilot projects to large-scale, multidisciplinary health and social care systems. Despite the acknowledged difficulties associated with comparing care systems, a number of common themes have emerged in the international literature on integration, which could provide important lessons for the UK. The phrase integration of health and social care has not been adopted globally and much of the literature refers instead to collaboration between sectors or disciplines. The term adult social care is also rarely used internationally; however, there is widespread use of and references to policies designed to deal with chronic and multiple conditions and the need for long-term care. Social care systems are not universal and in many countries government assistance is focused on those on low incomes.

Care pathways

Care pathways, also known as critical pathways, integrated care pathways, care maps or case management plans, are used to systematically plan a patient-focused care programme. These pathways are used throughout the world; De Luc (2001) identified 17 different terms to describe this concept. The objective of a care pathway is to improve the quality of care, optimise the use of resources and deliver better outcomes by designing and implementing a multidisciplinary health and social care plan or map. They are used as a vehicle to plan and deliver a care programme focused around the patient's needs and are generally based around a particular condition or a particular set of conditions. The care programme maps out what the patient can expect, ideally multidisciplinary in nature, and can provide a reliable, consistent record of treatment. The European Pathway Association (2005) defined a care pathway as:

> [a] methodology for the mutual decision-making and organization of care for a well-defined group of patients during a well-defined period.

The Association also identified four defining characteristics of a care pathway:

1. an explicit statement of the goals and key elements of care based on evidence, best practice and patient expectations;
2. the facilitation of the communication, coordination of roles and sequencing of activities of the multidisciplinary care team, patients and their relatives;
3. the documentation, monitoring and evaluation of variances and outcomes;
4. the identification of the appropriate resources.

There is a broad acceptance in the international literature that a care pathway approach, providing an outline of proposed care linked to evidence based interventions and clear time frames, has the potential to minimise variations in the quality of care. Although care pathways have been utilised in health care for some time, they vary widely in nature and scope. Internationally there is considerable variation in what is included in a care pathway and when and how they can be used to improve the quality of care.

The clinical use of pathways originated in the USA where managed care initiatives were developed to address rapidly increasing health care costs (Cheater, 1996). In the UK, however, their primary objective is to enhance the quality of clinical care (Riley, 1998). It has been suggested that Integrated Care Partnerships in health care continued to be promoted and supported as they somewhat uniquely incorporate both cost and quality outcomes (Ellershaw et al., 1997). Developing comprehensive clinical processes to address chronic conditions is widely viewed as an effective way of delivering cost-effective care. The emphasis is on working collaboratively within clearly defined parameters to improve performance.

The European Pathway Association (EPA) survey in 2005 noted that 23 countries were involved in integrated care pathways (ICPs) across the world with the median experience of pathways being five years. These figures reflected a significant increase in this way of working and suggested that the benefits of multidisciplinary collaboration were more broadly acknowledged and accepted. Integrated pathways are a mechanism to standardise clinical practice and this can lead to improved outcomes. The EPA (2005) found that clinical pathways were predominantly viewed by their users as a multidisciplinary tool to improve the quality and efficiency of evidence-based care, but were also employed by professionals as an important communication tool. In many respects clinical pathways are viewed as the vehicle to achieve clinical integration and seamless patient care across a range of providers. They are complex interventions for the design and delivery of care for a clearly defined group over an agreed period of time.

The integration journey of Canterbury District Health Board in New Zealand has been described as integration in action (Timmins and Ham, 2013). The development of care pathways was described as arguably one of Canterbury's most innovative and most effective changes, a concrete example of how integration works in practice. Introduced in 2008 they are local agreements on best practice, created by bringing together hospital doctors and GPs in order to design a patient pathway for a particular condition. They detail the extent to which treatments can be delivered in the community, and it is contended that the process of agreeing pathways matters as much as their content because it increases clinical buy-in and, therefore, supports effective implementation. By 2013 almost 500 pathways had been established and these are subject to regular review to ensure they reflect changes in evidence and practice. These initiatives have enhanced understanding between hospital and community based practitioners and have improved access to appropriate treatments.

In 2010, in response to increasing health care expenditure, the rising prevalence of chronic diseases, and an ageing population, the Basque Country in the North of Spain launched a strategy, 'Tackling the Challenge of Chronicity in the Basque Country'. A central component of this strategy was the promotion of integrated working between health and social care. Prior to this initiative, hospitals and primary care organisations were separate organisations each commissioning their own services. These organisations operated independently with their own vision and objectives. The strategy aimed to address this silo working with a two-pronged approach. Firstly, in order to promote seamless service delivery, clinical pathways were designed for chronic conditions such as diabetes, chronic obstructive pulmonary disease, and heart failure. A range of tools and interventions were designed to support this, including the introduction of nurse case managers and liaison nurses to coordinate and facilitate this initiative. Secondly, in a relatively radical approach, structural integration was facilitated through the establishment of integrated health care organisations (Nuno Solinis et al., 2013). These organisations amalgamated existing hospital and primary care structures into single organisations with the aim of achieving a more efficient, effective seamless service.

The initial pilot for this new structure, 'The Bidasoa Integrated Health Organisation', was created in January 2011 and was considered a landmark for the Basque Health Service in terms of building integrated care (Polanco et al., 2015). The first part of the initial pilot of this new system involved one hospital and three health centres serving a population of approximately 90,000 people. The success of this initiative led to the decision that the model should be spread across the region, with the objective that by the end of 2016, all primary and secondary care centres of the Basque health service would adopt this method of working. They used the following definition for care integration: the process that involves creating and maintaining, over time, a common structure between independent stakeholders (and organisations) for the purpose of coordinating their interdependence in order to enable them to work together on a collective project. By 2015 11 integrated health organisations had been established with plans for the development of a further two which would cover the whole population of the Basque region – each has a catchment area ranging from 30,000 to 400,000 citizens. Integration exists at different levels. At the strategic level, an integrated plan, setting common goals for both primary and secondary care, is agreed by the integrated health organisation. A more patient-oriented approach based on collaborative practices is sought, through deeper mutual knowledge and enhanced communication between professionals at different levels of care.

It has been contended that the establishment of these organisations has led to significant improvements in the organisation and delivery in the region. It is important to stress, however, that strong leadership and a major cultural change have also been central to success. This is usually accompanied by a clear vision of the need to manage population health in a holistic way, coupled with creating a culture of collaboration in primary and secondary care.

A review of innovative health care approaches for patients with multi-morbidity in 31 European countries (Noordman et al., 2015) examined the availability of integrated care programmes including care pathways. It noted that care pathways were usually a key component of integrated care, as 75 per cent of the integrated care programmes included a care pathway. The nature and scope of these pathways varied greatly; indeed, as already noted, the term care pathway has not been clearly defined and can cover a small specialised aspect of care, right through the whole chain of care. Whilst perhaps predictably, an upsurge of interest in integrated care has led to a growing interest in pathways of care, to date research has focused on disease-specific pathways rather than broader programmes. This study concludes that integrated care programmes are essential for the improvement of care for multi-morbid patients in Europe. Of all 31 countries reviewed, Spain had the largest number of integrated programmes. The integrated care programmes had the following common elements: patient-centredness; emphasis on coordination of care; enhancement of collaboration between (multi-professional) caregivers; multidisciplinarity, including aspects of both health and social care; and a focus on outcomes. Most programmes include a care pathway and a substantial number of the integrated care programmes specifically focus on the frail elderly.

In Sweden, condition-specific care pathways have been developed that include all the services provided for a specific group of patients in a defined geographical area. These are known as 'chains of care'. They specify the distribution of clinical work between health care providers and professionals and have a clear patient focus (Robertson, 2011; Ahgren and Axelsson, 2011). Integration of health and social care in Sweden has also included the restructuring of the health care services provided by the county councils and the introduction of a system of local health care which Ahgren and Axelsson (2011) describe as 'an upgraded family – and community – oriented primary health care within a defined local area, supported by flexible hospital services'. The aim was to create a service to meet the requirements of the local population and as a result there is no single model. Local health care has been important in facilitating collaboration between health professionals and social workers in the care of older people, dementia people with long-term mental health issues, addiction prevention, support for vulnerable children and young people, and health care for refugees. In the South of Sweden the Esther Model was set up to examine ways of improving care for older patients with complex needs (NHS England, 2016a, p. 39). This has resulted in some benefits such as a 20 per cent reduction in the number of hospital beds, and other improvements in cost-effectiveness. However, the experience in Sweden has also created a number of problems such as a lack of physicians in nursing homes. Challenges to integration have included some resistance from GPs, the policy shift towards free choice for patients, and the competing demands of managing competition alongside collaboration.

Financial framework

Whilst there are numerous ways of promoting the better integration of care, the use of financial incentives has been identified as an important way of achieving this goal. A broad range of financial incentives are deployed in many countries to encourage the design and implementation of integrated care schemes.

A series of financial payments for health care professionals were introduced by the Australian government in July 2005 to encourage the formation of Team Care Arrangements (TCAs) for dealing with chronically ill patients whose care involved at least three providers. Under this scheme health care professionals were remunerated if they were involved in the planning, delivering or reviewing of TCAs. These payments were included within Medicare, the universal health coverage system in Australia, The TCA document details the objectives and agreed actions of all of those collaborating in the care plan and is placed on the patient's records and reviewed and updated regularly. The underlying assumption is that the production of a TCA would facilitate greater integrated working and thereby improve outcomes for those with chronic conditions. To date evaluation of the initiative has been limited with some studies claiming that success may be limited due to the inflexibility of the policy (Young, 2013).

Over the past 20 years there has been a move towards integrating health and social care in Sweden (Aghren and Axelsson, 2011). The responsibility for care of older people, disabled people and people with long-term psychiatric conditions has transferred from the 21 county councils to the 290 municipalities. The aim of this move was to improve the integration between county council health services and social services in the municipalities and to improve collaboration between professionals. There is financial coordination in the form of pooled budgets. According to Aghren and Axelsson (2011) the financial coordination means that resources from the different organisations are pooled into a common budget for the local association. This budget may be used for different rehabilitation projects, which are managed by the association. These projects are usually aimed at individuals with multiple problems that require collaboration between professionals from the range of organisations.

In Canada, there have been numerous initiatives to enhance the integration of care which are designed around financial incentives. In Ontario's Family Health Team (FHT) model financial incentives are used to encourage doctors to work with Family Health Teams (FHTs). These multidisciplinary teams facilitate care providers to collaborate in the delivery of care to chronically ill patients. The scheme is based around an innovative blended funding model that involves payment by capitation, bonuses for achieving prevention targets, payments for increasing services available and a number of fees for service payments. Additionally, further incentives for doctors are provided by the Ministry of Health as they pay the salaries of interdisciplinary team members and provide the funding for the development of electronic medical records. The FHT facilitates the involvement of family doctors at all stages of patient care irrespective of whether the patient is at home, in a nursing home or in a hospital. For patients, FHT has the potential to provide seamless health and social care (Bienkowska-Gibbs, 2013). Hutchison et al. (2011) concluded that a growing, but relatively limited, body of evidence suggested that the financial models and incentives introduced in Ontario are improving preventive care delivery, chronic disease management, physician productivity, and access to care.

In Germany, the Gesundes Kinzigtal was developed in 2005 as a partnership between a network of physicians in Kinzigtal and a health care management company based in Hamburg. Gesundes Kinzigtal is responsible for organising care for almost half of the population of Kinzigtal in South-West Germany. The aim of this model is to keep the population healthy and reduce care costs. Gesundes Kinzigtal contracts with a range of providers to support prevention and self-management of health. The programme uses a shared cost savings contract to leverage health improvements by incentivising prevention activity and efficiency savings. Llano (2013) notes that initial results from the project counter any suggestion that financial incentives given to providers are too weak to result in greater efficiency. He cautions that whilst it is inaccurate to attribute the success of the system to any one particular component, financial incentives appear significant. Hildebrandt et al. (2012) highlighted the economic benefits of this approach and noted that the project had influenced the development of CCGs in England.

Concerns about the spiralling costs of health care were a major factor in developing incentives for health systems integration in the United States. It was believed that financial benefits would flow from integrated health systems because of economies of scale and cost reductions in both administrative and clinical areas. Duplication could be reduced and services streamlined into a more efficient, effective model. It has, however, been noted that the introduction of integrated processes can result in increased costs before they start to save money (Coburn, 2001). Integration must therefore be viewed as a long-term commitment rather than a short-term fix. Evidence has been produced of financial savings, though. In Denmark an integrated nursing home and home care service delivered cost savings of 21.6 per cent in net expenditure on elderly care in the municipality. In the Buurtzorg model in the Netherlands an integrated team of nurses, primary carers and the individuals and families provide care and support packages. An evaluation found that, as a result, the model created 40 per cent savings to the Dutch health care system (New Local Government Network, 2016, p. 51). There is also international experience of the use of integrated funds for health and social care. A study in eight countries found difficulties in implementing financial integration and budget holders' control over access to services while users' access to services often improved but, due to unmet needs being uncovered, costs actually rose (Mason et al., 2015, p. 6).

Information systems

There is general agreement in the international literature that information technology underpinned by robust governance is an essential component in integrated care systems. Indeed MacDonald (2015, p. 79) describes IT with sound governance as the most 'important tool' in the integration box. The ability to share clinical information in real time with all of those involved in decision-making including the patient and carer is described by him as 'critical'. He suggests attempts at integration in Australia failed to deliver as the IT platform was not fit for purpose. A significant enabler for integrated care was the facilitation of efficient exchange of information between different care providers.

PRISMA (Program of Research to Integrate Services for the Maintenance of Autonomy), established in Quebec, Canada, has been described as one of the most systematic and sustained bodies of research investigating the translation and outcomes of an integrated care policy into practice. Despite this, Stewart et al. (2013) note that while PRISMA has been underway since 1988, there has been no independent, systematic, holistic review of this work to draw out the lessons learnt. Their work aims to address this gap by providing an overview of PRISMA's body of work, and identifying the key themes that contribute to its success. They claim that despite the fact that the shared electronic health record was one of the six core PRISMA components, there was little discussion of its underlying technical structure, its implementation, or evaluation of its use. Given the growing importance attached to IT and the large-scale investments in new information technologies it is suggested that this is an area that requires urgent research attention.

In their review of the international literature on integrated health and social care Suter et al. (2009) identified quality information technology systems as one of the 10 principles associated with successfully integrating health care. Indeed it is claimed that many of the principles identified, such as performance management and delivering standardised care through multidisciplinary teams, were only possible if supported by a state-of-the-art system-wide approach that allows for reliable, effective access to data. Data should be accessible from anywhere in the system, including remote, rural areas, to facilitate the provision of seamless care. Information technology systems are often expensive, complex and time-consuming; therefore it is essential that the system designed and delivered is efficient and effective.

The Chronicity Prevention and Care Programme, which aimed to address the fragmentation in the health care system and encourage professionals to work collaboratively, was underpinned by a more global health care information system. Shared electronic health records facilitated remote care and direct access by citizens and service-users (Contel et al., 2015). Robust, reliable information is at the core of high quality integrated health and social care. Different systems must connect effectively to ensure the safe and reliable sharing of data. In the future the role of information technology is likely to expand and therefore it is essential that the potential of technology is fully investigated and understood. Information technology can be a major enabler to integrating care through facilitating the exchange of information between a broad range of care providers. Stewart et al. (2013) note that telehealth applications, email communication between health professionals and their clients, and in-home monitoring services can all support the provision of care in diverse locations. The significant technological improvements in the past decade have the potential to radically change how service users interact with health professionals. However, as IT systems can lead to new and unpredictable changes in behaviour, it is crucial that interventions are monitored and evaluated.

In the Basque region, in response to the desire to enhance the management of patients with complex health needs, continuity of care units were developed by organisations. These involve primary care doctors, specialists, case managers and social workers working in multidisciplinary teams to provide improved and seamless care to patients. The seamless care system has been underpinned by a fully developed shared electronic medical record system that facilitates the efficient and secure exchange of patient information (Polanco et al., 2015).

ICT solutions are clearly important enablers of information and knowledge sharing and are vital to the success of integrated health and social care initiatives. The ability to provide a seamless service will critically depend upon harmonised and widely adopted standards and electronic systems. Across the world, innovative health care systems acknowledge the need to invest in ICT systems and enhance the ICT skills of the workforce. Significantly, though, the technological issues are rarely the major barrier to more innovation in ICT enabled delivery of integrated care. Technology is an enabler to deliver a new vision of care, not the end in itself.

In Canada, PRISMA is a collaborative, integrated service delivery system developed to improve continuity and increase the efficacy of services, particularly for older and disabled populations. Evaluations of this system have suggested that its successful implementation is dependent on and requires the utilisation of a continuous information system and computerised tools to enable effective communications (Hébert et al., 2003). This system is based around the use of a Computerised Clinical Chart (CCC) that ensures complete, up-to-date, reliable information is available to all the practitioners and can inform the other clinicians of the client's progress and changes in the intervention plan. The shareable CCC is common to all the professionals and as such provides an interface between the clinical information and the management information.

It has, however, been suggested that the role that the shared PRISMA electronic health record played in facilitating integration and achieving the observed outcomes has not been robustly evaluated. Given the increasing focus and investment in IT systems, this was identified as a cause for concern (Stewart et al., 2013).

In their review of the Gesundes Kinzigtal integrated health care system in Germany, Struckmann et al. (2015) describe the electronic patient files that are shared amongst the participating health care professionals as an important achievement. They do, however, note that the programme would benefit from more advanced IT applications and e-health systems. The relatively poor infrastructure in some of the geographical areas and the attitudes of the older target population around IT mean that developments in this area have been hampered. In rural areas the telephone continues to be the preferred method of communication between the patients and health care practitioners.

Kaiser Permanente is the largest non-profit health maintenance organisation in the United States and is often cited as a highly successful virtual integrated system (Oldham, 2014). Integrated patient pathways are delivered through a team-based approach, multi-speciality medical centres and information exchange across a number of providers. The lynchpin of this system is the sophisticated electronic health record that facilitates effective information exchange and collaboration. The complete patient record available at the point of treatment can address some of the perennial issues around fragmented care. Additionally the data collected through this system can be used to assess interventions and promote evidence-based practice.

Two of the four case studies in the international integration study by Rosen et al. (2011) illustrated the benefits of improving the sharing and linking data to support integrated care, and demonstrated the numerous challenges associated with achieving shared access to clinical information. They noted that a broad range of skills were required to develop data linkages and web interfaces between different care settings. These include: the procurement and contract management of IT suppliers, technical expertise to customise products in order to meet organisational needs, leadership skills to encourage clinicians to adopt and use the system, and analytic skills to compare and evaluate clinician performance within data protection regulations. Despite these challenges they point to the fact that a number of UK Primary Care Trusts had put in place bespoke solutions by linking GP, community, hospital and some social care data.

Interestingly, in their 2014 study of providing care for older people with complex needs informed by seven international case studies, Goodwin et al. (2014) acknowledge the importance of an integrated IT system to facilitate service delivery, but suggest it should not be viewed as a prerequisite. Effective communication between organisations and professionals is essential but sharing information can be achieved through other 'old' technologies such as telephone and fax.

The absence of an effective IT system which facilitates the smooth transfer of information across a range of settings was identified as a major barrier to effective care transitions in Denmark (Lyngso et al., 2016). Participants reported that the IT solutions available were not adequate and there was considerable variation in the use of electronic systems. Data was shared within organisations but there was a limited transfer of information between primary and secondary care. Health care workers expressed a strong desire for a standardised electronic system, accessible across interfaces, as it was believed that this would help to drive integration.

Leadership

The significance of leadership for the delivery of integrated care is a key theme in much of the international literature. In times of organisational change and transformation, leadership is pivotal to setting the vision and blueprint for the future. Leadership requires the ability to inspire, motivate, galvanise, challenge misconceptions, and negotiate a shared understanding. Much of the available evidence on successful integration in health and social care highlights the importance of collective leadership and capacity building. Yet, in comparison to individual leadership, collective and shared leadership has been poorly explored and remains poorly understood. Health and social care is delivered by a large number of varied organisations that need to collaborate to ensure high quality patient care, with a focus on the whole system rather than their particular part. Leaders have to work together to build collective, collaborative systems. Studies on integrated health systems have stressed the need to engage clinicians and other frontline staff in owning the joint enterprise to improve and sustain care. High quality integrated care is dependent on a shared, collective, aligned, holistic vision which focuses on delivering a seamless service to the user.

In the international literature, leadership both within and between organisations emerges as a key determinant of successfully integrated health and social care. Leadership involves committed individuals but is also inherently collaborative, and based on building relationships. In this complex world of health care, collaborating and developing partnerships underpins effectiveness. It is generally not about a committed, dynamic individual or traditional hierarchical models, but about a more shared approach. It is distributed amongst a group of people rather than focused on the behaviour and characteristics of individuals. There is a growing consensus that in this complex, multi-layered area of care it is not feasible that one person will have the knowledge or expertise to address the issue. Innovation and problem-solving occurs when people collaborate across disciplines and share knowledge. The leader's role is to create an environment where all of the skills and knowledge of the team can be utilised, to be someone who can motivate and coordinate a team-based approach, and develop and empower individuals. The development of a vision and strategy requires a more collaborative approach to leadership that can utilise the entire organisation's human asset potential. Bengoa (2013) stressed the importance of promoting a distributed leadership approach when reflecting on his experiences of transforming health care systems in the Basque Country. In terms of change management, shared leadership was identified as one of four crucial strands of work necessary to achieve transformation. He noted that it is possible to develop a compelling narrative, and design a whole array of interventions, but it is unlikely that they will be successful if they are simply bolted on to existing management approaches. If initiatives are to attract the support of a wide range of health care professionals they should adopt a model where professionals are given the leeway to improve care processes in their local area. This bottom–up approach recognises and acknowledges local expertise and does not attempt to push a one size fits all agenda.

In a review of integration in action that involved an assessment of international case studies, Rosen et al. (2011, p. 8) concluded that excellent leadership was a prerequisite for successful initiatives. They noted:

> Skilled and trusted leaders with excellent communication skills are essential for developing and implementing integrative processes, and for winning support from professionals to change their practice.

In these case study organisations, leaders created a compelling vision of how coordination could be achieved across teams and organisations, and provided the leadership, infrastructure and support to achieve the vision. Usually leaders were clinicians who spearheaded the development of aligned professional working for agreed patient groups; they were also responsible for ensuring that the appropriate infrastructure was developed to deliver a high quality, accessible service. The authors suggest that the organisations that they led could be viewed as 'integrator organisations': a term coined by Berwick et al. (2008) for organisations contributing to the 'Triple Aim' of improved patient experience, population health, and reduced cost.

The quest for integrated health and social care in Canterbury New Zealand was reviewed by Timmins and Ham (2013). They stressed the crucial role played by people in ensuring transformation could take place. Whilst there were a small number of people at the heart of this change process, they did not act alone and could not have succeeded without the assistance of numerous other people throughout the health and social care system. Significantly this leadership was not based around one or two key actors but very quickly became collective, distributed and shared. The collective leadership involved managers, clinicians and a number of other key stakeholders. The creation of a vision was described as one of the three crucial enablers for change; however, it is noted that a vision can only have impact if it is acted on. In this case study the board had a coherent vision of what they were trying to achieve and implemented it by empowering staff to change their practices from the bottom up. A review of seven international case studies providing integrated care for older people with complex needs undertaken by Goodwin et al. (2014) suggested that integrated care might be achieved only if it was 'bottom up' through the development of specific 'micro-level' interventions by a small number of providers. This approach then may or may not lead to organisational integration. The success of these local initiatives is dependent on the local leaders who must have the vision, tenacity and determination to ensure that aims are achieved.

Leadership was identified as one of six dimensions key to the delivery of integrated care and support by Petch (2014). Transformational and distributed leadership underpinned by a shared vision is described as essential to success. It has become commonplace to emphasise the importance of leadership for the delivery of integrated care and support: 'In times of organizational transition … transformational leadership takes a central role in setting the vision and the out-line of the organization for the future' (Dickinson and Glasby, 2009). Leadership is more than management; it suggests a capacity to inspire, motivate and engage, to challenge embedded preconceptions and power dynamics, and to negotiate competing understandings and agendas.

Traditional notions of 'heroic leadership' as dynamic, decisive, authoritarian and competitive are not well suited to the environment of integrated care and support. Increasingly it has been recognised that the complex world of integrated working requires a different approach. This requires sophisticated skills of nego-tiation and consultation to enable collaborative agreement on the direction to be taken and to foster collective decision-making. Leaders need to be supportive of innovation, have an awareness and understanding of the complexity of inte-grated working, and be alert to the perspectives of all the different stakeholders involved. These new models of leadership have moved away from a focus on the 'heroic individual' to a more inclusive and organic approach. This has led to models of leadership based not only on the individual qualities of the leader but on how they enable the whole system to support innovation and work together as a team.

Transformational or dispersed leadership is characterised by a desire to create a sense of collective identity and ownership. Through acting as a role model, leaders seek to enhance people's motivation, morale and performance. Such an approach to leadership is designed to steer the development and delivery of a vision, to empower users and staff, to foster a strengths-based approach, to support positive risk taking, to encourage staff to reflect and challenge, and to encourage creativity. It requires a clear accountability framework, transparent governance, robust supervision, acknowledgement of the range of skills and experience in the workforce, and targeted professional development (Bogg, 2011). Effective leaders are usually characterised by their sustained long-term commitment, enthusiasm and involvement in integrated care locally, and by the trust and respect given by their peers that have built up over time. Leaders for integrated care and support need to embrace change and take the initiative rather than adopting a fortress mentality focusing on their own organisations.

Despite numerous initiatives to improve collaboration and facilitate coop-eration the Danish health care system is described as fragmented and disjointed (Lyngso et al., 2016). Research into health care professionals' views on the barriers to and facilitators of a more seamless system identified good leadership as one of five key themes. There was a broad agreement amongst health care professionals that committed leadership with clear communication processes was crucial when attempting to bring different organisations together. Success was viewed as dependent on managers and leaders consistently sharing and reinforc-ing their vision with everyone engaged in the process of change. Collaboration and building relationships were complex and time-consuming and it was essential that this was acknowledged by those driving the process of change.

Promoting a more integrated approach with an array of organisations with different cultures, values and objectives requires an approach which can make sense of change, ensure direction and create a sense of collective identity. Enhancing collaboration between health and social care providers has been a significant policy goal in Finland for the last decade. Primary health care centres have been established as a means of enhancing access to services and facilitating the development of integrated care. A number of these centres have focused on integrating a wide range of health services; others have included social care services. An evaluation of the Care and Home service in Helsinki, an integrated health and social care project, concluded that results from the project were mixed. It was suggested that a possible explanation for this was a lack of effective leadership (Valvanne, 2005).

Decentralisation

International examples such as Sweden, Denmark and Norway have demonstrated that decentralised systems can be correlated with high quality services (New Local Government Network, 2016, p. 25). Thus health and social care is the responsibility of regions and municipalities including major funding responsibilities. Norway has adopted light-touch regulation in favour of local determination and a focus on local solutions. In Denmark municipalities are responsible for primary care and for providing long-term elderly care, rehabilitation, supported housing and aspects of prevention (Bidgood, 2013).

Conclusions

From this review of international experiences four factors have emerged as being particularly significant: patient pathways; financial incentives; IT systems; and leadership. Following their successful adoption in Canterbury, patient pathways are at the forefront of changing service delivery. However, as MacDonald (2015) notes, they are not a one size fits all solution that can be implemented by those who want to redesign services to improve outcomes. Despite the lack of detailed, robust evidence of the effectiveness of integrated care pathways, there is significant support for this approach. Perceived advantages include improved patient care, reduced length of stay in hospitals, reduction in costs of care, improved patient outcomes, improved quality of life, and increased user engagement.

There is no one size fits all for care pathways and ideally they should be developed based on local needs and resources. They cannot be imposed and depend on the active involvement of professionals, carers and patients in their design, development and implementation. The sustainability of these care pathways is dependent on their recommendations informing commissioning and workforce development plans. Finally, if they are to be successful these initiatives must be locally led by those who have knowledge of local networks and are trusted by stakeholders.

Financial incentives are used in many countries to facilitate and encourage the implementation of integrated care approaches. The nature and objectives of these schemes vary widely and may aim to incentivise individuals to engage, improve IT systems, mandate multidisciplinary working or achieve agreed outcomes and targets. The structure, nature and outcomes of integrated working can be influenced by the use of financial incentives, but again crucially the literature suggests that there is no single transferable payment method and caution must be exercised when attempting to generalise or translate from one country to another. Health and social care budgets are often fragmented and are planned and delivered without any collaboration or alignment of objectives; integration requires all of those involved in the design and delivery of care to identify and build on synergies in their activities. As Mrinska (2010) has noted it is crucial to develop and incorporate rigorous analysis of the financial implications of integrating health and social care budgets, as to date there is little evidence on the effectiveness of financial systems that aim to necessitate fundamental changes around complex issues.

The introduction of information technology into health care has the potential to transform how services are designed and delivered. There is no doubt that IT solutions will play a significant role in future health care approaches and enable clinicians to make better decisions. Long-term institutional arrangements and investments in technology, capacity and skills will have to match the new ways of working. Effective IT systems allow health care providers to manage patient care through the sharing of health information. Well-designed IT systems can improve the quality and quantity of care and underpin an integrated system. They can ensure information is accurate, complete, accessible and enable health care providers and patients to make timely, appropriate decisions. If IT is to drive an integrated care strategy this may involve substantial cultural and behavioural change to support these new ways of working. It can no longer be seen as the preserve of specialists but instead is an enabler to enhanced care that must be embraced by all. This cultural change will involve strong leadership and a programme of education and training. Long-term strategies and investments in technology are required to drive substantial change and increase knowledge and capacity. The international examples demonstrate that there have been significant advances in IT that have the potential to radically improve the design and delivery of care. There is, however, huge variation in the way systems are used and developed. Additionally coordination can be hampered by a lack of IT infrastructure.

From the international literature on integration in health and social care it is clear that successful initiatives are associated with strong, committed leaders. These leaders were often long-established clinicians in their communities, with a track record of spearheading change and improvement. Nevertheless, the challenge of engaging their fellow clinicians, and working in independent practices, over whom they had no direct control, was considerable. The crucial role of professional champions in leading change and improvement in health and social care has been widely acknowledged. Numerous resources are available to develop leadership skills in doctors and other professionals, although these go only part of the way in promoting professional leadership of integration work. In the NHS there are, as yet, very few clinicians leading such networks or organisations, although the introduction of Clinical Commissioning Groups may help to develop a new generation of leaders. Leaders' attention should be focused on developing a full set of integrative processes, with mutually supportive links between clinical, organisational, informational and financial processes, in order to enable the delivery of integrated care for patients. Differences in the UK systems in terms of the universalist NHS, a comprehensive system of social care, administrative systems and devolved systems of delivery mean that caution must be exercised when attempting to transfer international lessons.

11 Conclusions

It is clear that there is a strong commitment by all governments in the UK to promoting the integration of health and social care, accepting the rationale for this policy, anticipating the benefits of integration, and supporting implementation of integrated practice. This policy has been endorsed at all levels of government including local government and non-departmental public bodies and is also strongly supported by advice, guidance, reports and analysis presented by representative and professional bodies. Closely associated with the adoption of a policy of integration has been the acceptance of another policy change, a shift in resources from acute care to community based care. Also implied is a change in the scale and functions of acute health care, the development of aspects of the provision of adult social care bringing closer together health and social institutions and also adopting change in commissioning structures and procedures, management and workforce development.

A widespread consensus on the rationale for integration has been established in terms of a holistic approach to people's needs, a necessary response to the numbers living with long-term conditions requiring more than episodic medical care and new models of care based on people in their own homes. A major development in recent years has been the introduction of legislation to put integration on a stronger statutory basis. Separate legislation with similar provisions now exists for England, Scotland, Wales and Northern Ireland. Rather than set out detailed prescriptions or lay out a plan for implementation, the legislation has tended to make it a legal duty for government to promote integration and/or establish integrated structures. Such legislation is significant in underpinning policy developments requiring public bodies to take action and also in raising the profile of integration.

A contemporary study of the implementation and promotion of integration must take into account the challenges produced by economic and demographic changes. This relates firstly to the economic challenge of the period of austerity, with deficit reduction impacting upon cuts in public expenditure. The position of local government finance has been identified as having major implications for resources for adult social care with direct consequences for integrated services. Expenditure on the NHS has also been affected but the UK government has offered more financial protection for health. Another aspect of the economic challenge is the actual expectation that the expansion of integration would lead to major cost savings and more efficient use of resources. The implications of Brexit, particularly for the workforce, add another socio-economic dimension for consideration. Humphries et al. (2016, p. 75) express concern not only at the impact of Brexit on the social care workforce but also at the risk of sidelining social care issues when the terms of Brexit are negotiated. A second challenge is noted as the continuing pressures on both health and social care exercised by demographic change. These pressures arise from increases in the numbers of older people and those living longer and increases in the number of proletariat with chronic and multiple conditions.

One of the main purposes of the book has been to describe and analyse the four systems of integrated care that have operated throughout the UK. Since 1999 Scotland, Wales and Northern Ireland are responsible for their own systems of health and social care and all are committed to systems of integration. There is significant policy divergence and difference in their structures. Northern Ireland demonstrates a very distinctive feature in having a form of comprehensive structural integration between health and social care. Scotland has developed a uniform system of statutory partnerships between health boards and local councils throughout Scotland, based on equality of status and representation. Wales has looser forms of partnership working between health boards and local councils. These devolved integrated structures differ from the pattern in England where more diverse forms of partnership and joint working exist. In England local partnerships are able to integrate services in a range of ways with more experimentation. Comparisons within the UK show differences in the breadth and depth of integration, including the position of children's services and relationships to acute hospital provision. There is also important divergence relating to: the legislative frameworks; the allocation of financial resources; eligibility for adult social care services; and charges for social care. To an extent there is sufficient divergence to state that in the UK there are four different models of integration requiring separate analysis and comparisons that can provide lessons for each other.

A major conclusion that can be drawn from an examination of integration across the UK is the significance in recent years of an experimental approach in England. This has involved major initiatives on a large scale through integrated care pilots, the Pioneer projects, the Better Care Fund, the Vanguard initiative, the city devolution deals introduced initially in Manchester, the Sustainability and Transformation Planning strategy and Integrated Personal Commissioning. This has meant a great deal of diversity in initiatives, with ongoing research and evaluations creating a knowledge and guidance base. The focus on experimentation has assisted in allowing the new CCGs to develop integrated approaches and involve HWBs. This has also encouraged the involvement of hospital trusts and voluntary bodies in integrated projects. The focus on experimentation and evaluation has encouraged work and analysis by research institutes, voluntary trusts such as Nuffield and the King's Fund and representative organisations such as the Local Government Association producing reports and guidance based on pilots and projects. It is still unclear from often short-term evidence whether any model of integrated partnership working can be articulated or designed which could be applied across England. The short-term nature of the operation of pilots and the special limited funding can affect the overall value of the experimentation approach. The National Audit Office concluded in 2017 that nearly 20 years of initiatives to join up health and social care by successive governments had not led to system-wide integrated structures (National Audit Office, 2017, p. 7). The commitment to continuous experimentation in England may also have served to avoid criticisms of the slow progress to a settled and uniform system of integration.

What has integration achieved? What is the impact? What works? What promotes integration? What barriers remain? These are very regular questions posed in studies of integration. There is largely a consensus from practitioners and academic studies on their responses to these questions with some exceptions. The evidence can be inconclusive, suggesting the strategies are not meeting objectives, but there have been improvements for users. Our assessment of these highlight the following:

- There is still a tendency for integrated initiatives to focus on joined-up structures and processes rather than outcomes, particularly as identified by service users and carers as well as practitioners.
- There have been few studies or commentaries in England giving support for full structural integration between health and social care nor for a centrally-led national organisation to achieve integration (ADASS, 2015, p. 8). There remains some uncertainty as to whether the evidence from the Northern Ireland model supports the contention that structural integration does not deliver effective service improvement. Glasby (2016) offers a view that it should not be assumed that changing structures can not be part of a broader solution but often it is not. A consequence is that integrated partnership working has become established as the preferred organisation model in Great Britain.
- Cost-effectiveness has also been disputed despite an earlier belief in integration working as a source of significant cost savings. There is less evidence for the expectation (Humphries, 2015) that integration will achieve substantial financial savings. The latest Pioneer initiatives have been experiencing more difficulty in projecting financial savings (Erens, 2015), while the new care initiatives' ambitions for savings have been seen as optimistic (National Audit Office, 2017, p. 9).
- There is evidence of strong support for multidisciplinary and joined-up working among staff and users. This is of some significance given the major changes in health structures in England. CCGs have fully engaged in integrated approaches and working with local authorities. In Scotland there is acceptance of equality in representation between health and social care in partnership governance.
- A significant development has taken place with the introduction of legislation putting integration on a statutory basis. Legislation has brought a compulsory framework and statutory basis, clarifying arrangements and resolving difficulties. It is widely recognised that legislation on its own will not produce the desired outcomes in practice and delivery.

- The balance of evidence suggests that integration can improve people's experience and outcomes and deliver efficiencies (Oliver et al., 2014).
- There is evidence of value and achievement of new initiatives, of reablement schemes, also rapid response teams, acute care at home and supported housing. The Care Quality Commission (2016) has noted that what marks many good and outstanding services is the way they reflect integrated relationships and practice.
- One somewhat neglected dimension has been an analysis of what areas of service provision demonstrate the most success for integration or even service areas that can be said to make the most use of integration or the subject of integrated development. There is clearly a focus on older people, the frail elderly or, more specifically, supporting those with chronic conditions, prevention and independent living. There has always been a strong voice for integration in the mental health sector. Integration in the areas of learning disability, physical disability and family and children's services has not developed so strongly but these services have a close link with social care and social work.

A theme in the book has been to identify and describe newer agendas which have had an impact on integrated practice. Most of these have a wider relevance but do have implications for integrated provision. This applies firstly to personalisation which itself has some different interpretations and meanings. In one interpretation personalisation is held to stress the importance of the individual and their family and carers getting joined-up support to deliver their wellbeing between two monolithic structures of health and social care (SCIE, 2013). The other and more significant meaning is personalisation meaning direct payments and individual budgets, giving people greater control over their care but bringing extra tasks for integrated approaches. Direct payments have had a much greater uptake in England proportionately than in the devolved administrations. The second important agenda has been user participation and co-production when the value of users and carers having a say in decisions about their care becomes paramount, in planning integrated services through care pathways and in evaluating the outcomes. User participation implies a much more bottom-up notion of integration than top-down approaches imply. Co-production means using participation as a resource to be a building block for integration and as a principle has other implications for governance arrangements. Thirdly is localism and the view that an integrated approach should be close to local needs, engage local councils, make use of local identity and be rooted in local accountability. In Great Britain integration is aligned to localism and local government, indicating the importance of place based planning. Many of the local initiatives in England in Pioneer projects have a strong local dimension, and locality bodies in the form of CCGs and HWBs, along with Sustainability and Transformation Plans, now play a major role in integration. Fourthly, the focus on prevention of loss of independence has been built into the narratives, aims and objectives of health and social care. Fifthly, although long acknowledged as an issue, more attention has been paid to the idea of a trained integrated workforce.

Stein (2016) asks why building a competent workforce has not been a priority with few examples of integrated care investing in education and training. The need for a new approach has been recognised, a workforce to work in different integrated ways (Local Government Association, 2016b, p. 46) and take on pivotal new roles. Among those suggested are care coordinators, care navigators, planning managers, network managers, and higher level qualifications for the care workforce. Also suggested were new professional roles, placing consultants in community settings or involving pharmacists in the community. Other ideas have referred to training to work in teams, developing new knowledge and skills for a multi-faceted and multidisciplinary approach, and launching initiatives to share skills. Lastly has been the transfer of resources from health to boost social care. Although there is a wide consensus that this offers a solution to the growing pressures on the health service, there is still insufficient evidence of a relationship between expenditure on social care or integrated care and the demand for health services. There remains a danger of concern with financial efficiencies and constraints diverting attention from integration.

There is still a need to develop a collective ambition to make further progress in better ways of working together and achieve more of a transformation to integrated care. Further action is required with a focus on:

- progressing the shift in resources and use from acute care to community based integrated care
- strengthening the provision of adult social care and counteracting loss of funding, problems with integration and outsourcing services, growing the workforce, and avoiding crises with the adequacy of provision on the brink
- making better use of information technology and sharing information
- relating to cognate services in more joined-up ways
- developing training and education in integrated competencies and task sharing as well as building better career paths in social care
- responding fully to user and carer desires for co-production and participation, in all four countries of the UK
- focusing the measurement of outcomes on quality improvement based on individual user and carer experience rather than quantitative assessed clinical outcomes.

To promote more focused engagement from GPs:

- better demonstrating the efficacy of integrated working and translating the lessons from innovations and pilots into guidelines, reforms and practice drawing on the sharing of lessons across the countries of the UK
- harnessing the strong commitment from governments in the UK to escalate the pace and scale of integration as a key contribution to crisis within the NHS.

This book demonstrates that integration of health and social care has been firmly established in the UK as a policy priority over the last three decades, attracting widespread support throughout the four administrations of the UK. There is broad consensus on the meaning and value of integration. There are, however, significant differences in the models of delivery across the countries of the UK coupled with diversity in approaches within England. There is substantial consensus on how to promote integration and the nature of barriers. However, there is still some debate on the achievements and outcomes of integrated working.

References

Abendstern, M., Hughes, J., Clarkson, P., Sutcliffe, C. and Challis, D. (2011) 'The pursuit of integration in the assessment of older people with health and social care needs', *British Journal of Social Work*, Vol. 41, No 3, pp. 467–485.

ADASS and NHS Confederation (2013) *Confederation Snapshot of How Integration Is Moving Forward*. Available at: http://www.adass.org.uk (accessed 17 June 2015).

ADASS (2015) *Distinctive, Valued, Personal: Why Social Care Matters: The Next Five Years*. Available at: http://www.adass.org.uk (accessed 7 May 2016).

Addicott, R. (2011) *Social Enterprise in Health Care*, London: The King's Fund.

Addicott, R. (2014) *Commissioning and Contracting for Integrated Care*, London: The King's Fund.

Age NI (2013) *Age NI's Response to Who Cares? The Future of Adult Care and Support in Northern Ireland: A Discussion Document*, Belfast: Age NI.

Ahgren, B. and Axelsson, R. (2011) 'A decade of integration and collaboration: The development of integrated care in Sweden 2000–2010', *International Journal of Integrated Care*, Vol. 11, No 5, http://doi.org/10.5334/IJIC.566.

Alakeson, V. (2013) 'The individual as service integrator', *Journal of Integrated Care*, Vol. 21, No. 4, pp. 188–197.

Allen, K. and Glasby, J. (2010) 'The (multi)-billion dollar question: Embedding prevention and rehabilitation in English Health and Social Care', *Journal of Integrated Care*, Vol. 18, No. 4, pp. 26–35.

Anderson, M. (1998) 'Social work and the integrated service', in M. Anderson, S. Bogues, J. Campbell, H. Douglas and M. McColgan (eds) *Social Work and Social Change in Northern Ireland*, Belfast: CCETSW.

Appleby, J. (2005) *Independent Review of Health and Social Care Services in Northern Ireland*, Belfast: DHSSPS.

Appleby, J. (2011) *Rapid Review of Northern Ireland Health and Social Care Funding Needs and the Productivity Challenge: 2011/12–2014/15*, Belfast: DHSSPS.

Armitage, G., Suter, E.,Oelke, N. and Adair, C. (2009) 'Health systems integration: State of the evidence', *International Journal of Integrated Care*, Vol. 9, No. 2, pp. 1–11.

Association of Directors of Adult Social Services (ADASS) (2010) *Where Next for Health and Social Care Integration*. Available at: http://www.adass.org.uk (accessed 7 August 2012).

Association of Directors of Adult Social Services Cymru (2015) *In Focus Newsletter Issue 8*. Available at: http://www.adass.org.uk (accessed 20 October 2016).

Association of Directors of Adult Social Services (ADASS) (2016) *In Focus Newsletter Issue 11*. Available at: http://www.adass.org.uk (accessed 20 January 2016).

Audit Commission (2011a) *Improving Value for Money in Adult Social Care*. Available at: https://www.audit-commission.gov.uk (accessed 5 February 2015).

Audit Commission (2011b) *Joining Up Health and Social Care: Improving Value for Money across the Interface*. Available at: https://www.audit-commission.gov.uk (accessed 5 February 2015).

Audit Scotland (2011) *Review of Community Health Partnerships*, Edinburgh: Audit Scotland.

Audit Scotland (2012) *Commissioning Social Care*, Edinburgh: Audit Scotland.

Audit Scotland (2014) *Self-directed Support*, Edinburgh: Audit Scotland.

Audit Scotland (2015a) *NHS in Scotland*, Edinburgh: Audit Scotland.

Audit Scotland (2015b) *Health and Social Care Integration*, Edinburgh: Audit Scotland.

Audit Scotland (2016) *Social Work in Scotland*, Edinburgh: Audit Scotland.

Baggott, R. (2004) *Health and Health Care in Britain*, Basingstoke: Palgrave Macmillan.

Baggott, R. (2013) *Partnerships for Public Health and Wellbeing*, Basingstoke: Palgrave Macmillan.

Ball, R., Forbes, T., Parris, M. and Forsyth, L. (2010) 'The evaluation of partnership working in the delivery of health and social care', *Public Policy and Administration*, Vol. 25, No. 4, pp. 387–407.

Barber, K. and Wallace, C. (2012) "Happily Independent" – configuring the Gwent frailty support and wellbeing worker', *Journal of Integrated Care*, Vol. 20, No. 5, pp. 308–321.

Bardsley, M., Steventon, A., Smith, J. and Dixon, J. (2013) *Evaluating Integrated and Community-based Care*, Oxford: Nuffield Trust.

Barker, K. (2014) *A New Settlement for Health and Social Care*, London: The King's Fund.

Bath and North East Somerset Council (2014) *Update on the Establishment of the Community Interest Company for the Provision of Community Health and Social Care Services*. Available at: https://www.democracy.bathnes.gov.uk (accessed 5 March 2015).

Beacon, A. (2015) 'Practice-integrated care teams – learning for a better future', *Journal of Integrated Care*, Vol. 23, No. 2, pp. 74–87.

Beech, R., Henderson, C., Ashby, S., Dickinson, A., Sheaff, R., Windle, K., Wistow, G. and Knapp, M. (2013) 'Does integrated government lead to integrated patient care?' Finding from the innovation forum', *Health and Social Care in the Community*, Vol. 21, No. 6, pp. 598–605.

Belfast Health and Social Care Trust (2012) *Annual Report*, Belfast: Belfast Health and Social Care Trust.

Bell, D., Bowes, A. and Dawson, A. (2007) *Free Personal Care in Scotland: Recent Developments*, York: Joseph Rowntree Foundation.

Bengoa, R. (2013) 'Transforming health care: An approach to system wide implementation', *International Journal of Integrated Care*, Vol. 13, No. 3, No 5, http://doi.org/10.5334/IJIC.1206.

Bengoa, R. (2016) *Systems, Not Structures: Changing Health and Social Care*, Belfast: DHSSPS.

Bennett, L. and Humphries, R. (2014) *Making Best Use of the Better Care Fund*, London: The King's Fund.

Beresford, P. and Carr, S. (2012) *Social Care, Service Users and User Involvement*, London: Jessica Kingsley.

Beresford, P. (2016) *All Our Welfare: Towards Participatory Social Policy*, Bristol: Policy Press.

Bernard, S., Aspinal, F., Gridley, K. and Parker, G. (2012) 'Benchmarking integrated care for people with long-term neurological conditions', *Journal of Integrated Care*, Vol. 20, No. 3, pp. 152–163.

Berwick, D. M., Nolan, T. W. and Whittington, J. (2008) 'Health affairs, the triple aim', *Care, Health and Cost*, Vol. 27, No. 3, pp. 759–769.

Bessos, K. (2015) 'Working together to improve health and social care outcomes in Scotland', *International Journal of Integrated Care*, Vol. 15, No. 5, http://doi.org/10.5334/IJIC.2040.

Bevan Commission (2011) *2008 – 2011 NHS Wales: Forging a Better Future*, A Report by the Bevan Commission 2008–2011. Available at: https://www.bevancommission. org (accessed 14 April 2015).

Bevan Commission (2013) *Increasing the Page in Integrated Care*. Available at: https://www. bevancommission.org (accessed 14 April 2015).

Bidgood, E. (2013) *Healthcare Systems: Sweden and Localism – An Example for the UK?*, London: Civitas.

Bienkowska-Gibbs, T. (2013) 'Integrated care programmes in Canada', *Eurohealth*, Vol. 19, No. 2, pp. 13–14.

Billings, J. (2005) 'What do we mean by integrated care? A European Interpretation', *Journal of Integrated Care*, Vol. 20, No. 6, pp. 346–358.

Birrell, D. (2009) *Direct Rule and the Governance of Northern Ireland*, Manchester: Manchester University Press.

Birrell, D. and Heenan, D. (2012) 'Implementing the Transforming Your Care agenda in Northern Ireland within integrated structures', *Journal of Integrated Care*, Vol. 20, No. 6, pp. 354–366.

Birrell, D. and Heenan, D. (2014) 'Integrated care partnerships in Northern Ireland: Added value or added bureaucracy?', *Journal of Integrated Care*, Vol. 22, No. 5/6, pp. 197–207.

Birrell, D. and Murie, A. (1980) *Policy and Government in Northern Ireland: Lessons of Devolution*, Dublin: Gill and Macmillan.

Blood, I. (2013) 'Integrating housing with care for older people', *Journal of Integrated Care*, Vol. 21, No. 4, pp. 178–187.

Bogg, D. (2011) 'Leadership for social care outcomes in mental health provision', *International Journal of Leadership in Public Services*, Vol. 7, No. 1, pp. 32–47.

Brand, D. (2012) 'Social and health care integration: (1) The individual dimension', *Journal of Integrated Care*, Vol. 20, No. 6, pp. 371–378.

British Association of Social Workers England (2015) *BASW Position on Social Work and Integration between Health and Social Care*, London: BASW England.

British Medical Association (BMA) (2011) *Doctors' Perspectives on Integration in the NHS, BMA Interim Report*, Health Policy and Economic Research Unit.

British Medical Association (BMA) (2016) *Integration in Wales*. Available at: https://www. bma.org.uk/collective-voice/policy-and-research (accessed 2 November 2016).

Brooks, N. (2002) 'Intermediate care rapid assessment support service: An evaluation', *British Journal of Community Nursing*, Vol. 7, No. 1(12), pp. 628–33.

Brown, L., Tucker, C. and Domokos, T. (2003) 'Evaluating the impact of integrated health and social care on older people living in the community', *Health and Social Care in the Community*, Vol. 11, No. 2, pp. 85–94.

Bruce, A. and Forbes, T. (2005) 'Delivering community care in Scotland: Can local partnerships bridge the gap?', *Scottish Affairs*, Vol. 52, No. 1, pp. 89–109.

Burgess, L. (2012) *Integration of Health and Social Care: International Comparisons*, SPICE Briefing, Edinburgh: The Scottish Parliament.

Burgess, L. (2016) *Integration of Health and Social Care*, SPICe Briefing, Edinburgh: The Scottish Parliament.

Bywaters, P., McLeod, E., Fisher, J., Cooke, M. and Swann, G. (2011) 'Good intentions, increased inequities: Developing social care services in Emergency Departments in the UK', *Health and Social Care in the Community*, Vol. 19, No. 5, pp. 460–467.

Camden and Islington NHS Foundation Trust (2013) *Our Services*. Available at: https:// www.candi.nhs.uk (accessed 12 February 2015).

Cameron, A. (2016) 'What have we learnt about joint working between health and social care?', *Public Money and Management*, Vol. 36, No. 1, pp. 7–14.

Cameron, A. and Lart, R. (2003) 'Factors promoting and obstacles hindering joint working: A systematic review of the research evidence', *Journal of Integrated Care*, Vol. 11, No. 2, pp. 9–17.

Cameron, A., Lart, R., Bostock, L. and Coomber, C. (2012) *Factors that Promote and Hinder Joint and Integrated Working between Health and Social Care Services*. Research briefing 41, London: Social Care Institute for Excellence.

Cameron, A., Lart, R., Bostock, L. and Coomber, C. (2014) 'Factors that promote and hinder joint and integrated working between health and social care services: A review of research literature', *Health and Social Care in the Community*, Vol. 22, No. 3, pp. 225–233.

Cameron, A., Lart, R., Bostock, L., Coomber, C. (2015) *Factors that Promote and Hinder Joint and Integrated Working between Health and Social Care Services*, London: Social Care Institute for Excellence.

Cameron, A., Lart, R., Harrison, L., Macdonald, G. and Smith, R. (2000) *Factors Promoting and Obstacles Hindering Joint Working: A Systematic Review*, Bristol: Policy Press.

Care and Social Services Inspectorate Wales (2014) *National Review of Commissioning for Social Services in Wales 2014*, Cardiff: CSSIW.

Care Quality Commission (2016) *Building Bridges, Breaking Barriers: Integrated Care for Older People*. Available at: https://www.cqc.org.uk (accessed 1 November 2016).

Care Quality Commission (2017) *The State of Health Care and Adult Social Care in England 2015–16*. Available at: https://www.cqc.org.uk (accessed 15 March 2017).

Carnes Chichlowska, S., Burholt, V., Beech, C. and Dobbs, C. (2013) *A Realistic Evaluation of Integrated Health and Social Care for Older People in Wales to Promote Independence and Wellbeing: An Interim Report*, Cardiff: Welsh Government Social Research.

Carpenter, J. et al. (2004) 'Integration and targeting of community care for people with severe and enduring mental health problems: Users' experience of the care programme approach and care management', *British Journal of Social Work*, Vol. 34, No. 3, pp. 313–333.

Cavendish, C. (2013) *An Independent Review into Healthcare Assistants and Support Workers in the NHS and Social Care Settings*. Available at: https://www.gov.uk (accessed 12 February 2015).

Cestari, L., Munroe, M., Evans, S., Smith, A. and Huxley, P. (2006) 'Fair Access to Care Services (FACS): Implementation in the mental health context of the UK', *Health and Social Care in the Community*, Vol. 14, No. 6, pp. 474–481.

Challis, D., Stewart, N., Donnelly, M., Weiner, N. and Hughes, J. (2006) 'Care management for older people: Does integration make a difference?', *Journal of Interprofessional Care*, Vol. 20, No. 4, pp. 335–348.

Cheater, F. (1996) 'Care pathways: Good tools for clinical audit? *Audit Trends*, Vol. 4, pp. 73–75.

Christie, C. (2011) *Commission on the Future Delivery of Public Services*. Available at: https://www.Scotland.gov.uk (accessed 10 March 2013).

Clift, E. (2015) 'How a rapid response team is supporting people to remain at home', *Nursing Older People*, Vol. 27, No. 10, pp. 16–22.

Close, P. (2010) 'From transition to transformation: Leading the management of change', in J. McKimm and K. Phillips (eds) *Leadership and Management in Integrated Services*, Exeter: Learning Matters.

Coburn, A. F. (2001) 'Models for integrating and managing acute and long-term care services in rural areas', *Journal of Applied Gerontology*, Vol. 20, pp. 386–408.

Cole. J. (2009) *Reconfiguring Health Services in Northern Ireland*. Presentation, Health Estates Conference, 23/24 April, Cardiff.

Collins, F. and McCray, J. (2012) 'Relationships, learning and team working in UK services for children', *Journal of Integrated Care*, Vol. 20, No. 1, pp. 39–50.

Connolly, S., Bevan, G. and Mays, N. (2010) *Funding and Performance of Healthcare Systems in the Four Countries of the UK Before and After Devolution*, London: Nuffield Trust.

Contel, J. C., Ledesma, A., Blay, C., Mestre, A. G., Cabezas, E., Puigdollers, M., Zara, C., Amil, P., Sarquella, E. and Constante, C. (2015) 'Chronic and integrated care in Catalonia', *International Journal of Integrated Care*, Vol. 15, No. 2. http://doi.org/10.5334/IJIC.2205

Cornes, M., Manthorpe, J., Hennessy, C. and Anderson, S. (2013) *Little Miracles: Using Communities of Practice to Improve Front Line Collaborative Responses to Multiple Needs and Exclusions*, London: King's College.

Cornwell, J. (2012) *The Care of Frail Older People with Complex Needs: Time for a Revolution*, London: The King's Fund.

Coupe, M. (2013) 'Integrated care in Hertfordshire: A case study', *Journal of Integrated Care*, Vol. 21, No. 4, pp. 198–217.

County All Party Parliamentary Group (2010) *The State of Care in Counties: The Integration Imperative*. Available at: https://www.countycouncilsnetwork.org.uk (accessed 5 March 2015).

County Councils Network (2016) *Health and Social Care in Counties: Funding, Demand and Cost Pressures*. Available at: https://www.countycouncilsnetwork.org.uk (accessed 5 March 2015).

Crossman, S. (2015) 'Integrating care across a challenged local health economy: The West Norfolk Health and Social Alliance', *Future Hospital Journal*, Vol 2, No. 2, pp. 102–106.

Curry, N. and Ham, C. (2010) *Clinical and Service Integration: The Route to Improved Outcomes*, London: The King's Fund.

De Luc, K. (2001) *Developing Care Pathways: The Handbook*, Oxford: Radcliffe Medical Press Ltd.

Department of Health (DH) (1998a) *Partnership in Action: New Opportunities for Working between Health and Social Services*, Discussion Document, London: The Stationery Office.

DH (1998b) *Modernising Social Services*, Cm 4169, Belfast: The Stationery Office.

DH (2000) *The NHS Plan*, Cm 4818, London: The Stationery Office.

DH (2001) *National Service Framework for Older People*. Available at: https://www.gov.uk (accessed 8 December 2014).

DH (2002) *Delivering the NHS Plan*, Cm 5503, London: The Stationery Office.

DH (2005) *Independence, Well-being and Choice*, Cm 6499, London: The Stationery Office.

DH (2006a) *Our Health, Our Care, Our Say: A New Direction for Community Services*, Cm 6737, London: The Stationery Office.

DH (2006b) *Our Health, Our Care, Our Say: Making It Happen*. Available at: https://www.dh.gov.uk/publications (accessed 22 February 2007).

DH (2008) *High Quality Care for All*, NHS Next Stage Review Final Report (Darzi Report) Cm 7432, London: The Stationery Office.

DH (2009) *Shaping the Future of Care Together*, Cm 7673, London: The Stationery Office.

DH (2010a) *Equity and Excellence: Liberating the NHS*, Cm 7881, London: The Stationery Office.

DH (2010b) *Liberating the NHS: Local Democratic Legitimacy in Health*, Policy Paper, London: The Stationery Office.

DH (2010c) *Liberating the NHS: Legislative Framework and Next Steps*, Cm 7993, London: The Stationery Office.

DH (2010d) *A Vision for Adult Social Care: Capable Communities and Active Citizens*. Available at: https://www.dh.gov.uk/publications (accessed 29 May 2012).

DH (2010e) Partnerships for Older People Projects, London: The Stationery Office.

DH (2011) *NHS Future Forum: Proposed Changes to the NHS*. Available at: https://www.gov.uk (accessed 29 May 2012).

DH (2012a) *Caring for Our Future: Reforming Care and Support*, Cm 8378, London: The Stationery Office.

DH (2012b) *Government response to the House of Commons Health Committee Report on Social Care*, Cm 8380, London: The Stationery Office.

DH (2012c) *The Functions of Clinical Commissioning Groups*, London: Department of Health

DH (2013a) *The Care Bill Explained*, Cm 8627, London: The Stationery Office.

DH (2013b) *Integration Pioneers Leading the Way for Health and Care Reform*. Available at: https://www.gov.uk (accessed 14 November 2013).

DH (2014) *Integrated Care Pioneer Programme. Annual Report*. Available at: https://www.local.gov.uk (accessed 23 August 2016).

DH (2016) *Health and Wellbeing 2026 – Delivering Together*, London: The Stationery Office.

Department of Health and Social Services (1972) *Health and Personal Social Services (Northern Ireland) Order*, Belfast: DHSS.

Department of Health and Social Services (1990) *People First*, Belfast: DHSS.

Department of Health and Social Services and Public Safety (2002) *Developing Better Services*, Belfast: DHSSPS.

Department of Health, Social Services and Public Safety (2005) *Caring for People beyond Tomorrow*, Belfast: DHSSPS.

Department of Health, Social Services and Public Safety (DHSSPS) (1990) *People First: Community Care in Northern Ireland in the 1990s*, Belfast: DHSSPS.

DHSSPS (2011) *Transforming Your Care: A Review of Health and Social Care in Northern Ireland*, Belfast: DHSSPS.

DHSSPS (2012) *Improving and Safeguarding Social Wellbeing: A Strategy for Social Work*, Belfast: DHSSPS.

DHSSPS (2013) *Who Cares? The Future of Adult Social Care and Support in Northern Ireland*, Discussion Document, Belfast: DHSSPS.

DHSSPS (2014) *The Right Time, The Right Place (Donaldson Report)*, Belfast: DHSSPS

DHSSPS (2015) *Review of the Commissioning Arrangements. Final Report*, Belfast: DHSSPS

DHSSPS (2016) *Systems Not Structures – Changing Health and Social Care*, Belfast: DHSSPS

Devaney, J. (2008) 'Inter-professional working in child protection with families with long-term and complex needs', *Child Abuse Review*, Vol. 17, No. 4, pp. 242–261.

Dickinson, H. (2014) 'Making a reality of integration: Less science more craft and graft', *Journal of Integrated Care*, Vol. 22, No. 5/6, pp. 189–196.

Dickinson, H. (2016) 'The evaluation of health and social care partnerships: An analysis of approaches and synthesis for the future', *Health and Social Care in the Community*, Vol. 14, No. 5, pp. 375–383.

Dickinson, H. and Glasby, J. (2006) *Free Personal Care in Scotland*, London: The King's Fund.

Dickinson, H. and Glasby, J. (2009) 'Introduction', in J. Glasby and H. Dickinson (eds) *International Perspectives on Health and Social Care, Partnership Working in Action*, London: Wiley-Blackwell

Dickinson, H. and Glasby, J. (2013) 'How effective is joint commissioning? A study of five English localities', *Journal of Integrated Care*, Vol. 21, No. 4, pp. 221–232.

Dickinson, H. and Neal, C. (2011) 'Single point of access to third sector services: The Conwy collaborative approach', *Journal of Integrated Care*, Vol. 19, No. 2, pp. 37–48.

Dickinson, H., Peck, E. and Davidson, D. (2007) 'Opportunity seized or missed? A case study of leadership and organisational change in the creation of a Care Trust', *Journal of Interprofessional Care*, Vol. 21, No. 5, pp. 503–513.

Donaldson, L. (2014) *The Right Time, The Right Place*, Belfast: DHSSPS.

Dornan, B. (1998) *Teamwork in Integrated Primary Health and Social Care Teams*, Research Report, Lisburn: Down Lisburn Trust.

Dow, J. (2010) 'From old patchwork to new patchwork? The Law Commission proposals for reform of Adult Social Care law', *Journal of Integrated Care*, Vol. 18, No. 4, pp. 16–18.

Dow, J. (2011) 'Health and wellbeing boards', *Journal of Integrated Care*, Vol. 19, No. 3, pp. 23–25.

Dowling, B., Powell, M. and Glendinning, C. (2004) 'Conceptualising successful partnerships', *Health and Social Care in the Community*, Vol. 12, No. 4, pp. 304–317.

Edmunds, C. and Kilbride, K. (2015) 'Collaboration, easy to say, difficult to do', *Journal of Integrated Care*, Vol. 23, No. 4, pp. 232–249.

Edwards, A. (2010) 'Working across the health and social care boundary', in J. Glasby and H. Dickenson (eds) *International Perspectives on Health and Social Care*, Oxford: Wiley-Blackwell.

El Ansari, W. (2011) 'When meanings blur, do differences matter: Initiatives for improving the quality and integration of care: Conceptual matrix or measurement maze', *Journal of Integrated Care*, Vol. 19, No. 3, pp. 5–22.

Ellershaw, J., Foster, A., Murphy, D., Shea, T. and Overill, S. (1997) 'Developing an integrated care pathway for the dying patient', *European Journal of Palliative Care*, Vol. 4, No. 6, pp. 203–207.

Ellins, J. and Glasby, J. (2011) 'Together we are better? Strategy needs assessment as a tool to improve joint working in England', *Journal of Integrated Care*, Vol. 19, No. 3, pp. 34–41.

Ellis, M., Curry, K. and Watson, J. (2013) 'Advancing the transformation of local services in Staffordshire', *Journal of Integrated Care*, Vol. 21, No. 1, pp. 34–41.

Erens, B., Wistow, G., Mounier-Jack, S., Douglas, N., Jones, L., Manacorda, T. and Mays, N. (2015) *Early Evaluation of the Integrated Care and Support Pioneers Programme: Interim Report*, London: Policy Innovation Research Unit.

Ernst and Young (EY) (2015) *Creating a Better Care System*, London: Ernst and Young.

European Pathway Association (EPA) (2005) *Care Pathways, Belgium*. Available at: https://www.e-p-a.org (accessed 25 May 2014).

Evans, S. (2014) *Delivering Excellence across the Health and Social Care System through Prudent Health Care*. Available at: https://www.prudenthealthcare.org.uk (accessed 30 August 2016).

Farnsworth, A. (2012a) *Improving Care for Mrs Smith*, Torbay and South Devon Health and Care NHS Trust.

Farnsworth, A. (2012b) 'Unintended consequences? The impact of NHS reforms upon Torbay Care Trust', *Journal of Integrated Care*, Vol. 20, No. 3, pp. 146–151.

Ferguson, I. and Lavalette, M. (2013) 'Crisis, austerity and the future(s) of social work in the UK', *Critical and Radical Social Work*, Vol. 1, No. 1, pp. 95–110.

Field, J. and Peck. E. (2003) 'Mergers and acquisitions in the private sector: What are the lessons for health and social services?', *Social Policy &Administration*, Vol. 37, No. 7, pp. 742–55.

Fillingham, D. and Weir, B. (2014) *System Leadership: Lessons and Learning from AQuA's Integrated Care Discovery Communities*, London: The King's Fund.

First and Deputy First Minister (2005) *The Review of public administration in NI a further consultation* Belfast, RPA.

Fisher, M. P. and Elnitsky, C. (2012) 'Health and social services integration: A review of concepts and models', *Social Work in Public Health*, Vol. 27, No. 5, pp. 441–468.

Forbes, T. and Evans, D. (2009) 'Partnerships in health and social care: England and Scotland compared', *Public Policy and Administration*, Vol. 24, No. 1, pp. 67–83.

Francis, J., Fisher, M. and Rutter, D. (2011) *Reablement: A Cost-effective Route to Better Outcomes*, Research Briefing 36, London: Social Care Institute for Excellence.

Freeman, T. and Peck, E. (2006) 'Evaluating partnerships: A case study of integrated specialist mental health services', *Health and Social Care in the Community*, Vol. 14, No. 5, pp. 408–417.

Fulop, N., Mowlem, A. and Edwards, N. (2005) *Building Integrated Care: Lessons from the UK and Elsewhere*, London: Nuffield Trust

Garthwaite, T. (2013) *Collaboration in Social Services Wales*, Cardiff: Improving Social Care in Wales.

Gilburt, H. (2016) 'Supporting integration through new roles and working across boundaries', London: The King's Fund.

Glasby, J. (2005) 'The integration dilemma: How deep and how broad to go?', *Journal of Integrated Care*, Vol. 13, No. 5, pp. 27–30.

Glasby, J. (2007) *Understanding Health and Social Care*, Bristol: Policy Press.

Glasby, J. (2016) 'If integration is the answer, what was the question? What next for English Health and Social Care', *International Journal of Integrated Care*, Vol. 16, No. 4, p. 11.

Glasby, J. and Dickinson, H. (2008) *Partnership Working in Health and Social Care*, Bristol: Policy Press.

Glasby, J. and Dickinson, H. (eds) (2009) *International Perspectives on Health and Social Care*, Oxford: Wiley Blackwell.

Glasby, J. and Dickinson, H. (2014) *Partnership Working in Health and Social Care: What Is Integrated Care and How Can We Deliver It?*, Bristol: Policy Press.

Glasby, J. and Miller, R. (2015) 'New conversations between old players? The relationship between general practice and social care', *Journal of Integrated Care*, Vol. 23, No. 2, pp. 42–52.

Glasby, J. and Peck, E. (2003) *Care Trusts, Partnership Working in Action*, Oxford: Radcliffe Medical Press.

Glasby, J., Dickenson, H. and Miller, R. (2011) 'Partnership working in England – Where we are now and where we've come from', *International Journal of Integrated Care*, Vol. 11 (Special 10th Anniversary Edition) Jan–Dec.

Glasby, J., Dickinson, H., Nicoll, T., Fleischmann, P. (2012) *Integrated Adult Health and Social Care Teams in Leeds*, London: Social Care Institute for Excellence.

Glasby, J., Peck, E. and Davis, M. (2005) 'Joined-up solutions to joined-up problems? Alternatives to Care Trusts', *Journal of Integrated Care*, Vol. 13, No. 1, pp. 3–5.

Gleave, R., Wong, I., Porteus, J. and Harding, E. (2010) 'What is 'More Integration' between health and social care? Results of a survey of Primary Care Trusts and Directors of Adult Social Care in England', *Journal of Integrated Care*, Vol 18, No. 5, pp. 29–32.

Glendinning, C. and Means, R. (2004) 'Rearranging the deckchairs on the Titanic of long-term care – Is organizational integration the answer?', *Critical Social Policy*, Vol. 24, No. 4, pp. 435–457.

Glendinning, C., Moran, N., Challis, D., Fernandez, J., Jacobs, S., Jones, K., Knapp, M., Manthorpe, J., Netten, A., Stevens, M. and Wilberforce, M. (2011) 'Personalisation and partnership: Competing objectives in adult social care? The individual budget pilot projects and the NHS', Social Policy and Society, Vol. 10, No. 2, pp. 151–162.

Goldberg, D. (2014) Can the NHS Deliver Integration? Lessons from around the World, Sussex: Good Governance Institute.

Goldman, C. (2010) 'Joint financing across health and social care: Money matters, but outcomes matter more', Journal of Integrated Care, Vol. 18, No. 1, pp. 3–10.

Goodwin, N. (2012a) Lessons from the Integrated Care Pilots. Available at: https://www.kingsfund.org.uk/blog/2012/04/lessons_integrated_care-pilots (accessed 29 May 2012).

Goodwin, N. (2012b) NHS Reforms: The Five Laws of Integrated care. Available at: https://www.kingsfund.org.uk/blog/2011 (accessed 8 May 2012).

Goodwin, N. (2013) 'Taking integrated care forward: The need for shared values', International Journal of Integrated Care, Vol. 13, No. 2, p. 4.

Goodwin, N., Curry, N., Naylor, C., Ross, S. and Duldig, W. (2010) Managing People with Long-term Conditions, London: The King's Fund.

Goodwin, N., Dixon, A., Anderson, G. and Wodchis, W. (2014) Providing Integrated Care for Older People with Complex Needs. Lessons from Seven International Case Studies, London: The King's Fund.

Goodwin, N., Smith, J., Davies, A., Perry, C., Rosen, R., Dixon, A., Dixon, J. and Ham, C. (2012) A report to the Department of Health and the NHS Future Forum, London: The King's Fund.

Goodwin, N., Sonala, L., Thiel, V. and Kodner, D. (2013) Co-ordinated Care for People with Complex Chronic Conditions, London: The King's Fund.

Government of Northern Ireland (1969) The Administrative Structure of Health and Personal Social Services in Northern Ireland, Belfast: HMSO.

Gray, A. M. and Birrell, D. (2013) Transforming Adult Social Care, Bristol: Policy Press.

Greenwell, S. and Green, J. (2015) 'Guest editorial', Journal of Integrated Care, Vol. 23, No. 4, pp. 178–181

Greer, S. (2004) Territorial Politics and Health Care, Manchester: Manchester University Press.

Gregory, M. (2015) 'Developing a patient care coordination centre in Trafford, England', International Journal of Integrated Care, Vol. 15, No. 2, pp. 1–9.

Greig, R. (2012) 'What progress did "Caring for People" instigate and achieve?', Journal of Integrated Care, Vol. 20, No. 2, pp. 125–131.

Gridley, K., Brooks, J. and Glendinning, C. (2014) 'Good practice in social care for disabled adults and older people with severe and complex needs: Evidence from a scoping review', Health and Social Care in the Community, Vol. 22, No. 3, pp. 234–248.

Griffiths, R. (1988) Community Care: Agenda for Action: A Report to the Secretary of State for Social Services (Griffiths Report), London: HMSO.

Hafford-Letchfield, T. (2009) 'Management and leadership from strategy to service delivery', in J. McKimm and K. Phillips (eds) Leadership and Management in Integrated Services, Exeter: Learning Matters.

Ham, C. (2009) Only Connect: Policy Options for Integrating Health and Social Care, London: Nuffield Trust.

Ham, C. (2015) Three Challenges and a Big Uncertainty for the NHS in 2015, London: The King's Fund.

Ham, C., Berwick, D. and Dixon, J. (2016) Improving Quality in the English NHS, London: The King's Fund.

Ham, C., Dixon, A. and Brooke, B. (2012) *Transforming the Delivery of Health and Social Care*, London: The King's Fund.

Ham, C., Heenan, D., Longley, M. and Steel, D. (2013) *Integrated Care in Northern Ireland, Scotland and Wales, Lessons for England*, London: The King's Fund.

Hammond, E. (2015) *Devo Why? Devo How?*, London: Centre for Public Scrutiny.

Harding, E. and Kane, M. (2011) 'Joint strategic needs assessment: Reconciling new expectations with reality', *Journal of Integrated Care*, Vol. 19, No. 6, pp. 37–44.

Hardwick, R. (2013) 'Integrated services for women through a One Stop Shop: A realist review', *Journal of Integrated Care*, Vol. 21, No. 5, pp. 263–275.

Health and Social Care Board (2016) *Integrated Care Partnerships, Interim Impact Report*, Belfast: HSCB.

Hébert, R., Durand, P. J., Dubuc, N., Tourigny, A. and the PRISMA Group (2003) 'PRISMA: A new model of integrated service delivery for the frail older people in Canada', *International Journal of Integrated Care*, Vol. 3, No. 1, http://doi.org/10.5334/IJIC.73.

Heenan, D. and Birrell, D. (2006) 'The integration of health and social care: The lessons from Northern Ireland', *Social Policy & Administration*, Vol. 40, No 1, pp. 47–66.

Heenan, D. and Birrell, D. (2009) 'Organisational integration in health and social care: Some reflections on the Northern Ireland experience', *Journal of Integrated Care*, Vol. 17, No 5, pp. 3–12.

Heenan, D. and Birrell, D. (2011) *Social Work in Northern Ireland: Conflict and Change*, Bristol: Policy Press.

Heenan, D. and Birrell, D. (2012) 'Implementing the transforming your care agenda in Northern Ireland within integrated structures', *Journal of Integrated Care*, Vol. 20, No. 6, pp. 359–66.

Hendry, A. (2010) 'Lanarkshire's managed care network: An integrated improvement collaborative', *Journal of Integrated Care*, Vol. 18, No. 3, pp. 45–51.

Henwood, M. (2006) 'Effective partnership working: A case study of hospital discharge', *Health and Social Care in the Community*, Vol. 14, No. 5, pp. 400–407.

Henwood, M. and Wistow, G. (1993) *Hospital Discharge and Community Care: Early Days*, London: Great Britain, Department of Health, Social Services Inspectorate.

Hildebrandt, H., Schultz, T. and Stunder, B. (2012) 'Triple aim in Kinzigtal Germany: Improving population health, integrating health care and reducing the costs of care', *Journal of Integrated Care*, Vol. 20, No. 4, pp. 205–222.

Hill, M. (ed.) (2000) *Local Authority Social Services*, Oxford: Blackwell.

HM Government (2007) *Putting People First: A Shared Vision and Commitment to the Transformation of Adult Social Care*, London: NHS/ADHSS.

House of Commons Health Committee (2012) *Social Care*, Fourteenth Report of Session 2010–12, Vol. 1, HC1583–1, London: House of Commons.

Hudson, B. (2002) 'Integrated care and structural change in England: The case of Care Trusts', *Policy Studies*, Vol. 23, No. 2, pp. 77–95.

Hudson, B. (2003) 'Care trusts: A sceptical view', in J. Glasby and E. Peck (eds) *Care Trusts: Partnership Working in Action*, Oxford: Radcliffe Medical Press.

Hudson, B. (2006) 'Integrated team working: You can get it if you really want it', *Journal of Integrated Care*, Vol. 14, No. 1, pp. 13–21.

Hudson, B. (2007) 'Pessimism and optimism in inter-professional working: The Sedgefield integrated team', *Journal of Interprofessional Care*, Vol. 21, No. 1, pp. 3–15.

Hudson, B. (2010) 'Integrated commissioning: New contexts, new dilemmas, new solutions?', *International Journal of Integrated Care*, Vol. 18, No. 1, pp. 11–19.

Hudson, B. (2011) 'All that glisters: Are the NHS reforms good for local government?', *Journal of Integrated Care*, Vol. 19, No. 2, pp. 4–12.

Hudson, B. (2015) 'Can GPs coordinate "whole person care"?', *Journal of Integrated Care*, Vol. 23, No. 1, pp. 10–16.

Hudson, B. and Henwood, M. (2002) 'The NHS and social care: The final countdown', *Policy and Politics*, Vol. 30, No. 2, pp. 153–166.

Humphries, R. (2015) 'Integrated health and social care in England – progress and prospects', *Health Policy*, Vol. 119, No. 7, pp. 856–859.

Humphries, R. and Curry, N. (2011) *Integrating Health and Social Care*, London: The King's Fund.

Humphries, R. and Galea, A. (2013) *Health and Wellbeing Boards, One Year On*, London: The King's Fund.

Humphries, R., Galea, A., Sonola, L. and Mundle, C. (2012) *Health and Wellbeing Boards: System Leaders or Talking Shops?*, London: The King's Fund.

Humphries, R., Thorlby, R., Holder, H., Hall, P. and Charles, A. (2016) *Social Care for Older People: Home Truths*, London: The King's Fund.

Hutchison, B., Levesque, J. F., Strumpf, E. and Coyle, N. (2011) 'Primary health care in Canada: Systems in motion', *The Milbank Quarterly*, Vol. 89, No. 2. pp. 256–288.

Hutchison, K. (2015) 'An exploration of the integration of health and social care within Scotland', *Journal of Integrated Care*, Vol. 23, No. 3, pp. 129–142.

Huxley, P., Evans, S., Munroe, M. and Cestani, L. (2008) 'Integrating health and social care in community mental health teams in the UK: A study of assessments and eligibility criteria in England', *Health and Social Care in the Community*, Vol. 16, No. 5, pp. 476–482.

Independent Commission on Social Services in Wales (2010) *From Vision to Action*, The Report of the Independent Commission on Social Services in Wales. Available at: https://www.wlga.gov.uk (accessed 23 January 2015).

Institute of Public Care (2017) *Outcome-focused Integrated Care: Lessons from Experience*. Available at: https://www.ipc.brookes.ac.uk (accessed 8 March 2017).

Institute for Research and Innovation in Social Sciences (2013), *Leading for Outcomes, Integrated Working*. Available at: https://www.iriss.org.uk (accessed 23 January 2015).

Ismail, S., Thorlby, R. and Holder, H. (2014) *Focus On: Social Care for Older People*, London: Health Foundation and Nuffield Trust.

Jenkins, L., Brigden, C. and King, M. (2013) 'Evaluating a third sector community service following stroke', *Journal of Integrated Care*, Vol. 21, No. 5, pp. 248–262.

Johnson, N. (1990) *Reconstructing the Welfare State: A Decade of Change 1980–1990*, Hemel Hempstead: Harvester Wheatsheaf.

Joint Improvement Team (2013) *Annual Report*. Available at: https://www.jit.scotland. org.uk (accessed 14 November 2013).

Jones, N., Thomas, P. and Rudd, L. (2004) 'Collaborating for mental health services in Wales: A process evaluation', *Public Administration*, Vol. 82, No. 1, pp. 104–121.

Jordan, B. and Drakeford, M. (2012) *Social Work and Social Policy under Austerity*, Basingstoke: Palgrave Macmillan.

Kaehne, A., Birrell, D., Miller, R. and Petch, A. (2017) 'Bringing integration home: Policy on health and social care integration in the four nations of the UK', *Journal of Integrated Care*, Vol. 25, No. 2, pp. 84–98.

Kassianos, A., Ignatowicz, A., Greenfield, G., Majeed, A., Car, J. and Pappas, Y. (2015) "Partners rather than just providers ..." A qualitative study on health care professionals' views on implementation of multidisciplinary group meetings in the North West London integrated care pilot', *International Journal of Integrated Care*, Vol. 15, pp. 1–15.

Kelly, J. (2015) 'Integrating occupational therapy services – playing the long game', *Journal of Integrated Care*, Vol. 23, No. 4, pp. 185–193.

Kingsmill, D. (2013) *The Kingsmill Review: Taking Care. An Independent Report into Working Conditions in the Care Sector.* Available at: https://www.yourbritain.org.uk (accessed 1 November 2013).

Klinga, C., Hansson, J., Hasson, H. Andreen Sachs, M. (2016) 'Co-leadership – a management solution for integrated health and social care', *International Journal of Integrated Care*, Vol. 16, No. 2, p. 7.

Kodner, D. and Spreeguwenberg, C. (2002) 'Integrated care: Meaning logic, applications and implications – a discussion paper', *International Journal of Integrated Care*, Vol. 2, No. 4, http://doi.org/10.5334/IJIC.67.

Law Commission (2011) *Adult Social Care*, Hc941, London: The Stationery Office.

Leutz, W. (1999) 'Five laws for integrating medical and social services: Lessons from the United States and the United Kingdom', *The Milbank Quarterly*, Vol. 77, No. 1, pp. 77–110.

Leutz, W. (2005) 'Reflections on integrating medical and social care: Five laws revisited', *Journal of Integrated Care*, Vol. 13, No. 5, pp. 3–12.

Lewis, J. (2001) 'Social services departments and the health/social care boundary: Players or pawns?', in I. Allen (ed.) *Social Care and Health: A New Deal?*, London: Policy Studies Institute.

Lewis, J. and West, A. (2014) 'Re-shaping social care services for older people in England: Policy development and the problems of achieving good care', *Journal of Social Policy*, Vol. 43, No. 1, pp. 1–18.

Llano, R. (2013) 'The "Gesundes Kinziigtal" integrated care initiative in Germany. Incentivising integrated care', *Eurohealth*, Vol. 19, No. 2, pp. 7–8.

Local Government Association (2013a) *Concordat for Integrated Health and Social Care.* Available at: https://www.local.gov.uk (accessed 3 December 2013).

Local Government Association (2013b) *Integrated Care Evidence Review:.* Available at: https://www.local.gov.uk (accessed 3 December 2013).

Local Government Association (2014) *LGA Adult Social Care Efficiency Programme, Final Report.* Available at: https://www.local.gov.uk (accessed 12 March 2015).

Local Government Association (2015a) *Guide to the Care Act 2014 and the Implications for Providers.* Available at: https://www.local.gov.uk (accessed 28 October 2015).

Local Government Association (2015b) *Adult Social Care, Health and Wellbeing: A Shared Commitment.* Available at: https://www.local.gov.uk (accessed 28 October 2015).

Local Government Association (2016a) *Charting Progress on the Health Devolution Journey: Early Lessons from Greater Manchester.* Available at: https://www.local.gov.uk (accessed 12 May 2016).

Local Government Association (2016b) *Combined Authorities: A Plain English Guide.* Available at: https://www.local.gov.uk (accessed 20 July 2016).

Local Government Association (2016c) *Integration: Delivering Better Outcomes for Citizens and Communities.* Available at: https://www.local.gov.uk (accessed 20 July 2016).

Local Government Association (2016d) *Care and Health Improvement Report, Final Report.* Available at: https://www.local.gov.uk (accessed 20 July 2016).

Local Government Association (2016e) *The Journey to Integration: Learning from Seven Leading Localities.* Available at: https://www.local.gov.uk (accessed 22 June 2016).

Local Government Association/NHS Clinical Commissioners (2015) *Making It Better Together: A Call to Action on the Future of Health and Wellbeing Boards.* Available at: https://www.local.gov.uk (accessed 18 August 2015).

Local Government Association/NHS Improvement (2016) *Health and Wellbeing Boards*, London: Local Government Association.

Locke, P. and West, K. (2016) 'Individualised funding for older people and the ethic of care', in M. Fenger, J. Hudson and C. Needham (eds) *Social Policy Review 28*, Bristol: Policy Press.

London Councils (2012) *Improving Health and Social Care in London*. Available at: https://www.londoncouncils.gov.uk (accessed 9 May 2013).

Longley, M. (2012) 'Wales', in C. Ham, D. Heenan, M. Longley and D. Steel (eds) *Integrated Care in Northern Ireland, Scotland and Wales*, London: The King's Fund.

Lotinga, A. (2015) 'Context matters: General practice and social work – the Birmingham story', *Journal of Integrated Care*, Vol. 23, No. 2, pp. 88–95.

Lotinga, A. and Glasby, J. (2012) 'New conversations with new players?: The relationship between primary care and social care in an era of clinical commissioning', *Journal of Integrated Care*, Vol. 20, No. 3, pp. 175–180.

Lymbery, M. (2006) 'United we stand? Partnership working in health and social care and the role of social work in services for older people', *British Journal of Social Work*, Vol. 36, No. 7, pp. 1119–1134.

Lyngso, A. M., Godtfredsen, N. S., Frølich, A. (2016) 'Interorganisational integration: Healthcare professionals' perspectives on barriers and facilitators within the Danish Healthcare System', *International Journal of Integrated Care*, Vol. 16, No 1, p. 4.

MacDonald, A. (2015) 'Innovation and experiences of care integration in Australia and New Zealand', *Future Hospital*, Vol. 2, No. 2, pp. 79–80.

Maker, J. and Lucas, L. (2015) *The State of Care in Counties: The Integration Imperative*, London: County Councils Network.

Mangan, C., Miller, R. and Cooper, J. (2014) 'Time for some home truths – exploring the relationship between GPs and social workers', *Journal of Integrated Care*, Vol. 22, No. 2, pp. 51–61.

Mangan, C., Miller, R. and Ward, C. (2015) 'Knowing me, knowing you: Interprofessional working between general practice and social care', *Journal of Integrated Care*, Vol. 23, No. 2, pp. 62–73.

Maslin-Prothero, S. E. and Bennion, A. E. (2010) 'Integrated team working: A literature review', *International Journal of Integrated Care*, Vol. 10, No. 2, http://doi.org/10.5334/IJIC.529.

Mason, A., Goddard, M., Weatherly, H. and Chalkley, M. (2015) 'Integrating funds for health and social care: An evidence review', *Journal of Health Service Research and Policy*, Vol. 20, No. 3, pp. 177–188.

Mathieson, A. (2011) *Integration of Health and Social Care – A Snapshot of Current Practice in Scotland*, Edinburgh: Royal College of Nursing.

Mays, N. (2016) *Evaluation of the Integrated Care and Support Pioneers Programme*, Policy Innovation Research Unit, London: King's Fund Integration Care Summit 2016.

McCoy, J. (1993) *Integration – A Changing Scene in Social Services Inspectorate. Personal Social services in Northern Ireland: Perspectives on Integration*, Belfast: Department of Health and Social Services.

McCririck, V. and Hughes, R. (2013) 'Local Education and Training Boards: Key messages for promoting integrated care', *Journal of Integrated Care*, Vol. 21, No. 3, pp. 157–163.

McKenna, H. and Dunn, P. (2015) *Devolution: What It Means for Health and Social Care in England*, London: The King's Fund.

McKimm, J. and Phillips, K. (2010) *Leadership and Management in Integrated Services*, Exeter: Learning Matters.

McKinsey Review (2010) *Reshaping the System: Implications for Northern Ireland's Health and Social Care Services of the 2010 Spending Review*. Belfast: Northern Ireland. Department of Health, Social Services and Public Safety.

McTavish, D. and Mackie, R. (2003) 'The joint future initiative in Scotland: The development and early implementation experience of an integrated care policy', *Public Policy and Administration*, Vol. 18, No. 3, pp. 39–56.

Miller, E. and Cameron, K. (2011) 'Challenges and benefits in implementing shared inter-agency assessment across the UK: A literature review', *Journal of Interprofessional Care*, Vol. 25, No 1, pp. 39–45.

Miller, R., Brown, H. and Mangan, C. (2016) *Integrated Care in Action*, London: Jessica Kingsley.

Miller, R., Dickinson, H. and Glasby, J. (2011) 'The care trust pilgrims', *Journal of Integrated Care*, Vol. 19, No. 4, pp. 14–21.

Miller, R., Glasby, J., Cox, B. and Trimble, A. (2010) 'A liberated NHS – but will it lead health and social care together or force them apart?', *Journal of Integrated Care*, Vol. 18, No. 6, pp. 41–44.

Minkman, M. (2012) 'The current state of integrated care: An overview', *Journal of Integrated Care*, Vol. 20, No. 6, pp. 346–358.

Mitchell, D. (2013) 'Reforming care legislation in England and Wales', *Journal of Integrated Care*, Vol. 21, No. 3, pp. 164–170.

Mitchell, F., Dobson, C., McAlpine, A., Dumbreck, S., Wright, I. and Mackenzie, F. (2011) 'Intermediate care: Lessons from a demonstration project in Fife', *Journal of Integrated Care*, Vol. 19, No. 1, pp. 26–36.

Monitor (2012) *Enablers and Barriers to Integrated Care and Implications for Monitor. Report by Frontier Economics,* London: Monitor.

Monitor (2014) *Annual Report and Accounts 2013–14*, Hc340, London: Monitor.

Moore, J., West, R., Keen, J., Godfrey, M. and Townsend, J. (2007) 'Networks and governance: The case of intermediate care', *Health and Social Care in the Community*, Vol. 15, No. 2, pp. 155–164.

Morris, J. (2012) 'Integrated care for frail older people 2012: A clinical overview', *Journal of Integrated Care*, Vol. 20, No. 4, pp. 257–264.

Mrinska, O. (2010) *Integrating Health and Social Care Budgets: A Case for Debate*, London: Institute for Public Policy Research.

National Audit Office (2012) *Healthcare across the UK: A Comparison of the NHS in England, Scotland, Wales and Northern Ireland*, HC 192 (2012–13), London: The Stationery Office.

National Audit Office (2013) *Integration Across Government*, HC 1041, London: The Stationery Office.

National Audit Office (2014) *Adult Social Care in England: An Overview*, HC 1102. Available at: https://www.nao.org.uk (accessed 28 January 2015).

National Audit Office (2016) *Planning for the Better Care Fund*, HC 781. Available at: https://www.nao.org.uk (accessed 17 November 2016).

National Audit Office (2017) *Health and Social Care Integration*: HC 1011 Session 2016–17. Available at: https://www.nao.org.uk (accessed 10 March 2017).

National Collaboration for Integrated Care and Support (2013) *Integrated Care and Support: Our Shared Commitment*. Available at: https://www.gov.uk/government (accessed 5 May 2016).

National Institute for Health Research (2011) *Government Response to NHS Future Forum*. Available at: https://www.nihr.ac.uk (accessed 21 April 2015).

National Voices (2013) *A Narrative for Person-Centred Coordinated Care*. Available at: https://www.nationalvoices.org.uk (accessed 3 March 2017).

Naylor, D., Alderwick, H. and Honeyman, M. (2015) *Acute Hospitals and Integrated Care*, London: The King's Fund.

Needham, C. and Glasby. J (eds) (2014) *Debates in Personalisation*, Bristol, Policy Press.

New Local Government Network (2016) *Get Well Soon: Reimagining Place-Based Health*, London: NLGN.

NHS Commissioning Board (2012) *The Way Forward: Strategic Clinical Networks*. Available at: https://www.england.nhs.uk (accessed 12 March 2015).

NHS Confederation (2010) *Where Next for Health and Social Care Integration?* Available at: https://www.nhs.confed.org (accessed 19 June 2012).

NHS Confederation (2013) *Transforming Local Care*, Community Health Services Forum Briefing, Issue 258. Available at: https://www.nhsconfed.org (accessed 15 January 2015).

NHS Confederation (2016) *New Care Models and Prevention: An Integration Partnership*. Available at: https://www.nhsconfed.org (accessed 21 June 2016).

NHS Confederation/Local Government Association (2016) *Stepping up to the Place. The Key to Successful Health and Care Integration*. Available at: https://www.nhsconfed. org (accessed 16 November 2016).

NHS England (2015) *Integrated Personal Commissioning Programme*. Available at: https://www. england.nhs.uk (accessed 23 August 2016).

NHS England (2016a) *Sustainable Improvement Team*. Available at: https://www.england. nhs.uk (accessed 18 August 2016).

NHS England (2016b) *Devolution: What Does It Mean from an England Perspective?* Available at: https://www.england.nhs.uk (accessed 13 April 2016).

NHS England (2016c) *New Care Models – Vanguard Sites*. Available at: https://www. england.nhs.uk (accessed 30 August 2016).

NHS England (2016d) *People Helping People: Year Two of the Pioneer Programme*. Available at: https://www.england.nhs.uk (accessed 25 February 2016).

NHS Evidence (2011) *Rapid Response Services: Intermediate Tier, Multi-disciplinary Health and Social Care Service*. Available at: https://www.arms.evidence.nhs.uk (accessed 15 June 2013).

NHS Future Forum (2012) *Integration: A Report from the NHS Future Forum*. Available at: https://www.gov.uk/government/uploads (accessed 30 January 2015).

NHS Health Scotland (2012) *A Fairer Healthier Scotland: Our Strategy 2012–2017*, Edinburgh: NHS Health Scotland.

NHS Improvement (2016) *NHS Improvement Business Plan and Objectives/NHS Improvement: Our Business Plan for 2016/17 and Objectives from Now until 2020*. Available at: https://www.improvement.nhs.uk (accessed 25 August 2016).

NICE (2015) *Older People with Social Care Needs and Multiple Long-term Conditions*. Available at: https://www.nice.org.uk (accessed 18 August 2016).

NIHR School for Social Care Research (2008) *Good Support for People with Complex Needs*, Social Policy Research Unit.

Nolte, E. and Pitchforth, E. (2014) *What Is the Evidence on the Economic Impacts of Integrated Care? Policy Summary 11*, European Observatory on Health Systems and Policies, WHO, Denmark.

Noordman, J., Van der Heide, I., Hopman, P., Schellevis, F. and Rijken, M. (2015) *Innovative Health Care Approaches for Patients with Multi-morbidity in Europe*, NIVEL, Netherlands. Northern Ireland Audit Office (2017) *Management of the Transforming Your Care Reform Programme*, NIAO, Belfast.

Northern Ireland Association of Social Workers (2014) *A Blueprint for Change. For Adult Services Social Work in Northern Ireland*, Belfast: NIASW.

Nuffield Institute for Health Joint Improvement Team (2011) *Delayed Discharge. Report of the Expert Group*. Available at: https://www.jitscotland.org.uk (accessed 28 October 2015).

Nuffield Trust (2015) *Improving UK Health Care.* Available at: https://www.nuffieldtrust. org.uk (accessed 28 October 2015).

Nuno-Solinis, R., Perez Vazquez, P., Toro Polanco, N. and Hernandez-Quevedo, C. (2013) 'Integrated care the Basque perspective', *International Journal of Healthcare Management,* Vol. 6, No. 4, pp. 211–216.

Oakley, P. and Greaves, E. (1995) 'Process re-engineering: From command to demand', *Health Service Journal,* 23 February, pp. 32–33.

OECD (2016), *OECD Reviews of Health Care Quality, United Kingdom: Raising Standards,* Brussels: OECD.

Office of National Statistics (2013) *'People, Population and Community, England and Wales, 2013'.* Available at: http://www.ons.gov.uk/peoplepopulationand community (Accessed 10 March 2017).

Oldham, J. (2014) *One Person, One Team, One System,* Report of the Independent Commission on Whole Person Care for the Labour Party.

Oliver, D., Foot, C. and Humphries, R. (2014) *Making Our Health and Care Systems Fit for an Ageing Population,* London: The King's Fund.

O'Neill, C., McGregor, P. and Merkur, S. (2012) 'United Kingdom (Northern Ireland): Health system review', *Health Systems in Transition,* Vol. 14, No. 10, pp. 1–91.

Oxfordshire County Council (2014) *Oxfordshire's Joint Health and Well-being Strategy 2015–19.* Available at: https://www.oxfordshire.gov.uk (accessed 30 June 2015).

Patient and Client Council (2012) *Care at Home: Older People's Experiences of Domiciliary Care,* Belfast: Patient and Client Council.

Payne, J. (2012) *Social Care (Self-Directed Support) (Scotland) Bill,* SPICe Briefing, Edinburgh: Scottish Parliament.

Peck, E. Tower, D. and Gulliver, P. (2001) 'The meaning of "culture" in health and social care: A case study of the combined trust in Somerset', *Journal of Interprofessional Care,* Vol. 15, No 4, pp. 319–27.

Perkins, N. and Hunter, D. (2014) 'Health and wellbeing boards: A new dawn for public health partnerships', *Journal of Integrated Care,* Vol. 22, No. 5/6, pp. 220–224.

Petch, A. (2011) *An Evidence base for the Delivery of Social Services,* London: Association of Directors of Social Work.

Petch, A. (2012a) 'Tectonic plates: Aligning evidence, policy and practice in health and social care integration', *Journal of Integrated Care,* Vol. 20, No. 2, pp. 77–88.

Petch, A. (2012b) *Integration of Health and Social Care, IRISS Insight,* No. 14. Available at: https://www.iriss.org.uk (accessed 23 January 2015).

Petch, A. (2014) *Delivering Integrated Care and Support,* Institute for Research and Innovation in Social Services. Available at: https://www.iriss.org.uk/resources (accessed 23 January 2015).

Petch, A., Cook, A. and Miller, E. (2013) 'Partnership working and outcomes: Do health and social care partnerships deliver for users and carers?', *Health and Social Care in the Community,* Vol. 21, No. 6, pp. 623–633.

Phillips, C. (2008) 'Improving primary care, integrating health and social care', in Institute of Welsh Affairs (ed.) *The Welsh Health Battleground,* Cardiff: IWA.

Plamping, D., Gordon, P. and Pratt, J. (2000) 'Practical partnerships for health and local authorities', *British Medical Journal,* Vol. 320, No. 7251, pp. 1723–1725.

Polanco, N. T., Zabalegui, I. B., Irazusta, I., Solinus, R. N. and Camara, M. D. R., (2015) 'Building integrated care systems: A case study of Bidasoa Integrated Health Organisation', *International Journal of Integrated Care,* Vol. 15, No. 2, http://doi. org/10.5334/IJIC.1796.

Public Accounts Committee (2017) *Integrating Health and Social Care,* London, HC 959 House of Commons.

Preston-Shoot, M. (2010) 'Repeating history? Observations on the development of law and policy for integrated practice', in J. McKimm and K. Phillips (eds) *Leadership and Management in Integrated Services*, pp. 20–34, Exeter: Learning Matters.

Priest, J. (2012) *The Integration of Health and Social Care*, London: British Medical Association.

Rabiee, P. and Glendinning, C. (2011) 'Organisation and delivery of home care re-ablement: What makes a difference?', *Health and Social Care in the Community*, Vol. 19, No. 5, pp. 495–503.

RAND Europe and Ernst and Young (2012) *Progress Report: Evaluation of the National Integrated Care Pilots*, London: Department of Health.

Randall, J. and Casebourne, J. (2015) *Making Devolution Deals Work*, London: Institute for Government.

Reed, J., Cook, G., Childs, S. and McCormack, B. (2005) 'A literature review to explain integrated care for older people', *International Journal of Integrated Care*, Vol. 5. No. 1, http://doi.org/10.5334/IJIC.119.

Redding, D. (2013) 'The narrative for person-centred coordinated care', *Journal of Integrated Care*, Vol. 21, No. 6, pp. 315–325.

Regen, E., Martin, G., Glasby, J., Hewitt, G., Nancarrow, S. and Parker, H. (2008) 'Challenges, benefits and weaknesses of intermediate care: Results from five UK case study sites', *Health and Social Care in the Community*, Vol. 16, No. 6, pp. 629–637.

Reilly, S., Challis, D., Donnelly, M., Hughes, J. and Stewart, R. (2007) 'Care management in mental health services in England and Northern Ireland: Do integrated organisations promote integrated practice?', *Journal of Health Services Research and Policy*, Vol. 12, No. 4, pp. 236–241.

Richards, J. (2000) *The Northern Ireland Model-Unifying Health and Social Services: What Can Be Read Across?*, Belfast: QMW Public Policy Seminar.

Riley, K. (1998) 'Care Pathways paving the way', *Health Service Journal*, Vol. 108,/March 1998, pp. 30–31.

Roberts, A. and Charlesworth, A. (2014) *A Decade of Austerity in Wales?*, London: Nuffield Trust.

Robertson, H. (2011) *Integration of Health and Social Care: A Review of Literature and Models Implications for Scotland*, Royal College of Nursing, Scotland.

Robson, K. (2013) *Public Bodies (Joint Working) (Scotland) Bill*, SPICe Briefing, Edinburgh: Scottish Parliament Information Centre.

Rosen, R. and Ham, L. (2008) *Integrated Care: Lessons from Evidence and Experience*, Oxford: Nuffield Trust.

Rosen, R., Mountford, J., Lewis, G., Lewis, R., Shand, J. and Shaw, S. (2011) *Integration in Action: Four International Case Studies*, London: Nuffield Trust.

Royal College of Nursing (2012) *The RCN in Scotland: Principles for Delivering the Integration of Care*, Edinburgh: Royal College of Nursing.

Rummery, K. (2009) 'Healthy partnerships, healthy citizens? An international review of partnerships in health and social care and patient/user outcomes', *Social Science and Medicine*, Vol. 69, No. 12, pp. 1797–1804.

Sandford, M. (2015) *Devolution to Local Government in England*, Briefing Paper 07029, London: House of Commons Library.

Scotland Public Bodies (Working Together) (Scotland) Act 2014.

Scottish Executive (2003) *Partnership for Care: Scotland's White Paper*, Edinburgh: The Stationery Office.

Scottish Executive (2005a) *Building a Health Service Fit for the Future* (Kerr Review). Available at: https://www.gov.scot (accessed 6 March 2015).

Scottish Executive (2005b) *Delivering for Health*. Available at: https://www.gov.scot (accessed 22 April 2016).

Scottish Government (2007) *Better Health, Better Care: Action Plan*. Available at: https://www.gov.scot (accessed 22 April 2016).

Scottish Government (2009) *Improving the Health and Well-being of People with Long-term Conditions in Scotland: A National Action Plan*. Available at: https://www.gov.scot (accessed 22 April 2016).

Scottish Government (2010) *Study of Community Health Partnerships – Research Findings No. 100*. Available at: https://www.scotland.gov.uk/publications/2010/05/06171436/1 (accessed 4 June 2012).

Scottish Government (2012a) *Integration of Adult Health and Social Care in Scotland: Consultation on Proposals*, Edinburgh: Scottish Government.

Scottish Government (2012b) *Evaluation of Integrated Resource Framework Test Sites – Research Findings*. Available at: https://www.scotland.gov.uk/publications (accessed 10 March 2013).

Scottish Government (2013a) *Integration of Adult Health and Social Care in Scotland: Scottish Government Response*. Available at: https://www.scotland.gov.uk (accessed 12 February 2014).

Scottish Government (2013b) *A Route Map to the 2020 Vision for Health and Social Care*. Available at: https://www.scotland.gov.uk/publications (accessed 23 May 2014).

Scottish Parliament Health and Sport Committee (2012) *Inquiry into Integration of Health and Social Care*, SP Paper 121, Edinburgh: Scottish Parliament.

Seddon, E., Robinson, C. and Perry, J. (2010) 'Unified assessment: Policy, implementation and practice', *British Journal of Social Work*, Vol. 40, No. 1, pp. 207–225.

Shaw, S. and Rosen, R. (2013) 'Fragmentation: A wicked problem with an integrated solution?', *Journal of Health Services Research and Policy*, Vol. 18, No. 1, pp. 61–64.

Skills for Health/Skills for Care (2014) *Working Together: A Summary of Health and Social Care Projects*. Available at: https://www.skillsforhealth.org.uk/service-area (accessed 10 November 2016).

Smith, D. and Wistrich, E. (2014) *Devolution and Localism*, Farnham: Ashgate.

Snape, S. (2003) 'Health and local government partnerships: The local government policy context', *Local Government Studies*, Vol. 29, No. 3, pp. 73–97.

Social Care Institute for Excellence (2012a) *At a Glance 54: Reablement: A Guide for Families and Carers*, London: Social Care Institute for Excellence.

SCIE (2012b) *At a Glance 52: Reablement: Key Issues for Commissioners of Adult Social Care*, London: Social Care Institute for Excellence.

SCIE (2013) *Integration, Collaboration and Pioneers*, London: Social Care Institute for Excellence.

SCIE (2015) *Community Led Care and Support: A New Paradigm*, London: Social Care Institute for Excellence

SCIE (2016) *Better Care Exchange – The Social Network for the Health and Social Care Sector*, London: Social Care Institute for Excellence

Social Services Improvement Agency, Legacy Report 2016-17, Cardiff: SSIA.

Somme, D. (2014) 'Integrated care in France: Dream or reality', *International Journal of Integrated Care*, Vol. 13, No.1, http://doi.org/10.5334/IJIC.1540.

Steel, D. (2013) 'Scotland', in C. Ham, D. Heenan, M. Longley and D. Steel (eds) *Integrated Care in Northern Ireland, Scotland and Wales*, London: The King's Fund.

Steel, D. and Cylus, J. (2012) 'Health systems in transition', *United Kingdom (Scotland) Health System Review*, Vol. 14, No. 9, pp. 1–150.

Stein, K. V. (2016) 'Developing a competent workforce for integrated health and social care: What does it take?', *International Journal of Integrated Care*, Vol. 16, No. 4, http://doi.org/10.5334/IJIC.2533.

Stewart, M. J., Georgiou, A., Westbrook, J. I. (2013) 'Successfully integrating aged care services: A review of the evidence and tools emerging from a long-term care program', *International Journal of Integrated Care*, Vol. 13, No. 1, http://doi.org/10.5334/IJIC.963.

Struckmann, V., Boerma, W. and Van Ginneken, E. (2015) The Gesundes Kinzigtal programme Germany, ICARE4EU.

Suter, E. Oelke, N. D., Adair, C. E. and Armitage, G. D. (2009) 'Ten key principles for successful health systems integration', *Healthcare Quarterly*, Vol. 13 (sp), pp. 16–23.

Swinkels, A. and Mitchell, T. (2009) 'Delayed transfer from hospital to community settings: The older person's perspective', *Health and Social Care in the Community*, Vol. 17, No. 1, pp. 45–53.

Syson, G. and Bond, J. (2010) 'Integrating health and social care teams in Salford', *Journal of Integrated Care*, Vol. 18, No. 2, pp. 17–24.

Taylor, A. (2015) 'New act, new opportunity for integration in Scotland', *Journal of Integrated Care*, Vol. 23, No. 1, pp. 3–9.

Thiel, V., Sonola, L., Goodwin, N. and Kodner, D. (2013) *Developing Community Resource Teams in Pembrokeshire, Wales: Integration of Health and Social Care in Progress*, London: The King's Fund.

Thistlewaite, P. (2011) *Integrating Health and Social Care in Torbay: Improving Care for Mrs Smith*, London: The King's Fund.

Thomas, A. (2015) 'Stranger danger! What's the real challenge in integration? A perspective from a housing association and care and nursing home provider', *Journal of Integrated Care*, Vol. 23, No. 4, pp. 194–205.

Thompson, J. (2016) *Transforming Health and Social Care – Services and Governance*, Research and Information Briefing Paper, No. 40/16 Northern Ireland Assembly, Belfast.

Timmins, N. (2015) *The Practice of System Leadership*, London: The King's Fund.

Timmins, N. and Ham, C. (2013) *The Quest for Integrated Health and Social Care: A Case Study in Canterbury, New Zealand*, London: The King's Fund.

Torbay Care Trust (2013) *Integrated Care Value Case*. Available at: https://www.eelga.gov.uk (accessed 21 January 2015).

Trench, A., Jeffrey, C. (2007) *Older People and Public Policy: The Impact of Devolution*, London: Age Concern.

Trivedi, D., Goodman, C., Gage, H., Baron, N., Scheibl, F., Iliffe, S., Manthorpe, J., Bunn, F. and Drennan, V. (2013) 'The effectiveness of inter-professional working for older people living in the community: A systematic review', *Health and Social Care in the Community*, Vol. 21, No. 2, pp. 113–128.

Tucker, H. and Burgis, M. (2012) 'Patients set the agenda on integrating community services in Norfolk', *Journal of Integrated Care*, Vol. 20, No. 4, pp. 231–240.

Tucker, S., Baldwin, R., Hughes, J., Benbow, S., Barker, A., Burns, A. and Challis, D. (2009) 'Integrating mental health services for older people in England – from rhetoric to reality', *Journal of Interprofessional Care*, Vol. 23, No. 4, pp. 341–354.

Valvanne, J. (2005) 'Integrating social and health care in practice – a Finnish project', in M. Vaarama and R. Pieper (eds) *Managing Integrated Care for Older Persons. European Perspectives and Good Practices*. National Research and Development Centre for Welfare and Health. European Health Management Association, Saarijärvi, Finland, pp. 200–219.

Van Herck, P. Vanhaecht, K. and Sermeus, W. (2004) 'Effects of clinical pathways, do they work?', *Journal of Integrated Care Pathways*, Vol. 8, pp. 95–105.

Wade, L. (2010) 'Integrated hospital discharge in Torbay: Results from a pilot project', *Journal of Integrated Care*, Vol. 18, No. 3, pp. 37–44.

Wales Audit Office (2015) *Supporting the Independence of Older People: Are Councils Doing Enough?* Available at: https://www.audit.wales (accessed 10 March 2015).

Walshe, K. and Smith, J. (eds) (2006) *Health Care Management*, Maidenhead: Open University Press.

Weatherly, H., Mason, A., Goddard, M. and Wright, K. (2010) *Financial Integration across Health and Social Care: Evidence Review*, Edinburgh: Scottish Government Social Research.

Weekes, S. (2006) *Report on the Integration of Health and Social Care Services in England*, London: UNISoN.

Welsh Assembly Government (2004) *Making the Connections: Delivering Better Services in Wales*, Cardiff: Welsh Assembly Government.

Welsh Assembly Government (2006) *National Service Framework for Older People in Wales*, Cardiff: Welsh Assembly Government.

Welsh Assembly Government (2007) *Fulfilled Lives, Supportive Communities: A Strategy for Social Services in Wales over the Next Decade*, Cardiff, Welsh Assembly Government.

Welsh Government (2010) Setting the Direction: Primary and Community Services Strategic Delivery Programme. Available at https://www.wales.nhs.uk (accessed 15 January 2015).

Welsh Assembly Government (2011a) *Health, Social Care and Well-being Strategies: Policy Guidance*. Available at: https://www.wales.nhs.uk (accessed 9 March 2015).

Welsh Assembly Government (2011b) *Sustainable Social Services for Wales: A Framework for Action*, Cardiff: Welsh Assembly Government.

Welsh Government (2013) *Social Services and Well-being (Wales) Bill. Explanatory Referendum*. Available at: https://www.cymru.gov.uk (accessed 15 January 2015).

Welsh Government (2014) *A Framework for Delivering Integrated Health and Social Care for Older People with Complex Needs*, Cardiff: Welsh Assembly Government.

Welsh Government (2017) *Reforming Local Government: Resilient and Renewed*. Available at: https://www.consultations.gov.wales (accessed 10 March 2017).

Welsh Local Government Association and NHS Confederation (2013) *Transitional and Longer Term Implications of the Social Services and Well-being (Wales) Bill 2013*. Available at: https://www.ipc.brookes.ac.uk (accessed 5 May 2015).

Welsh Local Government Association (2017) *Social Services*, Cardiff: WLGA.

West, T., Armit, K., Loewenthal, L., Eckert, R., West, T. and Lee, A. (2014) *Leadership and Leadership Development in Health Care: The Evidence Base*, London: The King's Fund.

Westminster Health Forum (2016) *Next Steps for Health and Social Care in Greater Manchester*, Proceedings of keynote seminar, Westminster Health Forum.

Wilde, A. and Glendinning, C. (2012) 'If they're helping me then how can I be independent?', The perceptions and experience of users of home-care re-ablement', *Health and Social Care in the Community*, Vol. 20, No. 6, pp. 583–590.

Wilderspin, J. (2013) 'Health and wellbeing boards and service transformation', *Journal of Integrated Care*, Vol. 21, No. 1, pp. 13–18.

Wilkes, L. (2014) *Break on Through: Overcoming Barriers to Integration*, London: New Local Government Network.

Williams, I., Dickinson, H. and Robinson, S. (2010) 'Joined-up rationing? An analysis of priority setting in health and social care commissioning', *Journal of Integrated Care*, Vol. 19, No. 1, pp. 3–11.

Williams, P. (2011) 'The life and times of the boundary spanner', *Journal of Integrated Care*, Vol. 19, No. 3, pp. 26–33.

Williams, P. (2012) 'Integration of health and social care: A case of learning and knowledge management', *Health and Social Care in the Community*, Vol. 20, No. 5, pp. 550–560.

Williams, P. (2014) *Commission on Public Service Governance and Delivery Summary Report*, Public Health Wales

Williams, P. and Sullivan, H. (2010) 'Despite all we know about collaborative working, why do we still get it wrong?', *Journal of Integrated Care*, Vol. 18, No. 4, pp. 4–15.

Wistow, G. (2011) 'Integration and the NHS reforms', *Journal of Integrated Care*, Vol. 19, No. 4, pp. 5–13.

Wistow, G. (2012) 'Still a fine mess? Local Government and the NHS 1962 to 2012', *Journal of Integrated Care*, Vol. 20, No. 2, pp. 101–114.

Wistow, G. and Waddington, E. (2006) 'Learning from doing: Implications of the Barking and Dagenham experience for integrating health and social care', *Journal of Integrated Care*, Vol. 14, No. 3, pp. 8–18.

Wistow, G., Gaskins, M., Holder, H. and Smith, J. (2015) *Putting Integration Care into Practice: The North West London Experience*, London: Nuffield Trust.

Woods, K. (2001) 'The development of integrated health care models in Scotland', *International Journal of Integrated Care*, Vol. 1, No. 2, http://doi.org/10.5334/IJIC.29.

Woolrych, R. and Sixsmith, J. (2013) 'Toward integrated services for dementia: A formal carer perspective', *Journal of Integrated Care*, Vol. 21, No. 4, pp. 208–220.

World Health Organization (2016) WHO Geneva. 15 April.

Young, R. (2013) 'Team care arrangements in Australia', *Eurohealth Incorporating Euro Observer*, Vol. 19, No. 2, pp. 11–12.

Index

A

Access 113
Acute Care 71, 89
Association of Directors of Adult Social
    Services 24
Association of Directors of Social Services,
    Wales 81
Austerity 91, 169
Australia 158

B

Balance between Health and Social
    Care 143–4, 173
Barker Commission 1
Basque Health Service 156–7, 161–3
Berlin Wall 17
Better Care Fund 56–7, 62, 145
Bottom-up 164
Boundary spanning 132
Brexit 169–70
British Medical Association 25

C

Canada 159–61
Care Act 43, 145
Care and Support Act 23
Care Coordination 134, 140
Care Coordinator 172
Care Pathways 154–8, 172
Care Quality Commission 1, 126, 146, 172
Care Trusts 17, 18, 20, 28–31
Caring for Our Future 23
Chronic conditions
    (see long-term conditions) 7, 58,
        72–3, 82–3, 120–1, 151, 161–2
City Devolution 59–60
Child and Adolescent mental health
    services 85
Children's services 125, 151

Clinical Commissioning Groups 22,
    43–5, 47, 51, 62, 115, 145, 147
Clinical outcomes 112–3
Collaboration 4, 5, 8, 58, 66, 86–7, 147
Co-location 36, 133
Commissioning 97, 103–4
Communication 2, 128, 146, 148–9
Community care 8, 15
Community Health Care 25
Co-production 74, 131, 172
Councils (see local councils)
Culture, values 131, 151

D

Darzi Review 19
Decentralisation 166
Delayed discharge 37–8, 82, 101–2,
    105, 112–3
Delivering the NHS 18
Dementia 121–2
Demography 7
Denmark 159–60, 165
Devolution 170, 174
Direct payments 88, 172
Domiciliary care 6, 30

E

England
    commissioning 21
    operation of Integration 28–42, 43–53
    partnerships 16–7, 32, 34
    strategies 15–6, 18–20, 170
    structures 10
Evaluation (see Research)

F

Finland 166
Flexibilities 16–18, 31, 138
Fragmentation 2, 150

Frail older people   83
Frameworks   78
Fulfilled Lives, Supported Communities
   (see Wales)
Funding / Financing   86, 127–8, 139,
   144–5, 167

G
Germany Gesundes Kinzigtal   159
Global development   153–4
Governance   77–8
Government policy   54–5, 140, 150,
   173
GPs engagement   4, 5, 38–9, 58, 72, 86,
   135, 148
Griffiths Report   15

H
Health and Well Being Boards   21, 44,
   46–50, 56, 151
Health and Social Care Act 2012   21,
   23–4, 28, 43
Healthwatch   47, 49
Holistic approach   2, 11, 81, 89, 131,
   157
Holland   160
Hospital discharge
   (see Delayed discharge)
House of Commons   24, 57
Housing   125

I
Independence, Well-being and Choice   19
Independent Providers   24
Inner North West London Project   51
Integration Achievements
   assessments   42, 62, 71–2, 74–5, 89,
      107–8, 114–5, 125–6, 151–2
   commissioning   33, 60, 115–6, 137–8,
      150
   definitions   3–6, 145–6
   enablers   133, 139, 141
   evidence base   101–2, 109–117, 136,
      149, 170
   financial benefits   71, 116–7, 171
   implementation   9, 138–9, 142,
      151–2
   processes   5, 79, 139, 153
   rationale   2–3
   structures   10, 68–9, 147, 169, 171

   scope   4, 34–5
   vision   67–8, 130–1, 146, 150
Integrated Authorities
   (see Scotland)
Integrated Personal Commissioning
   Programme   60–61
Integrated teams   35–6, 83, 104, 113–4,
   136–7, 161–2
IT Systems   8, 38, 85, 114, 128–9, 146,
   161–2, 167
Intermediate Care   39–40, 73, 84, 106,
   118
Inter-professional working   72, 104–5,
   135, 137, 143

J
Joint Commissioning   33, 103–4
Joint Future (see Scotland)
Joint posts   35
Joint Strategic Needs Assessment   39, 46,
   114–5
Joint working   114, 135, 171

K
Kaiser Permanente   162
King's Fund   25–6

L
Law Commission   27
Lead Commissioning   33–4
Leadership   87, 89, 129–30, 149–50,
   163–6
Learning disability   86, 122–3
Legislation   8, 150, 169, 171
Leutz   6
Local Government Association   25, 49,
   55–6, 116
Local Government Councils   48, 54, 77,
   81
Localism   74, 172
Long-term conditions
   (see chronic conditions)

M
Managing Clinical Networks   66
Mental Health   32, 35, 85, 106, 121,
   151
Modernising Social Services   17
Monitor   27, 46, 151
Multi-disciplinary teams   35–6

N

National Audit Office   27
National Collaboration for Integrated
   Care   55, 137
National Voices   27
New Labour   18
New Zealand   156
NHS   1, 17, 20, 23
NHS and Community Care Act   16
NHS Commissioning Board   45–6
NHS Confederation   25, 130
NHS Future Forum   21
NHS Improvement   46
NHS Improving Quality   54
NHS Plan   17
NICE   57
Northern Ireland
   Bengoa Report   107
   Development of Integration   93–6
   Devolution   92
   Enhanced Integration   102
   Health and Social Boards   94
   Health and Social Care Reform
      Act   96–7
   Health and Social Care Trusts   96–7
   Integrated Care Partnerships   100–101
   Mental Health   106
   Operational aspects   102–7
   Origins of Integration   92–3
   Patient and Client Council   99
   Programmes of Care   101–3
   Reablement   106
   Review of Public Administration
      95–7
   Structure   10, 96–7, 107
   Transforming Your Care   97–100
North West London Programme   146–150
Nuffield Trust   25–6

O

Older people frameworks   83
Our Health, Our Care, Our Place   19, 33
Outcomes   2, 66, 71–2, 117, 172
Oxfordshire HWB   49

P

Partnerships   34, 64–5, 80–2
Partnerships for Older People   120
Partnerships NHS Trusts   50
Personalisation   2, 133–5, 172

Person Centred Planning   2, 3, 8, 154
Physical disability   109
Pioneers   50–53, 112, 123–4, 172
Pooled Budgets   32–3, 127, 144
Prevention   2, 8, 117
Primary Care Trusts   17–18, 20, 32,
   35–7, 43–4
Professional cultures   142–3
Public Bodies (Joint Working) (Scotland)
   Act 2014(see Scotland)
Putting People First   19

R

Rapid Response   41–2, 118–9
Reablement   40–1, 73, 84–5, 106, 117–8
Rehabilitation
   (see Intermediate Care)
Research / evaluation   109–112, 136,
   140, 149, 170–1
Resources   2
Review of Public Administration,
   (see Northern Ireland)
Royal College of Nursing   67, 172
Royal College of Physicians   1

S

Scotland   64
   Community Care and Health Act   200
   Community Health Partnership   64–6
   Integrated Resources Framework   66
   Integrated Authorities   68–71
   Joint Future   63–4
   Parliament   65
   Policy   63, 67–70, 74
   Public Bodies Joint Working Act   64–71
   Strategies   72–3
   Structures   10, 68–72
Seamless service   2, 161
Seebohm Report   15
Self-directed support   73
Shaping the Future of Care Together   19
Social Care Institute for Excellence   26
Social Care Workforce   149
Social Enterprises   36–7
Social Workers   99, 105
Staff Satisfaction   119
Structural Integration   64–5, 94–7
Sustainability and Transformation
   Plans   61, 123, 172
Sweden   157–8

T
Toolbox for Integrated working   48
Torbay Care Trust   21, 30–1
Transforming Your Care (see Northern Ireland)
Training / Education   5, 9, 11, 131–3,
   139, 148–9

U
Unified Assessment   2, 7, 38–9, 60–1
User Participation   2, 134, 140, 150, 172
User Satisfaction   119

V
Vanguard   57–8, 123
Vision for Adult Social Care   9, 22
Voluntary Sector   26, 124–5, 151

W
Wales
   Care and Repair Cymru   85
   Care Council for Wales   81

Devolution   76
*Fulfilled Lives Supporting
   Communities*   78
Improving Social Care in Wales
   77
Frail Older People   83
   Funding   86
From Vision to Action   79
Policy   77–90
Public Services Boards   77
Setting the Direction   78
*Social Services and Wellbeing (Wales) Act
   2014*   82–2, 88
Structure   10, 76–8, 81, 90
Sustainable Social Services for Wales
   79
Voluntary Sector   84
*Wellbeing of Future Generations (Wales)
   Act 2015*   71
Williams Commission   90
World Health Organisation   154

Printed by Printforce, the Netherlands